Imaginary States

Imaginary States

Studies in
Cultural Transnationalism

Peter Hitchcock

University of Illinois Press
Urbana and Chicago

Library of Congress Cataloging-in-Publication Data
Hitchcock, Peter.
Imaginary states : studies in cultural transnationalism /
Peter Hitchcock.
p.   cm. — (Transnational cultural studies)
ISBN 0-252-02393-5 (cloth : alk. paper)
1. Culture. 2. Globalization. 3. Intercultural communication.
I. Title. II. Series.
HM621.H58   2003
306—dc21   2002005680

In memory of my father

Contents

Acknowledgments

I began this book several years ago as an attempt to work out what critical tools would be appropriate for literary and cultural analysis under the sign of globalization. While much of what I have to say about cultural transnationalism is in the spirit of that effort, the case studies themselves stand in sharp contrast to the theoretical focus I originally imagined. This is undeniably an effect of working on such provocative writers, but it also has to do with the thoughtful responses and inspiration that my friends, colleagues, and students have given me over the course of this project. Although they are not responsible for any errors in the theory and practice of these studies in cultural transnationalism, I would like to the thank the following people: Alex Alberro, Nora Alter, Emily Apter, Michael Bell, Craig Brandist, Jeff Derksen, Michael Gardiner, David Glover, Chris GoGwilt, Jim Groom, Susan Hegeman, Sherif Hetata, Michael Holquist, James Hurt, Marko Juvan, Cora Kaplan, E. Ann Kaplan, Chi-she Li, Vitaly Makhlin, Melissa Myambo, Margie Orford, Nikolai Pankov, Sonali Perera, Dominique Perron, Nicola Pitchford, Roger Rawlings, Alastair Renfrew, Domingo Sanchez, Zohreh Sullivan, Imre Szeman, Galin Tihanov, Anthony Wall, Candice Ward, Phillip Wegner, Donald Wesling, and Clarisse Zimra. A special mention goes to Robert Barsky, Amitava Kumar, Obioma Nnaemeka, Clive Thomson, and Lawrence Venuti, all of whom still subject themselves to my work despite the pressures of their own. I extend my thanks as well to Dick Martin of the University of Illinois Press, who has shown a remarkable patience with the process of this publication.

I am especially grateful to Kamau Brathwaite for permission to reprint his poetry here. I would also like to thank the following publishers for permission to reprint some previously published material: Indiana University Press for an earlier version of chapter 1 that appeared as "Antillanité and the Art of Resistance," *Research in African Literatures* 27, no. 2 (Summer 1996): 33–50; the editors of

Bucknell Review for a portion of chapter 3 that appears in "The Scriptible Voice and the Space of Silence: Assia Djebar's Algeria," *Bucknell Review* 43, no. 2 (2000): 134–49; University of Minnesota Press, for portions of chapter 5 that appear in my book *Oscillate Wildly: Space, Body, and Spirit of Millennial Materialism* (Minneapolis: University of Minnesota Press, 1999), 109–42; and Palgrave Publishers for part of the conclusion that appears in "The World According to Globalization and Bakhtin," in *Materializing Bakhtin,* ed. Craig Brandist and Galin Tihanov (London: Macmillan, 2000), 3–19.

This book carries a dedication to my father, who succumbed to a disease that, as yet, will not accept our best efforts to combat it. There are no words here that fight that particular struggle, but I hope in a small way this book might keep alive the principle of struggle itself.

Imaginary States

Introduction:
Imaginary States

How naturally we entify and give life such. Take the case of God, the economy, and the state, abstract entities we credit with Being, species of things awesome with life force of their own, transcendent over mere mortals. Clearly they are fetishes, invented wholes of materialized artifice into whose woeful insufficiency of being we have placed soulstuff. Hence the big S of the State. Hence its magic of attraction and repulsion, tied to the Nation, to more than a whiff of a certain sexuality reminiscent of the Law of the Father and, lest we forget, to the specter of death, human death in that soul-stirring insufficiency of Being.

—Michael Taussig, *The Magic of the State*

The challenge of cultural transnationalism as a methodology for cultural studies is the challenge of imagination itself, for while there are many different ways to think of the globe there is as yet no convincing sense of imagining difference globally. The question of persuasiveness is vital, because at this time the globalism most prevalent and the one that is busily being the most persuasive is global capitalism. To pose culture alone as a decisive blow to global modes of economic exploitation is idealist in the extreme (and misleading, since capital can also utilize cultural import/export and culture can exploit sans capital). Yet, because such exploitation depends upon a rationale, a rhetoric of globalism if you will, so culture may intervene in the codes of that imaginary, deploying imagination itself as a positive force for alternative modes of Being and being conscious in the world.[1]

Obviously, this method of approaching culture in a transnational frame is not unrelated to Arjun Appadurai's powerfully suggestive argument for "imagination as a social practice"—that imagination itself is "central to all forms of agency."[2] By turns polemical and profound, Appadurai's insistence on imagination as a crucial corrective to hasty global concepts of integration (for the sine qua non of imagination is *disjuncture*) raises the stakes in global cultural critique. But a number of problems remain in Appadurai's approach that are symptomatic of difficulties within transnational cultural studies as a whole. For one thing, the social practices of the imagination are coterminous with social Being and have not simply emerged in the schizo-culture of globalism (in this respect, imagination has been central to human agency all along). Second, despite imagination's centrality, its cognitive force is dependent upon myriad structures of power, production, and reproduction. Thus, as soon as one asks "Whose imagination?" the material possibility of agency must be radically particularized. Without this distinction, the only imagination at stake will be Appadurai's own in articulating a highly nuanced model of global cultural flows. Finally, despite the obligatory yet subjunctive nod to a Marxist base/superstructure model ("particular flows of capital may well profoundly determine the shape that ethnoscapes, ideoscapes and mediascapes may take" [47]) and the acknowledged influence of Deleuze and Guattari's schizo-analytic of capital, Appadurai balks at the idea that materialism has a rather compendious tradition of examining the imbrication of imagination with capital, which gives the impression that its present "scaping" is its own invention. Although Appadurai has clearly opened the way for critical transnationalism, I begin with the supposition that the imagination is undertheorized vis-à-vis the global, and that this limit has a material explanation with a history.[3]

To some extent, this is implicit in Appadurai's argument, for when the anthropologist reaches for fractals and chaos theory as critical tools (whose complex mathematical formulae have a highly specific systematicity), we understand anew that the challenge of transdisciplinarity in cultural studies is its ability to think through the actual differences in theoretical models it advocates. This is not an argument against the prescience of metaphoricity, for metaphors themselves are imaginative criteria of new methodologies. But the deployment of imagination within the terms of social practice demands a fairly detailed sense of its logical integrity, not least because so many have a stake in cultural studies *not* being able to think of disjuncture and difference in this way (a failure that would reaffirm the dominance of traditional disciplinarity). On the imaginative plane, there are positive signs of thinking difference globally, and these I shall gather under the rubric of cultural transnationalism. They are discrepant imaginings to be sure (as Taussig's view clearly is), but the term itself might be schematized as follows: (1) it represents an array of critical methodologies broadly associated with cultural studies that are attempting to rethink culture as an object of knowledge beyond its strict and restricting national base (Appadurai's contribution here is indisputable); (2) it refers to modes of artistic and imaginative expression that give vent to supranational and transnational yearnings; and (3) it connotes various ways of being transnational that as yet have no viable political, economic, and social framework to sustain adequately the possibilities they might embrace. In this introduction I will focus on (1)—but as a demand of the other two and as a lesson that will inform the following chapters.[4]

In the conclusion to *Culture and Imperialism,* Edward Said suggests that "the major task . . . is to match the new economic and socio-political dislocations and configurations of our time with the startling realities of human interdependence on a world scale."[5] I would like to indicate some of the ways in which cultural transnationalism might contribute to that vital endeavor. Culture can act as a conduit in producing a more agonistic sense of global consciousness than the pieties of unreflective multiculturalism. The "match," as Said calls it, can be achieved paradoxically only through a recognition of disjunction and difference in world cultures. Frankly, there can be no "global expertise" of these differences; indeed, the assumption of expertise or the worldliness of traditional cosmopolitanism usually masks some good old-fashioned hegemonic homogenization (in cultural studies this was once known as the "Benetton thesis"—in a series of ads Benetton, the clothing company, mixed different clothing colors and races to imply that all are really "equal" under the law of surplus value). The role of culture, then, must not only acknowledge difference but encourage a consciousness of the patent inequalities of the world system. To a certain extent, culture's "travels" do this ineluctably (such movement is sometimes parallel but not necessarily synonymous with the trajectories of migration, exile, diaspora, and trade—the latter has included not only things but people, from slaves to temporary workers). Yet it is only relatively recently that cultural critique has begun to come to terms with the vital implications of culture's movement as a measure of "human interdependence on a world scale." What blocks or inhibits greater understanding of this kind is, on the one hand, cultural diversity itself (vast stores of knowledge that cannot simply be learned or translated—even the modest prospect of thoroughly learning one's most immediate culture is daunting), and on the other hand, the mystifications that accompany the juxtapositions of the Nation State and the global economy. Even when knowledge of culture's movement is the explicit aim of cultural critique, it often collapses back into a more strictly Nation and/or nationalist framework, leaving the global to be networked by a seemingly more natural globalizing logic—capital. In this light, the Nation can be an alibi, or the very mark of cognitive impasse in a more radical reading of contemporary social Being.

The cutting edge of cultural studies precisely cuts against the inevitability of inhibiting national dynamics, but again it must be asserted that ultimately the requisite transformation of knowledge into more egalitarian forms of global interdependence cannot be achieved on culture's terms alone. To put it bluntly, the

answer to global capitalism will never be global culturalism. Recent cultural studies polemics (especially after the geopolitical realities of post–cold war "free market" capital) have seriously grappled with the culture/nation nexus and have provided an urgent provocation to reexamine cultural studies' governing paradigms.[6]
I am not going to cover these debates here (I have alluded to one already, and
other aspects will emerge later in this book), but I do want to situate them in a
general way before providing my own claims for the necessity of the imaginary
state. Then, in the final part of this chapter, I will link the question of imagination to the particular case studies I have in mind.

To imagine the world as other to the perquisites of the Nation State does not,
at first glance, appear a task of Sisyphean proportions. And yet, the Nation idea
in national formations not only remains a normative means of identification but
it exerts a tremendous ideological pressure on both political subjecthood and the
aesthetics of representation.[7] Clearly, the disciplinary distinctions accorded literature, language, and culture on the basis of national identity are as much a mainstay of the academy as they are part of the doxa of the public sphere, and there are
clearly good historical (and materialist) reasons for the synergy of disciplines and
nations. Transnational cultural studies, as I will argue, presents a formidable challenge to this orthodoxy, but this discipline's efforts come with a heavy and perhaps intractable set of practical and theoretical problems. These may be indicated briefly in the following questions: The major paradigm for transnationalism
has not been provided by culture, but by economics—how, then, can transnation-
alizing culture avoid, or indeed challenge, a form of economic worldliness that
currently gives to global capital its hegemonic stature? Does transnationalism, for
all its tenacious border crossing, merely replicate the will to hegemony formerly
predominant in colonialism and imperialism? Capital and cultural flows certainly interrupt one another, but does not the latter risk the political limits of culturalism as an ideology in the forms of its resistance? Who are the arbiters of cultural
transnationalism and how are their positions any less retrograde than the captains
of culture (the Eurocentrists, the Great Traditionalists) they would presumably
supersede? Does not any claim to transnationalism risk the elision of key specificities in individual cultures that do not require and do not need the mantle of globalism to understand their textures and logics? Cultural studies remains a generally tenuous field of study—could it be that the more the going gets tough, the
more the tough go global? Who would blame members of any "marginalized culture" for seeing in cultural transnationalism yet another round of domination, this
time in the guise of more egalitarian intercultural relations?

Cultural transnationalism certainly risks these criticisms (because of the truths
on which they are based), but pursuing it is a cognitive, epistemological, and by

all means political imperative. Mikhail Bakhtin once suggested that we have no alibi in Being—we cannot claim to be anywhere else than where we are in Being (there is a philosophical quandary here to which this study will return); but we have no alibi for not being cultural transnationalists either.[8] The main problem, however, is that we do not have, and perhaps cannot "have," the requisite cognitive tools for living the transnational effectively and affectively. Boldly stated, the crisis of globalization is a crisis of imagination, something that exists in the material limits of a global imaginary as currently construed. The imaginary states of my title are, in part, attempts to imagine this situation otherwise, not in any formulaic way, to be sure, but in a fashion that lends to transnationalism a positive resource of hope.

The main approach here to cultural transnationalism will focus on questions of representation and nonrepresentation in the interpretation of key examples of transnational culture. It will also provide analyses of the economy of cultural exchange in more literal objects of commodity circulation. By juxtaposing the work of cultural workers with an exploration of the macroeconomic realities of commodities in the world system, I hope to show that the transnational imperative is not something to be either feared or suppressed but rather something to be approached as a condition of possibility in the analysis of global difference. This should not imply that the methodology remains the same between literature and the commodity; nor will this study maintain that literature is basically a commodity before transnational critique. The juxtapositions of the literary with the commodity underline the importance of imagination to both the aesthetic and the economic in cultural transnationalism, a commonality with a distinctive set of cognitive limits on our worldly pretensions. The tension between the literary and the commodity exists in this study as counterpoint or contrapuntal contradiction: they urge the transcultural in transnationalism.[9] Before outlining the specific case studies, I want to map some of the critical parameters that inform the articulation and interpretation of imaginary states.

We know that there are definitive histories of the subject of the Nation State, the now infamous imagined community that gives to identity its political borders in the world system.[10] This subject is coded according to the terms of a Nation agenda, one which can vary considerably from case to case but basically affords the individual a legal, economic, and cultural affinity under the sign of Nation. Obviously, many of the world's population are not privy to this mode of subjecthood. For instance, there are migrant, diasporic, and refugee communities worldwide who do not necessarily share in the largesse of Nation as a primary principle of identification, and there are many "within" a nation who are actually outside the confines of its interpellation (marked by the intensities of preexisting social formations). The number of people who either are forced or choose to move be-yond and between national borders is reason enough to examine whether the Nation Subject remains an adequate identitarian formula. The alternatives, how-ever, are marked by fluid but no less contradictory forms of subjecthood.

In their collection of essays *Displacement, Diaspora, and Geographies of Identity*, Smadar Lavie and Ted Swedenburg argue for tactical identities in understanding the global realities of moving centers and populations.[11] Chela Sandoval's concept of "differential consciousness" is read in these terms, and clearly a more fluid non-essentialist sense of the mobile in cultural critique has much to recommend it.[12] For one thing, Lavie and Swedenburg come to grips with the local instantiation of the global, as diasporic, transnational, hybrid, and border identities resist and recode a late capitalism characterized by flexi-local strategies of accumulation. In particular, their argument highlights the interpellation of "Third World women" as the motor of a particular form of globalized value extraction. As my continu-ing work on Indonesian shoe production underlines, this "twist" in the codes of accumulation must renew our theorization of the conditions of gender and labor differentiation. Lavie and Swedenburg approach the problem through a discus-sion of hybridity and a novel elaboration of a third time/space, both of which are provocative components of materialist mapping.[13] Like Appadurai, however, we are also made to rethink the location of agency in the imagination of fragmented identities and this may require a more dialogic delineation.

Thus, to the extent that our identities are constructed along no single trajec-tory with no single fragment that could stand in for all the possible identities that we might express, we are all, ontologically if not subjectively, hybrids—complex articulations of border beings. This does not mean that a unitary sense of self does not exist, as if ideologies do not have something important to say about subject constitution, or as if certain modes of power do not have purchase on particular, centered subject positions. Neither does this mean that all forms of hybridity can be lined up as equally significant, as if each border being deserved accolades merely upon recognition of its multiple existence. Indeed, the only reason for this gen-eralization is its provocation. For if we are all hybrids of some kind, then we should beware of reveling in its matter-of-factness as its own reward. Multiple and dis-junct identities—gendered, raced, located, classed, sexed, etc.—certainly chal-lenge in profound ways many treasured and normative notions of self, but it is not hybridity itself that guarantees this challenge, in the same way that a unified subject cannot ineluctably express perspicacity. By noting hybridity as a general condition therefore, I wish to focus on particular forms of its articulation rather than, willy-nilly, its quotidian pervasiveness.

The disadvantage of such an approach is that it invites the charge that the radical import of hybridity is being diluted, abrogated by a neocolonial urge to see everything everywhere at once. Who is the "we" of the previous paragraph that feels so drawn to the hybrid that it must make the hybrid state all-inclusive so that, naturally, it includes itself? The advantage, however, lies in the disadvantage. By generalizing hybrid identity one can foreground particular components of its formation that exceed the fact of multiplicity (which, in its weaker multicultural manifestations, seems only to offer the unitary self its binary mirror: one of the meanings of multiculturalism is "more of the same"). But this is not a book about hybridity as such, nor is it about a necessarily insurgent mode of hybridization (even when I emphasize it in this way). It is, rather, about what conditions these different senses of self—not just the cultural logic of their production, but also the sociopolitical coordinates of their possibility. To this extent, cultural transnationalism is not about hybridity per se, but is first and foremost about the experience of globality.

To be sure, this is a mainstay of much contemporary cultural critique, as work like Lavie and Swedenburg's accentuates. The problem is that globality itself arrives as a contaminated and contaminating concept, one which not only elides the complex experience of the local or micro-communal but risks reproducing dubious forms of inclusivity that cultural critique often otherwise and/or steadfastly opposes. This difficulty has been compounded on a number of different levels simultaneously by the commodification of theory in and around higher institutions of learning; the principles of "culture" employed; and a political void created by the collapse of Eastern European socialist states and the end of the cold war. The latter has meant, for instance, that globalism can be projected as a kind of Western triumphalism in the apparent absence of significant mass movement alternatives. Obviously the preponderance of Endist philosophy is not unconnected to this phenomenon.[14]

The commodification of theory is a difficult issue that has only recently been analyzed in terms of properly "global" understanding (and is similarly a symptom of larger macrological developments). Cultural studies has attempted to address this in the full range of its practical and institutional logics. But it has also proceeded within a national framework that has tended to buttress the needs of individual states. Indeed, by dint of the ineluctable force of national education programs and requirements, cultural studies has had to accommodate theoretical and practical positions that have compromised its transdisciplinary predilections. It is only relatively recently, for instance, that the Birmingham Centre's model of cultural studies has been significantly challenged for its parochial and nationalist inclinations. In the rush to celebrate its decentered and decentering identity, its blindness to its own national possibility was not considered materially relevant. The result was a creeping universalism that projected what was essentially "the peculiarities of the British" (to rework an earlier New Left debate) onto what was otherwise a provocative set of critical interventions. Situating what was Birmingham is an important historical task in understanding what is and what is not possible in other spaces and places. I should add, however, that critical reevaluation is not denigration and that Birmingham has remained a profound inspiration to cultural studies' advocates.

At the same time, cultural studies has been read as a source of theoretical production. This is perfectly understandable as an academic reflex of disciplinary justification. Longevity within an academic institution depends upon complex articulations of field identity: an institutional base is hardly likely to be granted to a field that does not have a rigorous paradigm for its contribution to knowledge. On the other hand, the rise of cultural studies was tied to a particular moment of theoretical production, one in which theory itself seemed to mime the perquisites of commodity fetishism. The intensity of this effect certainly varied according to location and identification: it is chiefly relevant to Euramerican formations of cultural studies, although because of theory's global flows it has had significant impact in postcolonial states and elsewhere. In the United States, cultural studies has clearly fractured key assumptions about disciplinary boundaries between the humanities and social sciences and, of course, what the suitable objects of knowledge are for such cultural critique. With the backlash against theory, however, and an often hostile economic environment of privatization in the academy, cultural studies has been generally denied an adequate and sustainable rationale for existence in the United States. Ironically, its survival may depend on the generosity of academic technocrats who see in cultural studies an opportunity to merge and downsize other departments. Whatever cultural studies' fate in the United States, it is clear that it must separate its mission from the feared abstraction of the "high theory" while remaining dedicated to nuanced theoretical production of some kind.

This is most evident in the various definitions that have emerged for the word *culture* in cultural studies. I am not going to rehearse what is a fascinating and complex narrative of terminological waywardness, but clearly different formations of cultural studies have turned on the axis accorded "culture." Raymond Williams's celebrated distinctions in *Keywords*,[15] for instance, acknowledge the difference in use between its aesthetic or literary correlative and its deployment in the social sciences (principally, sociology and anthropology). The notion of culture as "a whole way of life" might seem to bridge such interpretations, but in practice Williams's own culturalist approach erred on the side of the literary and his critiques favored textualism even when those texts were not literary (his work on communications and media, for instance). Interestingly, in Perry Anderson's "Components of the National Culture" literary criticism itself is seen to provide a key ideological framework in the legitimation processes of bourgeois identity in Britain.[16] From this point of view, it is not the weakness of sociological paradigms in Britain that opened up a space for cultural studies, but the arena of contestation provided by the literary in national identity. (Anderson mentions F. R. Leavis in this regard.) For my purposes, the consonance of the literary with identity formation in specifically British cultural studies has produced unexpected consequences. Wherever you look today, you see the distancing of the British or Birmingham model of cultural studies accompanying a rejection of the literary as a modus operandi.[17] There is much to recommend this move but it can prove a burden in cultural transnationalism. Just as much of the intercultural trade in theory occurs by the book, so to speak, so a good deal of transgressive national critique occurs in the literary. Indeed, we sometimes need to remind ourselves that the leading figures in postcolonial and diasporic culture include creative writers, and not only anthropologists or sociologists. My point is this: Cultural studies practitioners must remain vigilant and reflexive about the interpretation of "culture" in their critique. But they must also understand that as long as culture engages imaginative processes, the marginalization of the literary or its reduction to sociological method seriously underestimates the value of the literary for knowledge. Part of my interest in "imaginary states" is to explore the concept of transgressive imagiNation; that is, the ways that the literary exceeds, challenges, demystifies, or transcodes the components of national identity. Concomitantly, this opens the possibility of a transgressive imagiNative, itself an imaginary state that negotiates the experience of globalism through the realities of the local.[18] The analysis of imaginary states does not constitute a literary method as such, but neither does it simply believe that purging the literary from cultural studies better prepares it for an understanding of the transnational (and this will be in evidence even when the literary does not appear at stake).

I have suggested that cultural transnationalism might usefully explore forms of differential cognizing in what constitutes the global at this juncture. But what are the imaginative criteria of such intercultural understanding? Is not the privilege that provides the grounds for such a question itself a measure of the impossibility of egalitarian cultural relations? Even if one agreed that we have superseded the model of world systems analysis as such (and this remains highly debatable according to the terms of debate), clearly geopolitical positioning determines to a significant and debilitating degree the kinds of questions asked, and power relations in general. Indeed, cultural transnationalism is not just a commentary or critique of power: it is also its very effect. Yet we must adhere to the positive valence of cultural transnationalism, the power of difference in discourse, in order to stave off the cynicism and myopia that deems *any* globalizing critique as the will-to-silence of a hegemonic elite.

Cultural transnationalism has much to say about (and in) moving cultures, including alternative measures of modernity that do not depend inexorably on a Euramerican model of cognitive cogency, that which has relied upon a relatively stable set of cultural markers broadly associated with the Cartesian "I" and its tradition. Certainly, the legacy of Euramerican theoretical tools should give everyone pause in the support of this endeavor, since these include a righteous flexibility often consonant with the terms of a democratic ideal, if not always practice. Here a critical distinction must be made in forms of cultural transnationalism. Because of the positioning involved, the interpretive act should not be made the equivalent of the creative/imaginative/artistic act—even when interpretation is offered from the same location.[19] Similar concepts may apply, particularly with regard to notions of native informant, diasporic intellectual, subaltern spokesperson, etc. Many of these issues are the mainstay of contemporary ethnographic and anthropological studies (indeed, in the work of James Clifford the question of positioning is used to differentiate the ethnographic and the anthropological[20]). But most interpretative acts occur within interpretive communities that do not necessarily match those of the artist. Thus, while academic exchanges are significant, indeed crucial to the development of cultural studies, we might usefully guard against the tendency to make the arguments of cultural studies a primary object of cultural studies. Otherwise, the meta-discursive can bend into hermeticism.

"Imaginary states" imagines the state otherwise. It is hopelessly idealist and politically disabling, however, to believe that by articulating identity against the Nation Subject in its Euramerican configuration one has confounded the logic of the national form. There are important ways in which postcolonial positioning can question the normalizing projections of Enlightenment subjecthood. But there are strong ideological, economic, and political reasons why postcolonial states reproduce national identity.[21] The community of nations still demands obeisance to an idea of Nation, even when this is merely a cover for forms that are properly transnational—think of the mode of disbursement employed by the IMF or World Bank. And even if this were not the case, the relatively recently formed economic blocs (NAFTA, ASEAN, CARICOM, EU, or their global lifelines, GATT and WTO) can always disassemble into national entities as their governments require—witness the handwringing of the UK vis-à-vis the EU. The critique of Euramerican models of nationhood must continue for many reasons, including that which forestalls any descent into a renewed or reformed colonialism and imperialism (obviously, Euramerican nationhood does not have a monopoly on either colonialism or imperialism but historically it has played a major role in the development of these forms of social subjection). Yet most nations bear the detritus and imprint of the idea of Nation, and that is the "bad new thing," as Bertolt Brecht would put it, that cultural transnationalism must constantly confront.

The idea of Nation, then, exerts specific imaginative constraints on cultural transnationalism. Perhaps itemizing one's international consumables in a form of Lyotardian laundry list still makes one a progeny of postmodern panache. Perhaps this act itself constitutes a properly political form of transnational cultural resistance (especially in comparison to old Nation formulae like "I'm Backing Britain" or "Buy American"). But however pinned to modernity the Nation has been, it can also attach itself to postmodern narrativity in alarmingly fluid fashion.[22] Indeed, the ideological purview of Nation is imbued with its own sense of border crossing that makes the ascription of intrinsic radicality to this move extremely difficult to gainsay. A successful ideology does not remain so by monologism, as Bakhtin/Voloshinov understood very well. It continually renegotiates the form of its hegemony in terms of current contingencies (which is also a lesson from Antonio Gramsci). Ironically, the political attraction of the contingent, provisional, and unfinished has been very alluring to the idea of Nation all along. The need to rearticulate Nation is a raison d'être of national governments. Thus, just as one must specify the condition of hybridity in counterhegemonic discourse, so one must pay careful attention to the tactical virtuosity of the Nation as idea. The reason Benedict Anderson explores the Nation as an "imagined community" is not because it does not exist, but because it requires a logic of imagination to suture its governing idea in the face of ongoing and massive contradictions.[23] What an imaginary state does is not replace the Nation as it is currently constituted but challenge its cognitive rationale. It does not overthrow governments or their institutional supports but picks away at the imaginative grounds for their subsistence as an alibi for more egalitarian modes of socialization.

There is no magic key to the ways in which the local and global are being imaginatively articulated, but if criticism is now confident in its identification of the ruse of imagination in the Nation, it should at least be willing to explore the alternatives to its totemic grip on the substance of Being. This is precisely the route taken in Michael Taussig's *Magic of the State*.[24] Taussig daringly takes on the imaginative aura of the state by proposing a fictive/ethnographic counterdiscourse. Shattering the decorum of academic ethnography, Taussig explores the contradictory space of the Nation State as a kind of spirit possession, where a logic of reason and violence conjoined defy the powers of material exorcism. The State's projection of power offers an uncanny attraction to its subjects, one in which even the experience of death is being emptied (the "death of death" as Taussig terms it [80]). By turns surreally modern and wistfully postmodern, Taussig struggles to articulate the spiritual conditions of the State's Being, a spirituality that has made the Nation as baffling as it is natural. Taussig describes his approach as "pilgrimage," which evokes both the sense of spirit and the investigative zeal of the traveling theorist. That we are not all on the road together is clear. Indeed, this explains in part both the prominence of anthropological and ethnographic research in transnational cultural studies and the vectors of power that can make even the imaginary state a symptom of elites on the move. But again this is a necessary risk as well as an explicable condition. We should not be surprised at this time that reflexive ethnographic fieldwork can epitomize the imaginary as method, for in the ruins of the colonial moment it was ethnography that first realized that its fieldwork is also "homework" as Kamala Visweswaran puts it, the process through which the West itself becomes the subject of its investigation "elsewhere."[25] The lessons of such reflexivity are many (and often the necessity for homework must preempt the fieldwork at stake), particularly since concepts of imagination do not arrive "free" of certain epistemological and aesthetic baggage which has been as much a part of the West's art of objectification, its orientalism, etc., as the force of arms was crucial to colonial invasion (Taussig points out that the liberal democratic state is always already a violent state).

The major theory of imagination is so tightly bound to Enlightenment philosophy that it is hard to use the word without conjuring immediately the entire framework and logic redolent in romanticism.[26] The Kantian imaginary, for instance, finds in the sublime the convenient if not always comforting benefit of projection; that is to say, aesthetic judgment itself is a creative power, not an intrinsic property of the object of that judgment. It is a projection as a mode of identification, an imaginary relation which is the vehicle for ideology and a circuitous path to its content. The imagination, in this mode, is an immense overreaching that compensates for an estrangement with nature. In the imagination, one can heal the affective faculty for the enjoyment of beauty in a world that increasingly denies that sensate Being. But not for long. One of the ironies of the romantic imagination is that the components that offered flights of fancy simultaneously reveal the weight of social obligation ("should not reality be more like this?"), and thus the sovereign Subject was all the more necessary to assert rational control, the mantle of reason. One does not erase beauty or the sublime, for their brief apprehension is part of the very machinery of Subjecthood, the Subject, as Foucault reminds us, of subjection. To disparage the imagination, therefore, is to undermine the ideological reflex of Subject Being. The rub, of course, is that in the imagination one might glimpse the eclipse of the very Subject which gives to imagination its logical necessity. As with classes, so with ideology—domineering modes of socialization foster their own gravediggers. And thus, while the Kantian imaginary develops the codes of refinement redolent of bourgeois taste, it also reveals the propensity for crisis and revolution, or the kind of imagination that writes the "Mask of Anarchy" (later in this work, I will link this imaginary to the rise of a specific commodity).

Or indeed, the imagination that powers *The Magic of the State.* I am not suggesting that a counterhegemonic imagination is necessarily romantic. Far from it. I would contend, however, that various modes of modernity, however different, seem to turn on an imaginary realm that threatens their Being. Surrealism, for instance, was an aesthetics of the Other that fought the Subject's inevitable invocation of the Same. This was its attraction for Walter Benjamin, and many others since, for the montage of fragments denies the whole that the Subject is not and blasts away at its fetishistic impulses. But this is also a quandary for a global imagination. We know that specific discourses of the Subject can project worldliness, but we seek identities or modes of subjective states of being that do not depend on the Subject's reason for their globality. The difficulty of such imagination is that, in the absence of a sustaining ideology of identity, its suprasensible desire can be adduced to the Subject once more, which recodes it in its own image, just as the world's rich diversity can be packaged as a multicultural curriculum in major institutions of learning.[27] Most global cultural critiques gesture to the realm of the imagination but are unsure of its implication for knowledge or for politics. For instance, in their excellent collection, Rob Wilson and Wimal Dissanayake opine that "the 'transnational imaginary' comprises the *as-yet-unfigured* horizon of contemporary cultural production by which national spaces/ identities of political allegiance and economic regulation are being undone and imagined communities of modernity are being reshaped at the macropolitical (global) and micropolitical (cultural) levels of everyday existence. Given these macroeconomic transformations underway, can there emerge strategies of 'transnational solidarity' within such a space?"[28] The *as-yet-unfigured* are the imaginary states of my title, for the insurgent imagination wants to figure a new sense of the world that is not and cannot be a New World Order. Yet without coming to terms with the imaginary, however this is construed, it is difficult to see Wilson and Dissanayake's subsequent question as anything but a luxury. In his Afterword, Paul Bové describes the moment of global/local as an interregnum, and it seems to me this is a valuable characterization.[29] The question of the transnational is set as a task not as a space that has in essence been cognitively mapped (to borrow from Jameson). The advantage of the global/local conjuncture Wilson/Dissanayake explore is the demand it makes on the faculty of imagination which, if anything, emphasizes that the imagination is indeed at stake in combating the illusory unities of global integration through capitalism. What conditions of imagination might further the claims of the transnational imaginary that is their central concern?

The transnational imaginary is structured by its cognitive impossibility much more than by its perceptual prowess. This difference itself may mark two quite distinct categories of experience. Our "being in the world," as Jameson puts it,[30] was determined by its representability—the maps were cognized and made visible by the aura of the knowable that demanded them. The modern, for better or worse (and usually the latter in the nexus of capital and colony), is characterized by a certain self-assuredness on the question of representation that is only challenged at its avant-garde and nonconformist edges (in the opposition to realism, mimeticism, and conventional representational aesthetics). But even these latter modernist moments of angst and activism appear decidedly realist from the wobbly vantage point of our contemporary media simulacra. For Jameson, the present provides for a "geopolitical aesthetic" shorn of its order of representation. The political unconscious is insistently disconnected from the mediatized image of events even as the imagination strives to allegorize their portent, in Jameson's model, in the service of a conceptual refashioning of being-in-the-world. This is a provocative theoretical move, although for readers of Jameson, the political gainsay is familiar; namely, the imagination of what is otherwise an unrepresentable totality. Savvy theorists visibly recoil at the proximity of global and total in Jameson's dialectics, but for my purposes it presents the following formulation. Imaginary states are certainly "attempts to think the world system as such," (4) but they are agonistically local *and* global in their cultural effects. While they are not allegories of dysfunctional national cultures, they do play out a desire to transgress the codes of Nation. Thus, the geopolitical aesthetic is not just about the underbelly of questionable modes of global integration, but it foregrounds in a positive way the perceptual limits on what "global" can mean at this juncture. We are already so used to reading this in terms of the contingent and the conjunctural (to ward off all those nasty predictive narratives) that the imagination seems frozen in cognitive hesitancy, anxious about any programmatic implications outside the direct concretization of the moment.[31] I believe, however, that imaginative constraints actually prefigure all this contingency theory and that the transnational imaginary is material evidence of, to reword James Clifford's assessment, our predicament of *global* culture.[32]

Cultural studies has become a major arena for theorizing the transnational imaginary not just because of its reflexive manner of investigation (which, sooner or later, was bound to be repositioned by critique of its national configurations) but because its conceptual rethinking of culture is itself a linchpin of interrogating forms of imagination. Accepting the limits of location that must accompany such cultural analysis, its geopolitical import might actually lie in its imaginary criteria, perhaps even in the traces of its own political unconscious, rather than in the tactical realignments evident in the manifest content of its high profile debates. For instance, the exchange between Ien Ang and Jon Stratton, on the one hand, and Kuan-Hsing Chen, on the other, in the pages of *Cultural Studies* represents a laudable attempt to come to terms with the exploded discourse of Nation in global analytics.[33] Ang and Stratton argue from a well-defined transnationalist position in which the disarticulation of Australia as a Nation State proceeds through a strategic defamiliarizing of its state-driven identification with Asia toward a more critical sense of what they call the "cultural imagination of 'Australia'" (19). Chen's response acknowledges the value of their desire to reconfigure Australian culture studies outside or at odds with the agendas of Nation, but he also profoundly doubts whether this constitutes a properly transnational cultural politics. Chen wonders aloud whether "'international' cultural studies actually means the nation-states of the English speaking settler's world" (40). Furthermore, Chen remains suspicious of a resistance to class analysis in transnational critique, which he links to a general aura of "post" polemics in American academe in particular. Like many intellectuals "outside the teaching machine" of the Euramerican axis, Chen is critical of those American theorists who are "willing to isolate themselves quite comfortably 'on campus,' creating this gigantic imaginary universe in which they unconsciously situate themselves at the center of everything they are talking about" (41). But while I would agree with the tendencies he sees (because of or despite my own location), it is not clear whether this argument is actually relevant to the particular form of transnationalism Ang and Stratton advocate. In addition, if we are to understand the material conditions of knowledge production, it will not do to conflate these with whatever economic or political power is structured in dominance at a particular locale.

The value of Chen's criticism, however, lies beyond his hasty generalizations about theory and location. Cultural transnationalism risks reproducing dominant modes of globalization merely by pluralizing its critical grid. As Chen points out (in part using Arif Dirlik, who is a progressive political voice despite his affiliation with an American university!), even postcolonial thought echoes the theoretical moves of incorporation through integration redolent in European models of worldliness. The danger is that recognition of the Other is a projection onto the Other, a projection that constitutes the subject as the very justification for its transnationalism. This is how Chen sees "Asia" produced in the Asianing of

"Australia" proposed by Ang and Stratton. In the main, however, the major differences in this exchange are not political but procedural. The two arguments
share similar objects of critique: global capital, the Nation State, and various lin-
eages of Eurocentrism. Substituting internationalist for transnationalist really does
not get us out of the woods where counterhegemonic discourses are concerned.
Nevertheless, the terminological disputes do hint at alternative visions of globalism which may ultimately prove to be mutually exclusive. It remains questionable at this stage, for instance, whether the theoretical procedures of postcolonialism actually undo the geopolitical structures of the world system (merely
stating that the latter do not exist does not prove the case in terms of global capital, or indeed with reference to the vestiges of a persistent military-industrial
complex). This is in part why postcolonial identity is a controversial theme of
this book. The answer is not better policing of the terms (and here I disagree with
all three thinkers), but a better understanding of historical process.

Seen in this light, cultural transnationalism is a provisional register of a process that history itself may do well to redefine. Perhaps we could acknowledge
this by using cultural transnationaliz*ing* rather than another *ism* whose half-life
is determined by theory's profusion (it has already been suggested that the use of
transnationalism itself signals the eclipse of postcolonialism as a theoretical concern). Alternatively, Jameson may blur significant distinctions in the stunning
sweep of his theoretical framework, but his notion of a geopolitical aesthetic
maintains an imaginative grasp of the historical complexity that overdetermines
theory itself (including his own). Ang and Stratton recognize the modest role of
theory in general and cultural studies in particular, but the challenge of transnationalism continues to be to unthink the processes through which hierarchical
concepts of the global are reproduced. This is where an agonistic or dialogic
imagination may intercede.

I have suggested that an imaginary state does not collapse the inequities of the
world system as currently construed, nor indeed the logics that gird the Nation.
It may serve as a guerrilla epistemology, however, in destabilizing the rationale
that gives to the Nation its form for Being. I should add that disrupting a particular principle of this kind does not deconstruct the uses of Nation. Aijaz Ahmad,
for one, has been at pains to point out that the Nation form has had a strategic
advantage at different moments in history in the liberation struggles of many of
the world's oppressed.[34] In the anticolonial movements that flourished in the
twentieth century, Nation discourses were mobilized in imagining communities
outside colonial "beneficence." There is always a strong odor of arrogance when
theorists boldly declare that nations are only a ruse of identity from which the
newly freed masses will awaken. While I strongly believe that we will never see

human emancipation globally while we depend on nations locally, the historical yearning of nations has clearly counteracted and defeated specific modes of domination. What the imaginary state does is exceed the logic of Nation whenever it ossifies into dogma or irrationality for its putative beneficiaries. Under the sign of globalization, the necessity for this form of polemical excess has emerged as paramount. The twilight of nations will be long, certainly longer than it takes to disarticulate the idea of Nation itself. The question is, how imagination can provide a progressive resource in that decomposition and facilitate the progressive transformation required.

Worlds of cultural difference are vast and amorphous; their very variegation defies assimilation. Imagination too is limitless in its application, but for cultural transnationalism its defining characteristics are more precise. In Raymond Williams's *Keywords* the explication for *image* is squeezed between *ideology* and *imperialism*.[35] I would not want to make too much of the coincidence of alphabetical order in Williams's tome, but it seems to me that an entire history of domination and resistance is written into the space that "image" occupies. As Williams notes, there is a significant historical tension between image as copying and its cognates in the imaginary and imagination. Yet for both ideology and imperialism, that structural difference in interpretation is either collapsed or masked so that, for instance, the social reproduction of relations of domination occurs as if the imaginary is the real without contradictions. If we think of Althusser's discussion of ideology as an imaginary resolution of a real contradiction, then the necessity of image between ideology and imperialism becomes clear.[36] But the compulsion to copy, or image, the relations of domination puts imagination at a premium, for it describes both the imaginative leap of the exploiter that such practices are not indeed exploitative and the propensity for collusion of the exploited who might imaginatively adapt to the conditions of exploitation. Williams concludes his entry: "It is interesting that the implications of imagination and especially imaginary are kept well away from the [mid-twentieth-century] use of image in advertising and politics" (158–59). Indeed. One of the most important contributions of cultural studies has been to elaborate the complex relations between the ideological possibilities of the imaginary and imagination with its function for image markets and political discourse. Media studies in particular has focused on this vital coordinate in cultural production and many of the key works in cultural studies are contributions to knowledge on the question of mediatization, or the imaging of the national and international public sphere. Yet there is also a sense in Williams's remark that cultural critique suffers from its devaluing of the mental conception of imagination vis-à-vis the more concrete structures of image production and dissemination. Again, this is not a desire to sublimate the social within the semiotic but to come to terms with the desires that imagine the world otherwise and by that act contribute to counter-hegemonic and alternative ways of being and seeing. Not all imagination is at stake here then, but those acts of imagination that offer a different transnational imaginary than the logic of image as desire only for the commodity form. In this way, while analyses of image markets will continue to provide cultural studies with a significant and effective raison d'être, much of the evidence for thinking globalization differently more generally comes in those creative discourses that exceed their national prescriptions in contradistinction to the cultural flows of trade.

Like Lavie and Swedenburg's analysis of third time/space, cultural transnationalism emphasizes the in-between and the conflictual. How borders are transgressed is as much an imaginative condition of possibility as it is a concrete articulation of social Being. In *Borderlands/La Frontera,* Gloria Anzaldúa struggles with the alienation that traditional *mestiza* consciousness brings.[37] Against this she invokes *Coatlicue,* the Serpent Skirt of Aztec mythology. (As Anzaldúa explains, "The suffix '*cue*' means skirt and is a word to describe a lady. '*Coatl*' not only means serpent, it also means twin" [95].) *Coatlicue* offers a powerful image of inspiration. The goddess is represented as a woman whose head is actually two rattlesnakes facing each other. She wears a necklace made of open hands and hearts (the one symbolizing giving, the other, pain—particularly of birth, but also of everyday life). She has snakes where her hands should be—indeed, the snakes act as claws. *Coatlicue* is a symbol of ancestral and local knowledge deployed by Anzaldúa to register her identification with Aztec culture but also her divided self within *mestiza* reality. Importantly, it is also a state of mind, something that allows those affected to take stock, to understand the situation they are in. Anzaldúa explains that "We need *Coatlicue* to slow us up so that the psyche can assimilate previous experiences and process the changes. If we don't take the time, she'll lay us low with an illness, forcing us to 'rest'" (46). *Coatlicue* is a mark of psychological paralysis, a kind of mental stasis that shakes one out of the torpor of acquiescence to the pain of the everyday or normalized. What Anzaldúa calls the "*Coatlicue* State" is this prelude to heightened awareness, a state in which her identity will either fragment or disintegrate in the face of adversity or reform with those fragments into a more resilient, conscious, and what I would call answerable, sense of self. If she does not answer to *Coatlicue* she will remain "a stone," frozen in the roles apportioned her. On this level, the imaginary state is a state of trenchant awareness.

Every increment of consciousness, every step forward is a *travesia,* a crossing. I am again an alien in new territory. And again, and again. But if I escape conscious awareness, escape "knowing," I won't be moving. Knowledge makes me more aware, it makes me more conscious. "Knowing" is painful because after "it" happens I can't stay in the same place and be comfortable. I am no longer the same person I was before.

No, it isn't enough that she is female—a second class member of a conquered people who are taught to believe they are inferior because they have indigenous blood, believe in the supernatural and speak a deficient language. Now she beats herself over the head for her "inactivity," a stage that is as necessary as breathing. But that means being Mexican. All her life she's been told that Mexicans are lazy. She has had to work twice as hard as others to meet the standards of the dominant culture which have, in part, become her standards. (48–49)

The "*Coatlicue* State" is only one form of creatively addressing the transnational, the hybrid, or the liminal selves of the interstitial, the in-between.[38] While it would not do to elevate this state into a transnational archetype, Anzaldúa's imaginary process of selving has some important lessons for cultural transnationalism in the present work. For one thing, whatever the lived reality of global capitalism, the cultural unconscious is not necessarily dependent on its iconography; indeed, to some extent, while the invocation of the ancient is not outside the forces of commodification, *Coatlicue* stands in an ambivalent relationship to commodity desire (it is the shock of the old). Second, whatever the inspiration of Aztec culture, the new hybridity of borderland identity is not posed as some existential nirvana, as if the old and the new, the original and the refashioned resolve their apparent duality in an unproblematic mental mix (Anzaldúa is insistent that facing pain is difficult and that the imaginary state that she describes has a "third perspective" beyond its component parts or their synthesis). Third, the mental struggle of being Chicana is constantly set as a task because knowing does not simply accommodate the self to its new situation, it provides questions. Fourth, this interpretation about the imaginary state affirms that "moving" is geographic and geopolitical, the "crossing" has a space at stake, but that territory problematizes what counts as "home" mentally and physically. Perhaps the imaginary state is always alien to an actual state (say, the United States in Anzaldúa's example) but its main act is its effort of understanding of being in the world. Finally, and most importantly, the "*Coatlicue* State" engenders the self in a profound way, using icons and symbols where language, as Anzaldúa points out, is a male discourse. Again, at a time when capital is interpellating "Third World" women as its major labor resource of superexploitation, feminist articulations of Being otherwise are at the forefront of imaginative alternatives. Here the imaginary is not a retreat from the real, but a ground for its conscious reconceptualization.

Anzaldúa's book is much more than the coordinates sketched here, but it does provide an ardent inspiration regarding my main theme. Writer/critics like Anzaldúa often set the terms of engagement for cultural transnationalism because they do not divide off their own experience of the liminal from an aesthetic and theoretical commitment to understanding its logic. Frankly, the question of multicultures within Nation States is as old as those states themselves: The vital fulcrum of analysis, however, is to what extent the new relations of globalization render the integrity of those States as currently construed effete. We are social beings and even as nomads we define ourselves in a roving community. These are what Salman Rushdie has referred to as "imaginary homelands," where past and present homes are rearticulated.[39] The world of the macropolitical rarely concedes that these homelands are viable, for their realization would entirely change how the world is ordered, how communities of interest define themselves in relation to others. The Nation's grip on the imaginary is not simply malevolent, of course; the identification frameworks provided do offer a logical consistency for many people on the globe. But, just as the Nation was born of the logic of modernity, so it is destined to die with its prescriptions. Cultural transnationalism is not a handy formula for what comes next, but it does betray an interest in imaginative explorations of possible worlds in which to live: communities that are imagined transnationally.

The Case Studies

Imaginary states embody something of what Stuart Hall calls "metaphors of transformation." He explains:

> Metaphors of transformation must do at least two things. They allow us to imagine what it would be like when prevailing cultural values are challenged and transformed, the old social hierarchies are overthrown, old standards and norms disappear or are consumed in the "festival of revolution," and new meanings and values, social and cultural configurations, begin to appear. However, such metaphors must have analytic value. They must somehow provide ways of thinking about the relation between the social and symbolic domains in this process of transformation. The question of how to "think" in a non-reductionist way, the relations between the "social" and "the symbolic," remains the paradigm question in cultural theory—at least in all those cultural theories (and theorists) which have not settled for an elegant but empty formalism.[40]

It seems to me that Anzaldúa's deployment of the "*Coatlicue* State" elaborates this desire for transformation in both her Being and her theory. She imagines an identity that is not bound by its prescribed roles in a masculinist, homophobic, classist, and bigoted social formation. Anzaldúa knows that to experience difference differently often questions a hegemonic rendering of the social and the symbolic. It does not guarantee an identity beyond, for instance, the Nation, State, or

Nation State (for this takes considerably more than the naming of an imaginary state), but it does serve to highlight conditions of emergence, and this is of considerable value in and outside forms of cultural theory.

What I would like to do now is sketch out some of the implications of this conception of the imaginary state for the case studies to follow. My primary aim is to clarify the conceptual range of imaginary states by addressing specific sociocultural trajectories. Each case study provides different lessons for cultural transnationalism in terms of both theory and practice and as such can be read as stand-alone pieces. Yet their combination might give a more elaborate sense of the "agonistic liminality" of alternative globalisms even within those worldly discourses like transnational capital that believe somehow the die is cast.

In many ways, the Caribbean is the archetype for nonprescriptive cultural transnationalism precisely because the exact conditions of its transnational emergence are unreproducible (and it is therefore a trenchant lesson in the differential logic of the global/local matrix). Mapped historically by ignoble vectors of power, its politics of identity, however nationally defined, hinges on the specificity of the tortuous journey Paul Gilroy describes as one from "slave ship to citizenship."[41] The spatial awareness of position and "home" is crisscrossed by traces of uprootedness and displacement, the mark not only of the Middle Passage, but also the violence of "discovery" (the annihilation of the Caribs and Arawaks) and the legacy of plantation economics and ideology. While the Caribbean archipelago is not unproblematically postnational, it nevertheless embodies four elements that are crucial to elaborating differential cognizing (hybridity, diaspora, postcoloniality, and fragmentation). Specifically, the first three chapters analyze key components of Caribbean nationhood in the writings of Glissant, Brathwaite, and Condé. I do not imagine these writers "talking" to one another in any formal or unified way (although they have sometimes addressed each other's work directly). I am more interested in their symptomatic displacement of conventional modes of narrativization of the Nation State. In my previous work I have suggested that Glissant's notion of "antillanité" (Caribbeanness) builds and breaks from the perquisites of Martinican identity through a variety of technical and artistic innovations (including *langage-choc, opacité populaire,* and a form of cognitive remapping that is itself a challenge to a Jamesonian interpretation). This study expands on that theme through a formal, textual, and historical account of the different and differentiating ways of narrating Nation currently imaginable in the archipelago.

Obviously, by highlighting writers from Martinique, Barbados, and Guadeloupe I have already registered a certain incredulity to normative island identification. These islands repeat disjunctively (in Benítez-Rojo's sense[42]) in the imaginative schema of the writers I discuss. For Brathwaite, a Nation Language is not just a poetic de-scription of colonial homogenization: It is part of an aesthetics of voice that constantly reconfigures the multicultural and crosscultural realities of Caribbean identities. He does not have some dubious liberal-pluralist gumbo in mind but offers a polemical riposte to the languages of authority that were installed by colonization, the Middle Passages that place diaspora under the sign of brutalization. Yet Brathwaite also goes on to elaborate how this might help identify his Bajan consciousness in situ, rather than just sublate it for some "greater" whole (again, the island repeats and does not simply deracinate the specificity of individual rootedness or localism). For Condé, this knot of representation is overcoded in two specific ways. On the one hand, the "exploded discourse" of modernity (as Glissant would call it) has offered a multiplicity, a créolité, that defies narrativization (which is to say that, in Condé's novel *Crossing the Mangrove,* the emphasis is on the process of crossing rather than a completed act); but on the other hand, decolonizing desire accentuates unfinished business that national identity often denies—gender hierarchization for one (although all three writers also consider this in terms of ethnicity and class). Condé imagines a state beyond France, but one that must answer its own patriarchal constructions. In a sense, this "answers" some of the masculinist logic in both Glissant and Brathwaite's thinking and complicates any hasty notion of Caribbean integration (economic, cultural, and political). Glissant's poetics of relation remain a challenge, however, not because their opacity hides plodding old patriarchy but because, like Condé and Brathwaite, Glissant cannot imagine a Caribbean identity that could possibly carry the burden of Nation as currently articulated. In event, this does not make the Caribbean some backwater of modernity, but imagines a Caribbeanness that either exceeds modernity's more pernicious reach or multiplies it in innovative ways. In the "imaginary states" of these writers, we begin to register a discrepant syncretism, one which insistently defies the constraints of conventional nationhood. This discrepant syncretism is a primary scene of investigation.

With the rise of multiculturalism seemingly commingled with the remains of former colonial literary formations, the postcolonial writer is often interpellated to fulfill a contradictory and impossible subject position. On the one hand, the writer is often celebrated as an insider vis-à-vis her native culture, as an informant who illuminates the very essence of what counts for a representative identity, as it were, from the outside. But this celebration is often transnational and is particularly prevalent in those national formations whose histories include imperial or colonial othering of those very "same" natives. On the other hand, the postcolonial writer so hailed is also the writer whose diasporic journey (often from the Rest to the West, but not exclusively so) immediately marks her or him as an outsider or as marginal to the culture she or he is read to "speak." It seems to me that part, at least, of this contradiction is founded not simply on the binary opposition of the Rest/West articulation, but on the fragile Nation logic that demarcates cultural cartography. Problematizing the postcolonial writer does not deliver her or him to the "true, true name" of an originary Nation or subsequent Nation State but demands a sensitive dependence to alternative imaginative criteria. Such has been my point about Anzaldúa, but it must be qualified and clarified according to specific conditions of emergence.

The next analysis builds on the lessons of the Caribbean critiques, particularly in terms of the crisis of the Nation idea, but also in relation to certain Western phantasms of the feminine. My work on "The White of Algeria" begins an analysis of a paradoxical space of silence (a corollary of the doubled/troubled meaning of "white" in Assia Djebar's use of this title in French, a presence as absence, a "filled" area that is also a blank). While most of this reading will elaborate the notion of the scriptible voice as a delegitimation of Nation as patriarchy, I will also frame Djebar's imaginative engagement in terms of a North African vacillation on the function of Islam for the State (set against the backdrop of historical crisis in the civil war). While Islam does not inexorably block capital accumulation (and therefore economic integration into primary and secondary world trade), it can be positioned ideologically as a national defense from various forms of Westernization. "The White of Algeria" is, in this sense, Djebar's rumination on whether Algeria can be written through a vibrant interrelation of indigenous and moving cultural relations (Berber, Arab, French, etc.) or whether it is to be written on or over by a geopolitical logic for which its "blank" state is a blank slate for some other national agenda. The chapter closes with an analysis of cultural reconfiguration in Algeria's crisis, one in which elements of diasporic métissage can be recoded as Nation defense while at the same time circulating within the complex discourses of cultural exchange. To some extent this plays out the dilemmas of Djebar's own migrant identity in France or the United States, but the point is to explicate the structural compulsions of transnational imagination (the imagiNation, let us say, of imagination).

The aim in the first part of the book is to read specific imaginative criteria as a challenge to the normative and sovereign subject of Nation identity. I am not, however, interested in advancing this argument as an either/or stratagem about nations. Simply put, however much I emphasize the restless liminality of the transnational imaginary, it is not simply outside a national, if not nationalist, identification. Algerianness can mean both Djebar's embrace of traditional Berber women's songs *and* the cut and mix polemics of an Algerian migrant youth sampling rap with Arabic in a Parisian banlieue (Gross, McMurray, and Swedenburg's analysis of Franco-Maghrebi identities is exemplary in this regard[43]). Similarly, in my previous work on the dub poet, Linton Kwesi Johnson, the Caribbeanness at stake in his art does not exclude Black Britishness but places it in a transnational dialogic about the function of national identity.[44] What cultural transnationalism emphasizes are the possible worlds in which globalization can be taken up, not some zero-sum game in which individual national identities are trashed over vague notions of world citizenry. Ultimately, of course, there is a political interest in deconstructing the policed boundaries of national formations (as Edward Said has argued, the integration of the globe entails a new sense of global responsibility, or answerability), since these often mask repressive forms of transnationalism. In addition, imaginary states situate the particular predicament of the local and the comparatively "fixed." For the critic in particular, all this talk of the transnational should not obviate a commitment to the micrological realities of the local, as if the roving identities of the migrant, the traveler, the diasporic, or the refugee are all that is left subjectivity. In this light, the second part of the book will focus on two forms of cultural reconfiguration that shift the perspective on cultural transnationalism to questions of the commodity. In these examples, the imaginary state is crystallized by an explosive commodity market as "emerging" economies are rapidly integrated into circuits of global capital. One difficulty for cultural transnationalism is to separate the euphoria of commodity aesthetics from the range of meanings in which nations are being redefined. The challenge, which again is set as an imaginative task, will be demonstrated in the "symptoms" of this section: the athletic shoe and coffee.

These case studies bring me back to the questions with which I began; namely, those which address the cognitive limitation in imagining the world outside its constellation for hegemonic economic exchange. I will not preempt their major argument here, but I do want to indicate why they appear alongside four chapters on literary transnationalism. Conventional representations of transnational culture often achieve prominence because they refuse or disavow the logic of imagination that makes them possible. This is particularly true of the commodity in transnational trade. The thingness of the thing is not just a problem of philosophy, from the Kantian sublime to the reverie of Baudrillardian simulacra, but a condition of cultural exchange. The accumulation of cultures as "things" does not automatically constitute cultural knowledge or an expansion of understanding of difference on a world scale. Various analyses of the museum or similar archives have addressed this elision in some detail. What I attempt in the first chapter of this section, "Chronotope of the Shoe," is an elaboration of a critical apparatus more adequate to the actual conditions of a global imaginary—that is to say, a time/space that allows accumulation to intensify through desire and disavowal. In the chapter on coffee, I consider whether what is everyday in a mass-consumable commodity is actually founded on a linchpin of the incomprehensible in the commodity as form. Both commodities at issue playfully disrupt borders and are transnational *avant la lettre,* but they obviously do not mirror the transgressive logic of my other examples in any simple way. Indeed, part of the challenge of "Imaginary States" is to come to terms with how cultural expression and commodity circulation can share the rubric of cultural transnationalism within the same cognitive space. It is not the case that capitalist commodities simply overreach or sublate the imaginative zeal of postcolonial creativity, but neither can my literary examples exist outside the aura cast by commodity desire. By this I mean more than the fact that words and books are also consumables: I wish to advance the idea that to think cultural transnationalism is to deconstruct both the Nation/Subject binary and that which would forever separate the imagination *about* the commodity from the imagination that in a significant way *grounds* the commodity. Obviously, this is a difficult maneuver since my chapter divisions themselves seem to preserve the antimonies that have advanced the sway of the commodity in our epoch. Yet the attempt, at least, is to see whether criticism can learn both from the perspicacity of artistic expression and from the effort of imagination required to understand what builds and undoes the Nation at this time in more conventional international trade.

   This theoretical move bears comparison to Adorno and Horkheimer's analysis of the culture industry and a more general Germanic strain of commodity aesthetics from the Frankfurt School to Wolfgang F. and Frigga Haug. Wolfgang Haug, in particular, has focused on the links between the production and control of sensuality and commodity markets, especially those that proffer a veneer of luxury or status.[45] Indeed, when we talk of globalization, we are simultaneously invoking a specific form of interrelation in cultures tied to the circulation of desire, commodity desire. If Haug's critique of the advertising industry is less interesting today, some thirty years after his initial research, it is because cultural studies and the social sciences read the connection between power and desire as much more unstable and much less likely to guarantee "control" within the culture industries. This is partly an effect of French poststructuralist thought with its concern for the volatility of meaning and signification, but it also reflects an acknowledgment of the massive differentiation among consumers and producers on a world scale that deeply problematizes capitalist logic and its alternatives. Just as postcolonial writing constitutes an agential discourse regarding how to "be" otherwise beyond colonialism (which I also read as a desire to think borders differently), so the analysis of commodity narratives can dispel the myths of global homogeneity under the sign of capital. Of course, worlds of difference can also be marketed through commodity aesthetics (the Benetton thesis once more), but imaginary states seem to question the logic of packaging itself, whether by country or consumables. By looking into the heart of capitalist logic, what Karl Marx calls "the metaphysical subtleties and theological niceties"[46] of the commodity, one finds the imagination that is at stake in culture is also at issue in the commodity form, and that cultural transnationalism must account for the crisscrossing vectors of transnational trade (Do commodities imagine nations? How?) and the more common conduits of cultural transaction. Of course, to make such links is itself an act of imagination that I hope will traverse these chapter divisions.

Eschewing handy formulae of cause and effect, I argue that cultural transnationalism can trace the logic of connection in globalization even if it cannot assume a political constituency from such emerging connections. In this respect, I trust cultural transnationalism is closer to dialogism than dogma. Perhaps Jameson is right to believe that the chief limitation to a properly transnational imaginary is a cognitive failure to think the totality.[47] Perhaps those theories of totality have cast a long and enduring shadow over alternative modes of "mapping." But the magic of the Nation State no longer seems so magical, while the global village of capital does not offer egalitarian community, and thus cultural transnationalism can only proliferate as people in various places and spaces try to imagine their logic of Being and connection otherwise, for this too is how we "entify life." The imaginary state always begins with the negotiated realities of the global/local nexus. It is to those realities that these studies are dedicated.

The Agon of the Archipelago: Three Forms of Crossing and Caribbeanness

The question "What is the Caribbean?" comes with the indemnity and contradictions of conventional categories of Being. It is not the truism of multiplicity that is at issue so much as the specific forms of disjunction and difference produced by Caribbean history, geography, and culture.[1] These are defining features of Caribbean identity, yet to provide a formula or definition of identity from them appears to betray the actual processes of island identification in the archipelago (that oscillate between "island" as isolation and as transnational). Politically and theoretically this raises a very difficult problem: on the one hand, to attack identitarian formulae associated with Western categories of Being, those in particular coterminous with colonization, slavery, and plantation rationality, would seem to be in the spirit of an ardent struggle of decolonization in which the Caribbean emerges as a deconstruction of a specific ontology of domination; on the other, the play of identities, the chaotic plurality that weighs on the *is* in "What is the Caribbean?" threatens to unravel even radical forms of subjectivity so that, unintentionally or not, the archipelago comes close to becoming once again that blank space of asubjectivity to be filled by discourses of appropriation and assimilation. The unraveling of the colonial "I" remains an imperative in the Caribbean because of the persistence of social structures of domination, not only in those islands that remain Western territories but also in those that assert postcolonial difference in the face of indifferent tourism and neocolonial desire.

But what of the Nation? Do we, by asking "What is the Caribbean *nation*?" subvert or confirm the contradictions of Being implied above? Again, the multiplicity of islands has followed different trajectories of independence and nation formation, reflecting both the function of elites in particular states and the long shadow of foreign influence. (So, even as one might make superficial comparisons between, say, Cuba and Jamaica regarding the development of sugar plantations, the national identities that emerged from colonialism can be sharply differentiated.) A politics of nation in the Caribbean has always had to begin with the legacies of class and ethnic composition bequeathed by structures of colonization and the economies of race that were fundamental to the policies of displacement, settlement, and eradication in the "New World." Every subaltern constituency has had to fight both the colonial idea and continuing *comprador* collusion in forming a nation (for instance, a national economy may be driven by export oligopolies controlled by the same family or corporate elites that prospered under "dependence"). And, of course, every attempt at more radical social democratization has made the Caribbean nation an integer of geopolitical machination (Haiti, Cuba, Grenada, etc.). Perhaps, this is merely to confirm Aimé Césaire's observation that "the *nation* is a bourgeois phenomenon"[2] and forever suffers from its ontology and episteme, but I also want to maintain a sense of radical dissembling and agency; that is, that the Caribbean is simultaneously the scene of intense rearticulations of national identity and identitarian formulae more broadly construed (particularly now, in the great wake of the cold war). The process of negotiation is the key issue: one "crosses" the Caribbean as one crosses out debilitating notions of subjecthood. According to this view, the agon of the archipelago is neither the end of colonialism nor the triumphant end of the Nation State. And yet Caribbeanness can promise precisely both.

It is partly for this reason that Antonio Benítez-Rojo has argued for a postmodern Caribbean, by which he means that the logic of island identity exceeds or repeats itself beyond normative notions of Self. The structural logic behind the "repeating island" is driven by the experience of plantation ideology, which supports his view that the "quickest route toward defining a substantial form of Caribbeanness is not the cultural one."[3] The plantation is a socioeconomic formation that places a heavy burden on unifying concepts of Caribbean culture as such: it codifies and separates, permeates and dissociates; it is a colonial engine of otherness. Yet the subsequent force of Benítez-Rojo's argument is to link this logic to what he calls the "supersyncretism" of the archipelago, the specific modes of combination made available through the collision of diverse cultures afforded by the colonial system. This simultaneous placing together and pulling apart has a corollary for Benítez-Rojo in Chaos Theory, although on this point one would have to offer several pertinent equivocations. If we are to argue for Caribbeanness as transgressive, as defying ontological orders of sameness or origin, does this imply a nonagential discourse, or multiple forms of agency? The beauty of Chaos Theory is that it can explain processes of indetermination in determination—that apparent structures of disorganization and unpredictability do indeed evince repetitive patterns and surprising models of dynamism. In *Oscillate Wildly* I considered some of these issues in terms of materialist theory and, like Benítez-Rojo, I found Chaos Theory provocative if not revolutionary.[4] My point here is to question the transformation of a scientific exploration into a cultural metaphor. There are ways indeed that the plantation may be seen as a "strange attractor," but given the history of oppression and brutality done in the name of plantation economics, the invocation of Chaos is an odd distractor which tends in its sweep to marginalize the agency that resolutely opposed and defeated colonial regimes in the Caribbean over at least two centuries. So, while I would argue for the pertinence of "the notion that there are fragments of a great number of possible orders coexisting in a space that has no law and geometry: the space of the heteroclitic, of chaos"[5] it is surely inadequate to the actual processes of human interaction. Can we hold to the idea of the Caribbean as a "heterotopia" of sorts without eliding the work of social change or the people for whom that work is set as a task?

On this point, Benítez-Rojo's account recommends itself again, for in a series of provocative readings he interprets writers like Guillén, Ortiz, Carpentier, and Harris as working through chaos, as imagining its possibilities without succumbing to the lethargy produced by its mere scientific inevitability. Since these writers are cultural producers (rather than mere describers), perhaps we should distinguish the principle of chaos from its strategies of deployment. The latter, I would suggest, are ways in which the Caribbean can be reimagined, methods of rearticulation dependent upon the precise position and moment of intervention (the "utterance context" to borrow from Bakhtin) and are in the main antihegemonic. One cannot live by chaos, but one can encourage its imaginary state in the face of the Order of Othering resplendent in the colonial and neocolonial imagination.

The strategies I have in mind cannot be schematized (except perhaps in Borges's ironizing quotation from a Chinese encyclopedia) but this is not just the virtue of what Benítez-Rojo calls "the decentered center of the paradoxical"[6] that the Caribbean can be read to represent. However much the Caribbean is a postmodern zone of engagement, the forms of deconstruction this necessarily engages do not subsequently add up to a unified set of tactics for cultural praxis. Furthermore, while the following readings of specific Caribbean writers is intended to be a contribution to our understanding of cultural transnationalism, the imaginary states implied are only aspects of a counterdiscourse, not that idealist terrain where culture announces itself as the preeminent form of social struggle (here I concur with Paget Henry and Paul Buhle's other cautionary account of C. L. R. James as "Caliban the deconstructionist"[7]). I will, nevertheless, argue for the crucial contribution of imagining Caribbeanness in disabling a persistent territorializing of the Caribbean basin in terms of social and economic subjugation. And, while this agon

in the archive is not easily reconciled with even the postcolonial aspirations of nation building, I will explore some of the lessons of such desire.

The push and pull across the space of Caribbeanness as concept and form of
national identity manifests itself in forms of paradoxical rootedness and wandering, nativism and nomadism. Even a manifesto of supersyncretism like *Éloge de
la créolité* (published in *Callaloo* as "In Praise of Creoleness") enacts a "double solidarity" that both defines and exceeds the Caribbean.[8] Bernabé, Chamoiseau, and
Confiant suggest that Caribbeanness is a geopolitical principle of unity in the archipelago, but it comes with the reality of a Creoleness which recognizes links with
African, Asian, Macarin, and Polynesian roots. A nation, under such circumstances,
must be a very fluid if not irrelevant notion of affinity. Creoleness expresses an
ambivalent nativism because it is formed primarily through the experience of ex-
ogenous peoples, those for whom exotopy or outsideness is a condition of forced
displacement or settlement (as they note, "We are fundamentally stricken with
exteriority" [76]). One could quickly respond that surely this is not unlike Americanness, which is not best described as disabling the Nation State? The authors
of *Éloge de la créolité* understand this very well and acknowledge a distinct overlap in the forms of hybridity that Creoleness and Americanness represent (93). Yet
these hybrid states depart significantly in terms of socioeconomic trajectories—
vectors of culture and commerce that differentiate the forms of combination possible. Even if one omits the literal fragmentation of Caribbean space, the islands
repeat (Benítez-Rojo) toward Africa and Asia, whereas national unity to the north
has depended on a hegemony of European affiliation, despite the mask this places
over American diversity. As such, Creoleness is posed as "the world fractured but
recomposed," (88) which implies a different identitarian notion from E Pluribus
Unum. Just as we are quickly understanding the Caribbean as postmodern *avant
la lettre* we must yet realize that it offers an alternative mode of globalization—
"to live a complex Creoleness is to live the world" (110).

The refracted whole of Creoleness as a "diversality" certainly recommends itself over the kinds of universality sedimented in Eurocentrism. Yet Bernabé, Chamoiseau, and Confiant also claim a foundational stance for Creoleness in the
development of Caribbeanness, so that the latter appears almost as an epiphenome-
non of the former. Just as there can be no single model of Caribbeanness, so the
motor of its diversity should not be ascribed to an omnivorous logic of cultural
expression. I believe Creoleness works better as an acknowledgment of the aggre-
gate of sociocultural forces in the Caribbean than as the actual expressive identity
that they may produce; that is to say, it can draw relevant attention to the key
components of the Caribbean as a contact zone but cannot exhaust or encompass the possible combinations that are in fact produced. To be fair to the authors

of *Éloge de la créolité,* they admit that *créolité* favors an initial grouping within the Caribbean, the "creolophone" peoples of Haiti, Guyana, Martinique, St. Lucia, Dominica, and Guadeloupe. They suggest that this will be a prelude to a larger union with the anglophone and hispanophone communities of the archipelago (certainly the political and economic momentum for this supersyncretic federation has intensified since the cold war and particularly as a result of greatly reduced U.S. financial backing in the Caribbean). To maintain a positive cultural valence to Creoleness, therefore, we should assert that its dynamism contributes to rather than defines Caribbeanness. The poetics of relation in the latter also offer an alternative socioeconomic dimension.[9] This is at the heart of "crossing," and so let me outline some of its possibilities before proceeding with the clarifications and qualifications that the case studies within this argument provide.

1. Caribbeanness is the conscience of a space. It is a spatial logic of connection, not an integer of geographical location per se. If one of the major problems in the application of Western theory in particular is that it *locates* the margin, Caribbeanness crosses the borders of that fixation. It does not simply imagine a territory, but destabilizes the territoriality of subjection.

2. Caribbeanness is a turbulent concatenation of rhythm and dissonance. It places great importance on musical lines but also on the cultures of orality that have sung them. It answers the deconstruction of writing with the deconstruction of voice, sounds that are nonrecuperable within a discourse of origins. It recognizes, as Brathwaite underlines, that the "hurricane does not roar in pentameters" and thus explores the explosive cadence of speaking without the Subject. This does not mean the obliteration of an individual voice (to hear Brathwaite recite a poem is to be schooled in the necessity of individuating voice) but it is instead a sonorous emphasis on dub identity and "versions" of the voice.[10] The repeating island has a correlative in the repetition of sound, in the echo of "noise" as Benítez-Rojo describes it. Orality and versions are key components of Caribbeanness. Both instantiate its vocal local while also throwing the voice beyond the strict confines of the Nation idea.

3. If Caribbeanness is about process, about an intercultural and transcultural dynamic, then this must inevitably weaken island identity and a nationalist political paradigm. Yet federalist maneuvers, like the formation of CARICOM in 1973, have met with mixed success because of interisland competition and because of external geopolitical "restructuring" of Caribbean relations (like CBI—the Caribbean Basin Initiative—a brainchild of 1980s Reaganism). Does this make Caribbeanness a debilitating ideological projection, an imaginary resolution of a real contradiction? Caribbeanness is not outside ideological refraction: This is precisely the risk of imagination as a social practice. But the question of the imagi-

nary here does not resolve itself into the negative associations of ideology as delusion, mystification, or misrecognition. The imaginary interrogates the legitimacy of the Caribbean's social orders: It is an integer of desire for new identities more than a rationalization of a specific status quo in subjecthood or statehood.

4. Caribbeanness describes a matrix of political possibilities, but to the extent that these are produced within a cultural politics, they do not form a blueprint for political change more broadly construed. I would suggest, however, that in its class, gender, race, and ethnic configurations, Caribbeanness explicitly contests the representation of the Caribbean as a conglomeration of neocolonial outposts, or as a placid object of the tourist's gaze. Challenges to gender inequality, for instance, are provocations both to local institutionalized patriarchy *and* to a pious Euramerican investigation of Caribbean women as oppressed victims somewhere else on the globe than in America or Europe. If Maryse Condé does not eulogize Caribbean (or, for that matter, African) gender relations, neither does she allow this to guarantee entrenched discourses of objectification that always find social strife elsewhere. Caribbeanness opens up political debate by considerably broadening who constitute the interlocutors. The point for cultural transnationalism is not to take over that "conversation," but to foster rather than inhibit its dialogic implications.

The following readings focus on three writers: Édouard Glissant, Kamau Brathwaite, and Maryse Condé. Given my argument for Caribbeanness so far, each writer interprets, extends, and contradicts the concept in specific ways. I am particularly interested, however, in how they politicize their aesthetic stance on Caribbeanness and directly challenge the inclusionary zeal of Western modes of appropriation (in a kind of normalizing multiculturalism for one). By choosing two francophone writers I may seem to be supporting implicitly Bernabé, Chamoiseau, and Confiant's claims for a French-derived *créolité,* but that is also where Brathwaite's intervention on questions of Creole remains pertinent. All three writers raise significant issues about "crossing," nation, and Caribbeanness as a logic of connection in their own experiences of displacement and diaspora. My interpretations are neither introductions to their work, nor a survey of even their most prominent writings to date. As cultural workers of great distinction, however, these writers offer profound lessons for transnational cultural analysis in general and the study of Caribbean culture in particular. I will begin with Glissant, space, and the Caribbean's relationship to postcoloniality.

1

Glissant and Opaque Space

A postcolonial Caribbean? Even if one sets aside the extremely complex colonial history of the Caribbean occupation or the anticolonial movements of the last two centuries or so (at least back to 1 January 1804), the question of postcolonialism remains problematic, for many of the islands of the Caribbean still labor under the paternalist ministrations of the Western colonizer: The béké still has a material presence in the Antilles today. Surely then it is a misnomer to call Édouard Glissant a postcolonial writer, since under departmentalization or the glitzier "economic assimilation" France exercises a neocolonial interest in Martinique and the other islands of the "French" Antilles? I am thinking, however, of Glissant as a theorist of the postcolonial condition in the making, as an agent provocateur of that being or becoming "Caribbean," as a *quimboiseur* (storyteller) of that state-in-process if not statehood.[1] Thus, while I am sure he disagrees with the term (and with good reason), I will use it to interrogate its parameters, its logic of space, its transformative possibilities. Glissant is an expert in thinking this cartography as an active component of the lived relations of the postcolonial subject—a subjecthood highly resistant to colonial rationalism. In this way, rather than codify postcolonial Being, Glissant opens up perspective on its internal logics, the fierce simultaneity of connection and delinking that characterizes its purview. While I will have cause to remark in some detail about the implications of Glissant's notions for race, gender, and class polemics, his first lesson is about the politics of space or, more specifically, the conscience of a space.

Martinican space is complex net of landscape and memory, or rather, memory *as* landscape. It would be relatively easy to sentimentalize that space, as if history were a search for that prelapsarian identity before it was colonized, departmentalized, or regionalized by a European order of Being (France). Glissant does not entertain that daydream (such folkloric reverie has a name, *doudouis-*

me). Even in his novel *La lézarde* (1958), where the central trope and character
is a river, the emphasis is not on its source, despite the glowing prose associated
with Thaël's mountain home, but on linking—on the way that flows connect
but also on the sense that they hold things apart (the crack, *la lézarde,* in consciousness).[2] To elaborate Martinican space Glissant does not propose just repossession (although obviously legal possession is a paramount issue) but a
material understanding of how a decolonization of the mind entails a spatial logic
of connection and separation (in the same way that the islands of the Caribbean are distinct land masses, yet strung together as an archipelago in the sea, a
collective chain of identity in difference—*un champ d'îles* (a field of islands) to
borrow from the title of one of his poetry collections). Glissant is not always
sanguine about the possibility that such an understanding can be communicated (this is one of the lessons of his novels *Malemort* and *Mahogany*[3]), partly
because memory has been experienced as a rupture, as a *dis*location (a pain suppressed or internalized as quiescence or ennui), and partly because there is no
discrete or coherent language in which landscape/memories can be written. But
if each sentence comes with its own crack or impossibility, it is also an opening,
or space for negotiation—so that the trauma that informs the African Caribbean's "irruption into modernity" (as Glissant terms it) is also the moment of
Martinican *histoire à faire.* History can be made, and otherwise. The task of the
writer in this sense is not to occupy the space of history, but to make space for
history. Bound by the contradictions endemic to language, the density of se-
mantic flux, Glissant yet pushes against a certain impossibility, that the text
embodies this conscience of a space.

Space in Glissant's work is initially thematized quite literally as landscape. It
is the mountains and salt plains of Martinique, it is the vital rivers that cut through
the earth to the sea, it is the rain forests, the silk-cotton tree, the (now absent)
acoma, the mahogany (all of which are operative symbols in Glissant's cross-cultural poetics, his poetics of the relation[4]), it is the cocoa tree and the sugarcane
(vestiges of slavery and dubious commerce), it is a flora and fauna of rich variety, and most of all it is a coastline that traces the sea even as it is traced by the
Caribbean's flow. Glissant follows Aimé Césaire is this project, for, like Césaire
in his elegant and polemical *Cahier d'un retour au pays natal* (Return to my native land),[5] landscape is an active component of self-analysis, not the frozen exoticism of a tourist snapshot: "The relationship with the land, a relationship that
is even more threatened because the community is alienated from the land, becomes so fundamental to this discourse that landscape in the work ceases to be
merely decorative or supportive and is inscribed as a constituent being. To describe the landscape is not enough. The individual, the community, the land are

inextricable in the constitutive moment of their history. Landscape is a character in this process. One must understand it in all its profundity."[6]

Clearly Glissant does not claim this geographical aesthetic as the monopoly of Martinican consciousness; what he does suggest, however, is that a sense of the land's integral formation of Martinican Being is essential to any notion of Antillanité at this historical juncture. The characterization of land textualizes space in such a way as to affirm that there is land at stake in Martinican identity, something that has previously been lived or represented as dispossession—that which you cannot or should not have. The diasporic intellectual, that often lauded but equally misunderstood hybrid of the (post)colony, has not turned her or his back on the essence of land in her or his political purview but frequently (and a list here would include Césaire and Fanon in one generation and Ngũgĩ, Spivak, Emecheta, Said, and many more in the contemporary moment) has gained perspective on a particular space in leaving it. There is a return, of course, either physical or imaginative (naturally, the contours of exile shift from writer to writer), but spatial thought remains endemic to what the writer is or must become.

The conscience of a space is discernible in many writers of the Caribbean, including most notably Carpentier, Harris, and Brathwaite, but there are several distinguishing features in Glissant's contribution to this epistemology, and these include aspects of his biography and Martinican history. Glissant was born in 1928 in Saint-Marie, tucked away in the hills of Martinique, far from the bustle of the colonial stage-post, Fort-de-France. A desire for formal education would eventually bring Glissant down to the plains, an inspiring experience, for at that time Césaire was teaching at the Lycée Schoelcher and Frantz Fanon was a student there. This influence on Glissant's political outlook cannot be overestimated (much of the decolonizing spirit in Glissant's subsequent poetics can be traced to the nexus of Césaire and Fanon's thought). Of course, the presence of a Vichy-controlled government on the island during World War II only sharpened his resolve about Martinican independence. While still a teenager he coformed a political and cultural activist group, Franc-Jeu, and provided significant support for Césaire's election campaign in 1945. The heady idealism of this moment, however, barely outlasted the war, and Glissant went on to take a doctorate at the Sorbonne in 1946, the year Martinique fell under the sway of France's *département* policy. Now he would learn about the representation of colonial and colonized space from the outside and this would become a time not just of learning but of literary production. Glissant's early conceptions of space date back to this time, not just in his essays, collected in *Soleil de la conscience,* but in his books of poetry and his first novel, *La lézarde,* which would win the prestigious Prix Renaudot in 1958. Just when it might seem that Glissant had established himself in francophonic

belles-lettres, his activism for the political group, Front Antillo-Guyanais pour
l'Indépendence, would earn him notoriety of a different kind. Seeing threats to
its colonies here, there, and everywhere, the French government refused to allow
Glissant travel documents for Martinique (or Algiers either). Between 1959 and
1965 Glissant could only imagine the landscape of his Caribbean. But, I would
argue, Glissant experiences the disruptions of exile in two stages. The first would
include analysis of his realization of space as crucial to the termination of colonialism; the second stage, however, would necessitate a confrontation with the
political inertia taking hold of many Martinicans. Glissant's return to Martinique
shatters many of his political illusions not just about the process of decolonization but about the mindset appropriate to that transformation (this is something
of Condé's experience on returning to Guadeloupe in 1985). While the argument
here will remain necessarily speculative about the detours in Glissant's thinking,
I am interested in the ways in which Glissant negotiates the disjunction between
his own activism (literary, organizational, etc.) and the more general aura of quiescence he perceives in Martinique's "regionalized" and "assimilated" contemporary condition. Is the spatial conscience he offers simply abstract (in that long
tradition of French aesthetics whose avant-gardes could often only dream of an
active presence in mass consciousness)? If so, would not this feed suspicions that
postcolonial discourse itself is an elitist conversation among privileged intellectuals that, in the final analysis, can offer little or nothing to dislodge the ruling
orders of the West (colonial or otherwise) or can inspire those whose agency would
precisely undo that rule (the rule that says that no other order will do)?

Glissant's spatial awareness draws attention to the Caribbean's cartographic link
and separation from Western orders of experience. The link, not surprisingly,
begins with enslavement and displacement, with annihilation (of Arawaks and
Caribs) and occupation, war and dependency. It was not easy for colonial hegemony to hide or erase the memory of more than ten million slaves from Africa
and thousands upon thousands of cheap laborers from Asia. The emergence of
modern space simultaneously meant the emergence of the Caribbean archipelago as a vast string of labor camps, a serpentine sweatbox called upon to sate the
avaricious empires of Europe. The Martinican slaves were "freed" in 1848 (although they were escaping and mounting revolts before that official liberation),
but the memory of servitude continues to inform or deracinate all attempts to
make a new collectivity, a new sense of self.[7]

Although a close reader of negritude, Glissant does not primarily propose a spiritual return to an African homeland (yet he remains deeply interested in the African roots of culture in Caribbeanness), nor does he suggest a sweeping decolonization through language (a pure Creole would be a contradiction in terms), but

an alternative knowledge of the community self must begin with the land, which offers its own forms of delinking. Commenting on the Martinican experience of space alongside that of Africa, Glissant notes: "We, as islanders, don't know that dizziness of the land [the vertigo of African space] we prevent this giddiness by shrinking it, we must contract our space in order to live in it. Our scope is determined by the sea, which both limits and opens one's mind."[8] The mode of identification emerges in a relationship with the land; indeed, Glissant explicitly states that memory itself is conditional upon such identification ("it is like plowing the earth and planting one's tree"[9]). The land is a repository of memory. In *L'intention poétique* (Poetic design), for instance, Glissant suggests that the ancestors, the heroes of Martinique's past, can be conjured from the soil—their lives are precipitate in the rocks scattered around the island and await Martinicans to invoke them. Similarly, in *Pays rêve, pays réel* (Dream country, real country), Glissant notes that "La terre seule comprend"[10] (only the land understands). The land is a source of knowledge and connectedness. As Wilbert Roget has argued, this theme is consistent between Glissant's essays and his novel writing in particular (indeed, a similar case could be made for the poetry, especially that of the 1950s) and constitutes a mythopoetic chain of Being.[11] For Glissant the quintessence of this relationship is the tree, as metaphor and as a reality of landscape.

The cliché about the tree of knowledge does not begin to comprehend the memory/landscape logic that Glissant builds into his poetics. Glissant names his first journal "Acoma" after the tree that once graced the Martinican forests. His first novel, *La lézarde* (*The Ripening*) insistently makes the scenery, and trees in particular, a register of a character's realization of place (the *fromager*, the silk-cotton tree, for instance, becomes a point of rendezvous, for plotting, for decision making, and so on, so that it is hard to separate the landscape from the political intrigue—which will lead to an assassination—being played out upon it), a word that "takes root" as it were, in the narrator:

> there is in me this root which I try to pull out, but it is too firmly lodged and my strength fails me. When I can place my hands on its rough surface, when I can pull with an irresistible force, when my memories are quiet and strong, scattered into words and richly-flavored, then the place will appear to me in the precise quality which is its own; and all the miseries by any reckoning will not exhaust the account, and all the beauty here destroyed by the urgency of struggle and birth, all this will appear on the beach of an immense world as a tree whose foliage draws gently on its sap, like a banyan tree whose innumerable branches wrap the sea as it wishes.[12]

This is not some romantic reinvestment in the primordial force of nature (the eloquent riposte to the rationalistic plod of modernity), but a poetics of location.

Simply put, since the genocide of the Amerindians there has been no population on the island with a symbiotic relationship with the land: for the slaves, it was something they were forcibly brought to and placed upon; for the owners, the békés, it was a means to an end; for the indentured servants, it was something they worked around; for no one has it been an inextricable part of their Being, the very fabric of their subjectivity, their island identity. This is the first lesson of Glissant's polemic: that independence, true independence, not masked neocolonialism, assimilation, or cultural imperialism, begins with a psychic rootedness in the land, an intricate and alternative consciousness of possession (something that must pre- and postdate legal possession). Again, if Africans were literally uprooted through the violence of colonial logic, then Glissant's response is forceful connection, not necessarily with a mythic African past (for much history was also butchered in the Middle Passage), but with the world where he finds himself, the landscape where he can lose the Self of a different order of Being, the one imposed by colonialism that produced the Other through an ontology of dispossession.

Rootedness of this kind appears as a powerful symbol of Antillanité and stands in sharp contrast to the ideology of return found in Rastafari, the roots that lead from the Caribbean to Ethiopia. This is not to say they are simply antithetical, for both are forms of counterhegemonic discourse, but their difference does underline that Caribbeanness is not experienced univocally or unproblematically. One must add that Glissant's landscape identity can be read within an economy of masculinism, an ideology of penetration and phallic law that would seem to mitigate against the disarticulation of the Law of the Father resplendent in the colonial Self. I will comment further on the implications of a gendered reading of postcolonial politics and poetics in due course, but here let me point out that Glissant consciously reads rootedness against the grain of its almost inevitable logic of phallocentrism so that it is the system of roots, connections, and the regenerative cycles of the tree that are ultimately emphasized over and above the phallic certitude of, for instance, the trunk. Beneath the ground the roots spread out (in that tangled complexity of the rhizome articulated by Deleuze and Guattari—thinkers familiar to Glissant[13]) and defy the ability to totalize their connectedness. In Glissant's fiction in particular, the tree is a witness to history, but it defies any interpellation as history, the history of colonial rights from which it dissembles and against which it survives.[14]

Glissant's novel *Mahogany* underlines that the tree does not simply embody the positive elements of anticolonial insurgency. Frederick Ivor Case has suggested about Glissant's conception of landscape that "the land gives direction but confers ownership on those who establish a relationship that is both economic and moral"[15] but one should add that this moral question is not self-evident or generated by just "being there." Mahogany (which in French of course is phonetically very close to "my agony") is an American tree and, as Alain Baudot notes, is "a landmark, the emblem of a space recorded in time, at once witness and guarantor of successive generations."[16] In Glissant's novel it is witness to successive acts of resistance and escape (at three moments, 1831, 1936, and 1978) by three characters whose names form its name in a variety of ways, Gani, Maho, and Mani. The mahogany functions as a place of refuge and as a point of reference, it orients the characters and readers in Martinican space: "Un arbre est tout un pays, et si nous demandons quel est ce pays, aussitôt nous plongeons à l'obscur indéracinable du temps, que nous peinons à débroussailler" (13). (A tree is a whole country, and if we ask what is this country, we immediately plunge into the ineradicable obscurity of time that we work to clarify.) Yet the tree does not just mark the escape (*marronnage*) crucial to Martinican identity, but measures various stages of defeat and death—the escapees do not survive the escape. In addition, "my agony" is a secret knowledge barely perceived or understood by those who must relate to it, indeed, those who are the bearers of its deepest implications. The various narrators in the book do not announce a unanimity about the significance of the history experienced or recorded but instead offer a vision of contingency in identification: "Parfois nous perdons la trace. Parfois elle se dédouble. Le plus souvent elle se perd dans une touffaille de végétation où nous enfonçons nos corps, plus raides que nos esprits" (251) (Sometimes we lose the trail. Sometimes it is divided in two. Most often it is lost in thick vegetation where we push our bodies, which are stiffer than our spirits)—this, too, will characterize the multiple voices of Condé's *Crossing the Mangrove* in their struggle to articulate its anti-hero, and indeed the nature of the mangrove itself. The contingency is compounded in the last sentence of the novel: "Selon la loi du conte, qui est dans l'ordre des arbres secrets, je vivrai encore longtemps" (252). (According to the law of the narrative, which is in the order of secret trees, I will live again for a long time.) The mystery is not offered as mystification, but as opacity, and it is to that aspect of Glissant's theory that we now turn.

Opacity for Glissant is not just an aesthetic prerogative, that is, that his fiction, drama, and poetry are self-consciously difficult as a mark of experimental élan, or avant-gardist pretension, but is a fairly developed cultural technique of decolonization. First, opacity resists the notion that the Other can be assimilated to the colonial Self—it is a direct intervention against the logic of recognition and denial that structures colonial authority, even accepting Homi Bhabha's rejoinder that such a logic is not monolithic, but is in fact febrile or ambivalent.[17] This is not a question of "native" inscrutability but a problem of unresolved identity formation in Martinican experience. If Glissant's prose is opaque it is both because assumed transparency has provided a window for colonial control (power as knowledge) and because he struggles to find a language adequate to the depth of the rupture in identity endemic to what constitutes a Martinican voice. If there is an authenticity to this language it is only in the recognition that such authentication is deformed in the very tenor of its syntax, in the very texture of its existential crisis. Indeed, the actual process of writing as Glissant describes it is *in*authentic, for the writer is a "forceur de langage" (DA 22), one who is trying to bring a language to existence (and therefore develops a forced language) rather than one who expresses a language. As Michael Dash has noted, "Its [Glissant's writing] main attribute is not destined to be clarity or accessibility. It is the articulation of a collective consciousness trying to be, to find expression" (CD xxvi)—to which we might add Glissant's suggestion that "Il y a poétique forcée là où une nécessité d'expression confronte un impossible à exprimer" (DA 236–37) (There is a forced poetics where a need to express confronts what is impossible to express).

A second point about opacity is that it is predicated on a counterdeformation, in this case by disrupting the fluidity and expressibility of the French language itself. For the Martinican there is something in the country's culture that French, as it is, cannot express. In perhaps a familiar move, the colonial language itself must be deracinated, made strange in order to make it new: "The Antillean writer will have to disintegrate—break up—the French language and try to restructure it for his own use. This is a must. The French language cannot be used as it is. It is absolutely necessary to violate it at the written level. It is absolutely necessary to obligate it to express something other than what it is equipped to do."[18] The perquisites of this guerrilla writing are outlined in *Le discours antillais* and are worth quoting at length.

> Against the sterile neutrality of expression which constrains Martinicans, the work of the writer is perhaps to "provoke" a *langage-choc,* a *langage-antidote,* not neutral, through which the problems of the community can perhaps be expressed. This work can require that the writer "deconstruct" the French language which he uses (and which is one of the "fundamental facts" of the situation); first through a demystifying function in relation to any fetishistic use of this language, then by a search for *lignes de force,* or defining structures, cultural projects, whose nature through the very interior of the French language would be to facilitate (by clarifying them) future uses of a (written or) revitalized Creole.
>
> . . . It is not a question of creolizing the French language but of exploring the responsible use (creative practice) that Martinicans could make of it.
>
> The function of the writer as a researcher and explorer in such a context often isolates him from everyday language and, consequently, from the "average" reader. (DA 347)

This is fascinating for several reasons, not least of which is the implication that the writer must, in fracturing French, confine himself to oblivion in his own culture. It comes as no surprise perhaps, even with the inevitable irony that accompanies it, that Glissant's writing is best known and most actively read within the French intelligentsia whose enthusiasm, like mine, is almost beside the point. As Glissant has commented elsewhere, his Martinican readers exist in the future. While Glissant is certainly not cut off from his most immediate audience (his work for the Institut Martiniquais d'Études, which he founded, has allowed him a pedagogical base and public forum for his ideas), in general his writing is not best described as populist and in that respect bears a remarkable (and perhaps unfortunate) resemblance to the forays of previous French avant-gardes (including notables like André Breton, whom Glissant met in Martinique in the 1940s) who struggled in a sometimes obtuse manner to marshal popular sentiment. I will maintain, however, that the opacity that Glissant here describes is *popular* (*une opacité populaire*), to the extent that it seeks to express a general and genuine dilemma in Caribbean identity, something that Glissant certainly shares with the other writers of the archipelago, but also, even when unspoken or unread, with large numbers of its population. Glissant's French often actively resists the normalizing of French on the island and challenges the notion that French, as it is, is somehow the natural mode of expression. In opposing the neutralizing tendencies of French, however, Glissant does not offer a creolized French (or, indeed, a francophonic creole). In part this is because he believes the colonizing impulse of French can be weakened from within French itself. Yet Glissant also believes there is a fundamental dysfunction in contemporary Martinican Creole that he describes as "the language of neurosis." Once a secret language, Creole no longer corresponds to the lived reality of Martinicans. For Glissant, its power and intelligibility have weakened in direct proportion to Martinique's dwindling productivity and the more this occurs the more verbal delirium (*le délire verbal*) Creole invites. French may well be the "langue imposée," but Creole is the "langue non-posée" (nonsituated). The objective conditions for Creole's revitalization do not exist in Martinique today, although in Glissant's comments about bilingualism and multilingualism he obviously maintains a future for some form of Creole discourse.

Opacity's third dimension is its diversionary provenance. Glissant claims that diversion emerges in the disorder created by unchallenged processes of colonization. The reason for this constrained opposition lies in the mode of oppression itself: "Le détour est le recours ultime d'une population dont la domination par un Autre est occultée: il faut aller chercher *ailleurs* le principe de domination, qui n'est pas évident dans le pays même" (32) (Diversion is the ultimate resort of a population whose domination by an Other is hidden: It then must search *elsewhere* for the principle of domination, which is not evident in the country itself). With the precise enemy seemingly unlocatable, the population may resort to diversionary tactics (Glissant uses the example of the creative capacity in Haitian Creole, a language of the trickster, to accentuate this point). Glissant also cites the ideology of return redolent in the work of Césaire and George Padmore as diversionary, a camouflaged response to the real differences that exist between Caribbean and African populations. Caribbean negritude becomes a displacement for a concrete politics of opposition and which actually proves more inspirational within African discourses of liberation. Glissant comments only that this is a "peculiar fate," but clearly he wants to distinguish Antillanité from Pan-Africanism to maintain the integrity of both. Even if Glissant's own theorization of Antillanité is not diversionary (and the skeptic may maintain it is, in light of the difficult path to mutual responsibility and support among Caribbean nations today—despite or perhaps because of Caricom), then one might productively view *opacity* as diversionary according to Glissant's own definition. He avers that "Le Détour *mène donc quelque part,* quand l'impossible qu'il contourne tend à se résoudre en 'positivités' concrètes" (33) (the strategy of diversion *can therefore lead somewhere* when the obstacle for which the detour was made tends to resolve itself into concrete 'positivities'). The positivities obtain, I would argue, in the resituation of a responsible cultural and political subjectivity that Glissant's writing promotes and to some extent enacts. The opacity here is a form of praxis, a practical investigation of (post)colonial potential, the *pulsion* within the French language taken to an extreme anticolonialism. Of course, if it leads absolutely nowhere then we are confronted with a diversion of the negative kind, but Glissant remains realistic (and humble) in his understanding that the intellectual herself cannot preempt the concrete possibilities in which opacity might become an operative politics beyond poetics. The point in suggesting the quasi-oxymoronic "common opacity" is to underline the density and richness of a discourse that signifies a widespread disjunction in Caribbean Being: How can one write what is unwritten in speech that is simultaneously, since it is a submerged or repressed narrative, largely unspoken? Caribbean writers have produced several provocative responses to this dilemma (Brathwaite's nation language, Bernabé, Chamoiseau, and Confiant's créolité, and Derek Walcott's creative schizophrenia, for instance), but it is Glissant who has, more than any other of his generation, attempted to foreground the depth of this disjunction, this splitting or crack in Caribbean consciousness which, for better or worse, conditions the very possibility of Caribbean self-realization and self-determination. In this light, the *opacité populaire* is something akin to what Glissant has written of René Char: "a form of self expression which lies somewhere between that of the pastoral poem and the maxim. . . . the phraseology is familiar and the formulation is enigmatic yet evocative; and this draws him close to the very source of the wisdom of the people, to the world of the writings based on popular oral traditions in which the poet works the raw material of words with same simplicity as a potter works his clay."[19] This is what Glissant terms oral literature (which he compares to oraliture, the Haitian neologism), a literature that is fragmented but, because it draws on the culture of orality, is shared: "La littérature n'est pas diffractée seulement, elle est désormais partagée. Les histoires sont là, et la voix des peuples. Il faut méditer un nouveau rapport entre histoire et littérature. Il faut le vivre autrement" (DA 142: CD 77) ("Literature is not only diffracted but it is henceforth shared. In it lie histories and the peoples' voice. We must reflect on a new relationship between history and literature. We need to live it differently"). Glissant's opacity lies in his negotiation of the difference of oraliture, and of the need to live difference differently. Perhaps paradoxically (given traditions of opacity), Glissant has always sought to produce a communal voice (a measure of what Bakhtin in a different context calls the "we-experience" or more generally the dialogic[20])— le nous—a first-person-plural interlocutor who strives, as in La case du commandeur, not to idealize a community, but to imagine, in all its complexity, why that community has not been.[21]

We are thinking, then, of ways in which Glissant's theorization of Caribbean discourse might be appropriately described as a postcolonial intervention, an insurgent discourse with an alternative sense of nationhood and spatial connection. Among the other elements that are crucial in this regard are the function of history and the place of orality, both of which define the problem of independence in Martinican space. Much of what Glissant says about history he shares with Asian, African, South American, and African American scholarship; namely, that the terms of historical debate are often loaded from the start by the continued reliance on classical Western forms of temporality with their elaborate but necessarily contaminated philosophies of choice intrinsic to the colonial "adventure." The quarrel reminds us of the problem of culture and culturalism and the exclusionary practices that attend certain of their definitions. In this light, Glissant remains appropriately suspicious of French narratives of Martinican history, "centuries, wars, reigns, crises etc." because it is assimilationist—it cathects Martinican Being with French nationhood: It refuses what Glissant calls the "overdetermination" of Martinican history, its inscription through slavery and the plantation.

In this Glissant may sound positively poststructuralist, for it has been poststructuralism that has, more than any other theoretical paradigm, shattered the totalizing pretensions of history and the periodization that girds its image of Europe in the world (or sometimes Europe as the world). Again, however, this would suggest that the disarticulation of Eurocentric thought, in this case, the deconstruction of a Hegelian Absolute Spirit, is primarily a European or North American reflex which, even when it is propelled in part by diasporic intellectuals of postcolonialism (Bhabha, Spivak, Said, etc.), fails to account for the ways in which the various peripheries defined in such discourse have, to borrow from Ngũgĩ wa Thiong'o, "moved the centre." While no one should doubt the familiarity of Caribbean writers with Western thought, one wonders whether such notions as "history is sea" (Walcott), "history is voice" (Brathwaite), or "History is fissured by histories; they relentlessly toss aside those who have not had the time to see themselves through a tangle of lianas" (Glissant, CD xxix) need poststructuralism in its current constellation to understand them.[22] To assume that need, at least, would surely be yet one more White Mythology.[23]

Note that this is a similar criticism to that found among feminist historians: Too much of the conceptual apparatus in history produces margins that elide the specificity of alternate or varied modes of pastness. For Glissant, Hegel's categorizations are particularly egregious in their import, for much of Africa and the Americas are condemned to the twilight of either ahistory or prehistory (like totalizing conceptions of culture, this leaves the peoples of the Caribbean effectively nonhistorical). Glissant does not propose an instantaneous history to fill the void of History but some perspective on how to approach *la trace* of Martinican history through what Dash calls "imaginative reconstruction" (CD xxxii). *If* Martinican history is experienced as "nonhistory," Glissant argues, it is because the historical consciousness at issue was founded on "brutal dislocation," "the context of shock, contraction, painful negation, and explosive forces" (CD 61–62) endemic to the slave trade. The memory of this is something that invites suppression, something that exists either as *boises* ("shackles"; CD 237) in the subconscious, or as a text written into Martinique's "mobile landscapes." This memory is not deposited as a chronology, or as a sequence that exists in linear time, but as a fractured simultaneity, as a "composite" or what Alain Baudot calls a "History in layers."[24] The narrative conflations, or parallel cycles, of *Mahogany* are evidence of this simultaneity in novelistic discourse. In *Discours antillais* Glissant elaborates this sensibility:

> Today we hear the blast from Matouba, but also the volley of shots fired at Moncada. Our history impresses us with stunning unexpectedness. The emergence of this diffracted unity (of this concealed connection in histories) that shapes the Caribbean at this time surprises us before we have even thought about this link. That means

also that our history appears at the edge of what is tolerable, an emergence that must be related immediately to the complex threads of our past. The past, to which we were subjected, which has not yet emerged as history for us, is, however, there (here), it troubles us. (CD 63; see also DA 132)

History emerges in a Caribbean dialectic of nature and culture (hence landscape/memory) and is materialist precisely because of the specificity of that relationship. Thus, although Glissant is explicit in his condemnation of Marxist historiography (for it too has been seen to be a harbinger of exclusionary totalities), his eye for the interrelationships of discursive and nondiscursive realities bears the hallmarks of a materialist concern for history's making and a perception of the real foundations of historical change, even if these foundations differ in degree from the perquisites of Marxist lore. Therefore, when I describe Glissant as a revolutionary writer, it is very much in the spirit of a Césaire or a Fanon (Martinicans of greater repute, to be sure) for whom Marxism was not a digestible doctrine but a raw material to be made anew.

For Glissant, the trauma of the Middle Passage creates in the Caribbean an exploded discourse and an imploded history—the latter is (as Glissant borrows from Brathwaite) submarine. It is this submerged quality that links the islands (once again, history is sea) and traces, if not defines, the notion of Antillanité. Conventional histories of the Caribbean are divisive in the sense that they present its narrative primarily in terms of the colonial borders within it, or the immediate shadows cast by its postcolonial constituencies. Glissant wants to maintain the sense of discontinuity in the processes of decolonization but simultaneously assert the common modalities of identity that flow between and within the islands of the archipelago. Part of the commonality at issue is the trauma of implosion, and Glissant acknowledges the psychological model of neurosis this invites. But rather than dwell on that negativity, Glissant suggests that the "shock" of history provides the means for a trenchant "transversality"—a mutual recognition of interest that is the seedbed for solidarity in diversity, not uniformity or divisions based on colonial compartmentalization.[25]

Orality, of course, plays a fundamental role in this sense of history (just as it decenters the ruling aesthetics of literature) but immediately places Glissant's efforts in doubt. In a footnote he asks, "C'est le moment de se demander si l'écrivain est (en ce travail) le receleur de l'écrit ou l'initiateur du parlé? Si le procès d'historicisation ne vient pas mettre en cause le statut de l'écrit? Si la trace écrite est 'suffisante' aux archives de la mémoire collective" (DA 132) ("Now one should ask whether the writer is [in this process] a 'fence' for the written or an origin for the spoken? If the process of historicization does not raise doubts about the status of the written? If the written record is 'adequate' for the archives of collective memory?" [CD 64]). While not all Glissant's answers to these questions are satisfactory (perhaps because he is a writer first), they nevertheless provide a framework that productively links the elements discussed so far, the landscape, opacity, and historical consciousness.

The vessel of history in Glissant's fiction is often the *quimboiseur*, particularly the figure Papa Longoué, who is a form of textualized griot within his narratives. As a spokesperson who is written, Longoué's "voice" is at once paradoxical and insurrectionary within the texts. He is a spiritual maroon (escapee) whose body exists in the present but whose mind is a repository of all that has been sensed in slave history, right down to the smells in the slave ships. Longoué is not interested in the petty provincialism of Fort-de-France (like Glissant, he is a product of the hillsides), but instead seeks to impart the "longue-durée" of Martinican Being. In Glissant's novel, *La case du commandeur,* Longoué has an epigraph that states "la parole a son histoire qu'il faut fouiller longtemps comme un plant d'igname loin au fond de la terre" (speech has its history that must be excavated [and thought out] over a long period of time, just as one would dig up a yam deeply rooted in the earth [4]). There is then no quick fix or transparency that reveals or produces Martinican history just as, in *La case du commandeur* the meaning of the word *Odono* does not bloom before the reader's eyes: It is the knot of existential crisis that impels the narrative as it breaks apart the Celat family in their quest to decipher it. The voice of history here is what fragments consciousness or enacts a displacement (seen, for instance, in the mythification of Africa in Pythagore Celat's tortured obsessions)—a voice that defies the ability of the speaker to speak it, and of course the writer to write it. Another raconteur in the novel is Anatolie Celat, for whom history is the means not of understanding, but of seduction. The patchwork tales he tells come from his grandmother Eudoxie and, as Barbara Webb has pointed out, stands in for the novel as a whole, *une histoire éclatée,* with no beginning and certainly no definitive meaning.[26]

The opacity of *La case du commandeur* is also evident in Glissant's *Quatrième siècle* (The fourth century), which is a much more obvious tribute to Papa Longoué's powers of narration. As in Glissant's play *Monsieur Toussaint,* here the writer attempts "a prophetic vision of the past" through the words of his central character. Much of the text is concerned with the lessons learned, or not, from Longoué, particularly by Mathieu, whose knowledge is that of conventional intellectualism. Mathieu appears elsewhere in Glissant's fiction and, as a historian attempting to complete a history of Martinique, is clearly Glissant's alter ego on the limits of conventional historiography. That is not to say, however, that Papa Longoué provides either an embodiment of historical memory or indeed *mar-*

ronnage. His declining powers are very much what this story is about, and his death on the eve of Martinican departmentalization, suggests that the mode of his memory may well be a thing of the past.

In a perceptive argument, Bernadette Cailler has questioned Glissant's "exaltation" of the maroon, the "negator" in the figure of Longoué. She asks, "How is it possible for an author, as Master of the Word and manipulator of narrators, narratees, characters, plots, beginnings, endings, imagery, ideology, et cetera, to take up the cause of the oral, collective, popular discourse (even if the idea of a *we* subject and object of discourse permeates the announced intention and, in various sections of the "creative" work, the text itself)?[27] As we have noted above, Glissant is aware of the impossibility implied in his inscription, but the point is worth pursuing because it draws attention to Glissant's precise sense of "oral literature" or "oraliture." The prime characteristic of the national literature Glissant fosters (and I will return to the question of nationalism in the conclusion) is its "irruption dans la modernité" (DA 192) ("irruption into modernity" [CD 100]). What this term points to is a doubling of necessarily irreconcilable aims: first, literature's capacity to connect or inflect the rich history of myth in oral discourse; second, literature's potential to destabilize the colonial imaginary from within its own language (through what Glissant terms demystification). While writing cannot suture the "lézarde" (crack) that separates these aims, it must, according to Glissant, "nourish" the oral or fall prey to the intimation of transcendence (or, one might add, solipsism) common to bourgeois ideologies of the author and authorship. Yet, just as we have noted a contradiction in the opacity of a "popular" discourse, so Cailler points to a possible fetishizing of heroes in the mythology of the maroon, an obsessive interest that even the contradictory subjecthood of Papa Longoué does little to allay.[28]

Despite this caveat, there are several ways in which Glissant has attempted to instantiate, or bring about, an oral conception of literature. The first, most obviously, concerns his theorization of, and production of, theater as a significant cultural mode of intervention. Theater in performance is popular not because of its function as entertainment but because it counteracts the notion that folklore can be revived unproblematically; instead, it attacks "alienated forms of representation" (including folkloric expressions), since folklore itself can only be "lived" as nostalgia and offers instead "a willed effort toward consciousness itself that produces community" (CD 214). This may sound like a little touch of Brechtian poetics in the night[29] but the point is to emphasize the strategic value in tackling the "void" of alienation Glissant perceives in contemporary Martinican culture, the "happy zombie" syndrome. The political efficacy of the opacity in *Monsieur Toussaint* can only be realized in performance through a collective dynamism that is not guaranteed. As Glissant notes, "The problem is not one of whether or not the form is accessible, but whether or not the representation is adequate" (CD 217).

While it is not Glissant's intention to transcribe Creole into his fiction (because Creole is "nonsituated") he nevertheless creolizes his writing through his use of the rhythms and locutions of everyday speech. The inclusion of dialogue in a discourse does not ensure that it is dialogic, since this depends on a more expansive notion of addressor and addressee, but there is, at least, a conscious attempt to draw on the productive heteroglossia in the clash of languages that Martinican multicultures represent. This creolization also draws its sustenance from another "voice," the land which, as Dash has suggested, "offers the creative imagination a kind of meta-language in which a new grammar of feeling and sensation is externalized" (CD xxxv). This reminds us again of the fundamental observation by Brathwaite regarding Caribbean poetry that "the hurricane does not roar in pentameters."[30] Similarly, the structures of Glissant's discourse are inspired by his landscape even as they entertain different orders of mimesis (one might say that Mont Pelée does not roar in pentameters either). The question of oral literature here then is one of embeddedness, for a collective voice emerges in the recognition of a fundamental relationship to the land, in common. Cailler, therefore, is right to aver that the communal "we" narrator, le nous of La case de commandeur, is something of an empty gesture, for by itself it would be just another flash of technical virtuosity or idiosyncratic stylistic.[31] The point, however, is that le nous symbolizes, rather than idealizes, a community that has not been, and oral literature marks that lack even as it strives to voice the "prophetic vision" required to produce a "we" that might mean something more than that absence.

The textualizing voice, then, is a political aesthetic that eschews the privileges assumed in the dominant language (in this case, French) for a contextual specificity rooted in the lived existence of the otherwise colonized population. Certainly, it is a form of resistance literature, but it is also marked by a powerful desire for cross-cultural connection across the languages of Caribbean space. This aspect of Glissant's poetics, the question of métissage, is the one in which his cultural polemic gains its strongest currency. It is a multiculturalism in situation.

Métissage is a condition and process of solidarism, epitomized in the dilemma and potential of Creole. The trenchant dissonance that Glissant achieves in French is in part inspired by the creativity of creolization, créolité, even if it is not synonymous with it. Its practical essence is its orality, its connection to the rhythms of speech that connects the chain of Being that is the archipelago. The dilemma is based on the internal marginalization of Creole within the Caribbean, the prejudice against formal instruction in Creole's various traditions, and the point mentioned earlier regarding Creole's productive correspondence (Glissant's belief is that Creole can only be successfully taught when it is linked to collective responsibility, a concern that emerges in the community when language is part of the productive process, both of things and of identity; otherwise, Creole is a "language of agony"). This aspect of Creole's impasse is problematic, however: One could argue that it smacks of a "chicken and egg" logic that in fact rationalizes Glissant's expertise in French. Does not the choice of French over Creole impede the principle of métissage in the Caribbean?

One answer comes in *Éloge de la créolité* ("In Praise of Creoleness") by Jean Bernabé, Patrick Chamoiseau, and Raphael Confiant (but again, is the level of discussion generated by the fact that this work too is published in French?).[32] For these authors the question is not one of either/or between Creole and French so much as a forceful productivity in the principle of creoleness (créolité) itself. While this would seem to place Glissant in the same spectrum as Césaire (accepting, of course, Glissant's postnegritude positionality) it does not preclude his contribution to the emergent culture at issue: His French functions within the same counterepisteme, it is French against what Bernabé, Chamoiseau, and Confiant call "Frenchification." Similarly, Césaire's predilection for French is not seen as "anticreole" but as "ante-creole"[33] with negritude itself as a conceptual clarification entirely necessary for a new sense of connectedness. The usefulness of Bernabé, Chamoiseau, and Confiant's statement is that it integrates a critique of French into a broader sense of Caribbean space (which again is the meaning and message of Glissant's *Caribbean Discourse*) with all the exuberance of a postcolonial manifesto:

> Creoleness sketches out the hope for a first possible regrouping at the center of the Caribbean archipelago, that of the Creole-speaking people of Haiti, Martinique, St. Lucia, Dominica, Guadeloupe and Guyana, a drawing together which is only the prelude to a larger union with our English-speaking and Spanish-speaking neighbors. This is to say that for us, the acquisition of an eventual monoinsular sovereignty would only be one stage (which we hope would be as brief as possible) on the road toward a Caribbean federation or confederation. Such a union is the only means of fighting effectively against the different blocks of hegemonic calling that divide the planet among themselves. In this perspective we affirm our opposition to the present-day process of integration without popular consultation of the people who live in the French *départements* of America into the center of the European community. Our solidarity is first and foremost with our brothers of the neighboring islands and secondly with the countries of South America.[34]

This, then, is a politics of métissage, to which Glissant contributes an aesthetic purview, a poetics of relation. The pulsion of Caribbean solidarism is not just measured in political declarations, formal or otherwise, but in the internal logic of connection (significantly, Creole is for Glissant "not a language of Being but a language of the Related,"[35] its discourse *explodes*. The centrifugal element in Caribbean discourse is precisely its dialogism, its will to an expansive definition and recognition of what is shared or exchanged in communication. As Bernabé, Chamoiseau, and Confiant note, "Collective memory is our emergency,"[36] that points not only to that dialogic expansion, but also to the sense that one must act on this recognition or risk losing that spatial connection (very much in the spirit of Benjamin's point about a memory seized "in a moment of danger"[37]). The cultural project of métissage must be multivarious because there is no single strategy of interrelation *and* because the principle of solidarity itself cannot confederate cultures or states: It is a basis *for* struggle, not an assumption about the product of that struggle. Ultimately, despite their optimism, the authors acknowledge some of Glissant's skepticism when they note: "We believe that a creative use of interlect [which signifies both multilingualism and intellectual exchange] might lead to an order of reality capable of preserving for our creoleness its fundamental complexity, its diffracted referential space."[38] The subjunctive here is an important reminder that créolité, space, difference, and opacity cannot in themselves guarantee a new order of Being; they can, however, inspire it.

Métissage splinters philosophies of the Same just as it obliterates the last vestiges of the infamous Code Noir. But it also allows Glissant to integrate various aspects of his theory of relation and creolization:

> If we posit métissage as in general an encounter and synthesis between two different entities, then creolization appears to us as a metissage without limits—that is, something whose elements are multiplied and whose results are unforeseeable. Creolization diffracts as well. It is linked in this regard to the explosion of the lands, which are no longer islands. Its most evident symbol is the Creole language, whose genius is perhaps its constant openness to change without ever becoming fixed. Creolization transports us into the adventure of multilingualism and the unprecedented explosion of cultures. But the explosion of cultures does not mean their dispersion or their mutual dilution. It is the sign of their consented partition.[39]

The question of consent is an important one; it is a reminder about the mutual recognition of diversity in cultures and languages, something that has not been the hallmark of the imperial and colonial moments in European identity. In his essay, "Beyond Babel," Glissant details the variegations accorded *relation* in history, including dominant, contagious, tangential, subversive, and intolerant relations. He also provides a summary of the plethora of linguistic situations discernible in contemporary formations of the state. The message of both aspects of his analysis is clear: "Their complexity rules out any summary or reductive assessment of the strategies which might be employed."[40] Yet, if métissage is intrinsically nonformulaic, how can one trace its efficacy in the production of Antillanité or Caribbeanness? Outside the intense "crossbreeding" of Creole and French, how does Glissant explain the potential of linguistic affinities across cultures?

In part this depends upon a distinction between *langue* and *langage* first made in *Le discours antillais,* but then, as Frederick Ivor Case has noted, given a further provocative resonance at a colloquium in Toronto in 1989. Thus, "*La langue* is the means of expression" whereas "*le langage* is the manner of expression and the collective attitude with regard to the *langue* that is used." The difference is an important one that is often overshadowed by a more Saussurean emphasis on *langue* and *parole.* The twist, as it were, is reported by Case: "[Glissant] said that although he does not express himself in the same *langue* as Brathwaite, Walcott, and Lamming, he writes the same *langage* and thus reveals a common relationship that transcends French and English."[41] Although this courts the twin demons of idealism and universalism, the distinction accentuates the concreteness of the Caribbean situation. The experience of no one country or no one writer can stand in for the diversity that marks the whole, but "the manner of expression and the collective attitude" is based on a recognition of that whole as a diversity worth fighting for. Whether as "Créolité" or Antillanité, a similar *mode* of identity is being articulated or desired. Again, for Glissant the idea and the space of the Caribbean mutually define one another: "Qu'est-ce que les Antilles en effet? Une multi-relation. Nous le resentons tous, nous l'exprimons sous toutes sortes de formes occultées ou caricaturales, ou nous le nions farouchement. Mais nous éprouvons bien que cette mer est là en nous avec sa charge d'îles enfin découvertes" (DA 249) ("What is the Caribbean in fact? A multiple series of relationships. We all feel it, we express it in all kinds of hidden or distorted ways, or we fiercely deny it. But we experience this sea within us with the force of newly discovered islands" [CD 139]).

The "we" of this last quote brings me back to the question of postcolonial subjectivity once more, for it would seem that Glissant's Caribbean discourse is a model polemic for identity production. The discourse is marked by an internal distanciation of colonial language; a displacement of temporal logic for a politics of space; a fervent belief in opacity as a subversion of colonial and neocolonial representations of the subject as transparent and assimilable; an affirmation of diversity and multiplicity as highly resistant to philosophies of the Same or the universal; various textual strategies that draw on the dissonant and dissident characteristics of oral culture; a practical application within the public sphere to matters of education (bilingualism), cultural production (theater), and indeed political platforms; and a struggle for a popular consciousness that challenges the "inexorable" slide from colonialism to dependency that has characterized much of anticolonial history. But does the difference that *traverses* the laudable components of Caribbean discourse ineluctably inflect the "we" of Glissant's *énoncé?*

This is not the moment when the White European Male dutifully returns the postcolonial letter of revolutionary spirit with a powerfully hierarchized qualification that proceeds to reassert the very mode of authority from which the postcolonial subject must delink. I am, however, interested in the antiuniversalism of this discourse, its specificity, as a means to address the extent to which it "explodes" some mythologies within cultural critique. If one accepts that the "we" here refers to Caribbeanness, an Antillanité that is itself fissured by difference, then how would this difference be experienced differently by a range of Caribbeans who might take up this position of identity and identification? How might that familiar although not fatuous mantra of race, gender, and class be operative within this position of fractured identification? And how might this "we" speak to questions of nation and nationalism, questions that must inevitably be raised if a cross-cultural discourse is to cross or create borders within the context of its deployment?

Cailler's earlier point about the heroification of the maroon rebel remains pertinent, despite her own qualification.[42] There is now more than a little evidence from other anticolonial histories that such struggle does not in and of itself displace masculinist ideology from within its own history. In Glissant's case this is not just a difficulty within his novelistic discourse (Françoise Lionnet has remarked on the "basically lifeless, distorted, or stereotypical representations of female protagonists"[43] in Glissant's writing) but is part and parcel of créolité and Caribbeanness as currently construed. In this the "father" figures inevitably loom quite large: as Bernabé, Chamoiseau, and Confiant note, "Césairian Negritude is a baptism, the primal act of our restored dignity. We are forever Césaire's sons."[44] Clearly, the issue is not about the central importance of Césaire to Caribbean anticolonialism but whether the restoration of dignity can be separated from masculinist forms of pride. One critic, for instance, appears to celebrate a patrilineal cultural progression even as she points to the patricide it implies: "It seems that the fathers must be killed by their prized sons so that these may fertilize their literary field; could it be that, after Césaire, Glissant's turn will come soon?"[45] This logic, of course, could be extended to the present piece, since it also depends to a great degree on the isolation and celebration of Glissant at the center of an anticolonial episteme. Do women writers of the Francophonic Caribbean (particularly those of Martinique and Guadeloupe) simply mime this paternal metaphor, or does woman's *marronnage* construct a different sense of Caribbean discourse?

The work of Maryse Condé, particularly her *Parole des femmes* (Women's speech) but also much of her fiction, suggests a complementary if not antagonistic sense of self, but in general Antillanité is not an object of gender criticism (despite or because of this it is crucial to the agon of Caribbeanness as my subsequent argument on Condé will underline). In her essay on Glissant, "Name of the Fathers, History of the Name: Odono as Memory," Priska Degras says only that the name of the father, the problem of the Name, in Glissant's work is not about "phallic narcissism" and, even though Odono "incorporates all the Names of the Fathers," the implication of Father's Name for women's subjectivity is never questioned.[46] Instead, and the pronoun object is notable, there is the following: "Edouard Glissant's writing can lead the way down the obscure and difficult path that so many of us have taken and not only bring forth, from the ancient hollow of opacity and misery, islands of light into this chaotic ocean of the world but also bring forth to the light of day that which, in the bottomless ocean of time, constantly tortures and torments us."[47] And then, a few lines later, "Glissant's words, already so far ahead of us, await us like the words of someone who divined there in the depths that which we have yet been unable to see. These patient, obstinate, rigorous, brilliant, and burning words,"[48] et cetera. The way that such issues are raised by Degras (and earlier by Cailler) only to be drowned in effusive praise should make one suspicious; again, not because Glissant is undeserving of these adjectives but because doubts are being raised and dismissed without any explanation. Could this itself be a measure of a gendered cultural unconscious? If Caribbean discourse is a people's discourse, at what moment in Glissant's elaboration of that discourse are those people gendered or is passage down the well-lit path that Degras describes equally accessible whatever crisscrosses one's Caribbean identity?

For postcolonial feminisms such questions are the sine qua non of anticolonial autocritique, but they are often met by the peremptory "first things first." This is reminiscent of Nasserism's valiant displacement of British colonialism in which women fought for that victory but were then told that statehood must have its priorities. The point here is that woman's consciousness is crucially inscribed in Caribbean identity. In their anthology on Caribbean women writers, Pamela Mordecai and Betty Wilson note the following concerns in the various narratives they present: "There is an agenda which refers directly to issues of value: the worth of male to female persons and vice versa; the worth of black persons (or other persons of colour) to other black persons and to white persons and vice versa; the worth of persons who have-not to other persons who have-not, and to persons who have, and vice versa; and finally, the complex of these criss-crossing valuings, for no-one is sexed without race, or 'raced' without class."[49]

While there is no single work comparable to *Le discours antillais* or *Éloge de la créolité,* this agenda of value is prominent in Caribbean women's writing, including francophonic literary production. Simone Schwarz-Bart's novels, *Pluie et vent sur Télumée Miracle* (Rain and wind on Télumée Miracle) and *Ti-Jean l'horizon* (Ti-Jean the horizon), and Myriam Warner-Vieyra's works, *Le quimboiseur l'avait dit* (The storyteller said it) and *Juletane*,[50] all explore this agenda of Caribbean identity, even when not set explicitly among the islands themselves. While there is some evidence of this in Glissant's fiction, particularly in *Mahogany*, such an agenda does not complicate in a significant way the contours of Caribbean discourse as he articulates it. Feminism does not explode his discourse, but it could certainly make it more explosive.

Of course, a poetics of relation is necessarily abstract and, although the level of concretization is quite marked, in general *as theory* the principle of relation does not have to instance every possibility for relationality. Yet it would appear difficult to realize any significant level of Antillanité if the material conditions of the Caribbean (the realm of difference that structures everyday interaction) are merely synonyms for the ground of solidarity that relation points toward.

Race and race difference, for instance, are crucial forms of identity production both within the discursive violence of colonialism and in the anticolonial movements that have disarticulated that discursive formation. Race continues to be a primary category for understanding the fabric of the modern Nation State (particularly bourgeois liberal democracy, although it has no monopoly on racial ideologies of legitimation), whether in formation or dissolution, stability or convulsion. The fact that race is arguably a genetic classification, whereas nation is supposedly a political and social entity, only adds to the insidious nature of national history in general, and colonial history in particular. Glissant knows this history very well, especially as it produces the modern Caribbean archipelago. In one of the appendices to his play *Monsieur Toussaint*, Glissant details how the discourse of race was deployed to smooth the contradictions of French control in the Caribbean.[51] What has always seemed to threaten the regulative discourse of the Nation State (given its racial underpinnings) is miscegenation (the problem of the "one drop rule" in the United States is a good example; indeed, for empirical background to the forceful polemic found in Cornel West's *Race Matters*[52] one could begin with the racial ideologies resplendent in the history of the census). It was in response to the ambiguities and complexities precipitate in miscegenation that Louis XIV introduced his infamous "Code noir" in 1685. The question of legal freedom remained firmly in the hands of the slaveowners, but the burgeoning population of mulattoes skewed the ideologies of natural or assumed entitlement. In a desperate attempt to maintain some semblance of racial privilege, a classificatory table was introduced that divided up degrees of blackness into 128 parts. As Glissant comments, "even the *sang-mêlé* with 127 white parts and 1 black part was considered a man of color."[53] To counteract and subvert this logic of racial purity, Glissant's Caribbean discourse emphasizes "mixture," or métissage. If essence is the colonial gambit, then créolité is its postcolonial Other, a strategy that confounds the binary logic of superiority/inferiority intrinsic, as Abdul JanMohamed has explained, to Manichaean orders of domination.[54] But, métissage depends upon a particular form of identification, one that is inseparable from the history of slavery itself (CD 231–32). What happens to the question of "rootedness," however, when applied to those peoples of the Caribbean who did not experience the rupture Glissant identifies? Does the influx of indentured servants in the nineteenth century disrupt the litany at issue? If métissage is a way out of the political and epistemological traps of the black/white dichotomy, does this encompass or differentiate the diasporic Asian communities (West, East, South) that have an active presence in Caribbean becoming? Despite the explicit relationship of rootedness and *marronnage* with slave history, the racial mix becomes a catchall for any racial constituency: "the immediacy of the natural order of things, the necessity of joining cultural elements that are African, European, and Indian whose impact must succeed without mishap; this is the vocation of a universality that is organic and no longer an ideal."[55] Yet it is an organic universality that elides the recognition that Glissant's writing develops about a specific relationship to the land in Martinican consciousness. Surely, given Glissant's definition, diasporic Asians, for instance, experience the conscience of a space in a different way?

There are a number of answers to such questions, each of which is, of necessity, prospective if we use the relative lack of formal response in Glissant's poetics. The simple answer to the last question would be "of course," but would this fundamentally alter the tenor or the implication of Glissant's argument? *Caribbean Discourse* is primarily an ethnographic critique that depends for its integrity on a demythification of identity formulae, even racial ones. Its cultural program (although hardly programmatic) emphasizes metamorphosis over autogenesis, a contingent "we" over a stable "I," a paratactic *langage* over a univocal *langue,* and a fervent openness to the heterodox over a self-consuming philosophy of the Same. Despite this mobile thought, or what Glissant calls "circular nomadism" (by which he means that the transversality of thought occurs in a definite space—it is not circular argument or cosmopolitan wandering in the usual sense) the qualification that race differentiation supplies is significant, since it points to an unresolvable diversity in the experience of the past and therefore in the construction of pastness. Thus, when Glissant defines *Antilles* in three ways (as the Caribbean islands, francophone islands, and anglophone islands) perhaps the multivalency should "take root" in Antillanité (Caribbeanness) so that the political unconscious (the mark or scar of slavery) does not devolve into a hierarchy of racial interest reminiscent of the colonial moment itself. Tensions are unavoidable because, as Benítez-Rojo notes, the Caribbean is the "scene of the most extensive and intensive racial confluence registered by human history."[56] Benítez-Rojo's provocative "answer" comes in the form of a more expansive notion of race memory very much in the spirit if not the statement of Glissant's métissage:

> In the Caribbean, skin color denotes neither a minority nor a majority; it represents much more: the color imposed by the violence of conquest and colonization, and especially by the plantation system. Whatever the skin color might be, it is a color that has not been institutionalized or legitimized according to lineage; it is a color in conflict with itself and with others, irritated in its very instability and resented for its uprootedness; it is a color neither of the Self nor of the Other, but rather a kind of no-man's land where the permanent battle for the Caribbean Self's fragmented identity is fought.[57]

In this sense of Caribbean space, identity is both demasculinized (even if inadvertently) and raced differently (the instability Benítez-Rojo notes does not miraculously sublate the race question, but reads it across its diversity). Thus, if race does not disable Caribbean identity, it renders it internally contradictory and potentially antagonistic. While the binary of Prospero and Caliban may well have been displaced, the "color line" announced by W. E. B. Du Bois is not simply eclipsed in the moment of Caribbean identity, for it is a margin produced both within what the Caribbean peoples have become and by the effete if still functional race ideologies that marked the "expansion" of Europe in the first place.

If the last point reminds us of the economic order of colonization, it must be said that Glissant is highly resistant to a class analysis of that order. This is not the product of what he calls a preference for a "neutral context" in which "no one dares to mention the class struggle except in low and muffled tones" (CD 254). It is, rather, a constituent in his general distrust of totalizing epistemes or *universal generalisé* that have produced an "intellectual mimeticism" in the Caribbean. In fact, Glissant provides a fairly detailed analysis of the Martinican economy from the moment of the plantation through to the stasis of "nonproductivity" that he sees as characteristic of "assimilation" today. One could argue that it is precisely this economic critique that separates his "poetics" from either the mindless formalism of the European traditions or the toothless culturalism of the Same.

Rather than use statistical evidence to track the (mis)fortunes of the Martinican economy, Glissant uses a systemic approach that foregrounds a worsening process of dispossession. His argument is based on a shift in primary production (particularly in sugar) toward tertiary and service-oriented business. Most, if not all, of these structural adjustments have been initiated in France and have effectively stifled "direct or self-generated" investment in Martinique (if capital accumulates, the surpluses are circulated elsewhere, but Glissant notes that the culture of dispossession has induced a fear of surplus from the outset). Those who sell services have done quite well, as has anyone who has not bucked the assimilationist agenda (the tourist franc being at a premium), but this has produced economic and social dislocations—the "isolation" of "what remains of the productive social strata" (again, Glissant strains not to use terms like "class" and "class fractions" to avoid the language of Western political economy). The net effect has been the institutionalization of a "nonfunctioning elite" and the development of a "dependent mentality." While the cultural theorist might quibble with the idiosyncracies of his analysis (consumerism as nonproductive, etc.), Glissant's reading of the "state" of Martinique identifies about as good an example of neocolonialism as one can find (although he cites another one, United States "presence" in Micronesia).

The division of labor and class character of Martinican society is complicated by several mediating factors: the alignment or "assimilation" of professions with business organizations of the metropole; the ethnicization of labor that tends to emphasize racial divisions within employment even with the "blurring" of these communities through interracial relations; a proletarianization within the "service" sector along the lines of other business hierarchies; the education and emigration of comparatively large numbers of youth for the metropole; little labor mobility between the islands (francophonic or otherwise); and the formation of a bureaucratic elite who are rewarded for their well-oiled administration of the "region" or *département d'outre-mer*. With class consciousness (a class for itself) at relatively low levels, Glissant terms the Martinican a "dispersed proletarian," which in part reflects the divisions outlined above, but more forcefully implicates Martinique's general subservience to the machinations of France. Clearly there has been significant resistance in Martinique to the tenets of *département* status— in protests over food, production reorganization, and income inequality—but none of this has facilitated a more general rejection of colonial administration or capitalist relations of production and exchange (although of course the former negritude movement had highlighted precisely these issues).

The main reason for the dispersed proletarianization of Martinique is that the machinery of domination wears a face of humanity and good sense. That is to say, French hegemony is achieved through a discursive deployment of benign dependency. Glissant comments, "the French system has produced an abstract and refined conception of this new form of colonialism: the urgency to persuade, to extract consent from the subjugated people, to subtly scorn (whereas the Anglo-Saxon visibly scorns) is both the symbolic and the major hidden reality of such a policy, which could have been applied only to small countries" (CD 50). To combat this requires not only conventional party political organization (of the sort Glissant practiced with the Front Antillo-Guyanais) but strategies of discursive disarticulation. Thus, while class differentiation is systemic to the organization of Martinican society, the overdeterminations of neocolonial rule do not obviously support a single-issue constituency, except of course nationhood—to which the discursive concept of Antillanité inexorably leads.

If indeed the economic organization of Martinique necessitates discursive intervention (for such is the thesis of *Caribbean Discourse*), then the interpellation of Martinique as a nation requires substantial qualification and explanation. Glissant is well aware that independence based upon conventional nationalist narratives is in danger of reproducing the very identity formula intrinsic to Western conceptions of the State. Antillanité, then, is transnational at the same time as it opens up the possibility of Martinican self-realization: "Caribbeanness, an intellectual dream, lived at the same time in an unconscious way by our peoples, tears us free from the intolerable alternative of the need for nationalism and introduces us to the cross-cultural process that modifies but does not undermine the latter" (139). Cultural creolization augurs "a new conception of nation" based not on exclusion but instead "is a form of disalienated relationship with the Other, who in this way becomes our fellow man" (250). This is a form of discursive resistance that graces the page much better than it does the populace. For instance, how does the discourse know that there is a correspondence between the dream of the intellectual and the unconscious of the people? Can we assume that modified nationalism is any better than its notorious predecessors? What actually disalienates the Other without either internalizing the Other to the Self or maintaining the Other as a condition of self-identity? If we bracket the notion of fellow human being, don't we still have the problem that this person is internally diverse, which would leave nationhood with the somewhat familiar formula of unity in diversity, an ideology of nation made infamous just north of the Antilles?

Several predicaments seem to follow from this: the predicament of nationhood formed in response to what has actually defined the history of nationalisms; the predicament of the intellectual who must imagine a community that he cannot represent; the predicament of a discourse that recognizes colonial domination as also nondiscursive; the predicament of a cultural discourse, a "poetics," that must internally distanciate the will to universalism redolent in fully fledged culturalism; and these are, perhaps, all predicaments of delinking that must justly claim autonomy economically, politically, and culturally from the sordid histories that inform it at the same time that it admits the inevitability of contamination that must, perforce, condition the very texture of any cross-cultural poetics so conceived. If Caribbean discourse is a text, or at least textualized, then there is no outside the realm of this predicament: It makes the *post* in *postcolonial* less an "end" than a condition of possibility—ironically, the only impossibility is the "end," in the sense of a complete, unconditional closure.

Of course, any liberation movement or discourse (the two can be mutually implied, however separable) has predicaments that prescribe the limits of its liberty, and Glissant, like most revolutionary writers in situ, knows the constraints that one must strain against. The detour, through intimations of gender, race, class, and nation, might strike one as obvious and dangerous: obvious, since they might all be deemed prefatory to the position taken up to make the statement (Glissant's, on Antillanité); and dangerous, because, in recapitulating them after an elaboration of the statement, the tendency is to suggest their absolute intractability, their haunting presence in and through *any* form of postcolonial discourse—precisely the character of *universal generalisé* that renews Europe and Europeanness rather than, say, the Caribbean and Caribbeanness. Yet, if all the problems of the postcolonial subject were transparent to itself, then surely that subject would be European, in terms of the Cartesian ego and its attendant if not obligatory certitude? In this respect, Glissant's project of Antillanité not only opens up perspective on the constitutive characteristics of Caribbean transversality but also on the epistemological and ontological dross of the European moment, a Europe that, as Cornel West suggests, may have ended in 1945, but for Martinique began again in 1946.

I have only begun to hint at the many lessons Glissant holds for a cultural transnationalism regarding the irreducibility of postcolonial subject positions, the alternative modalities of connection and solidarism implied, the paradoxical production of history through spatial identification, and the poetic *de*scription of what constitutes material evidence or effects. The nature of the questions asked hardly makes of Glissant a paragon of postcoloniality; indeed, the colonial situation of Martinique deliberately exacerbates the problems of definition and process. That this process is called "postcolonial" might be a sympathetic corollary of the politics of naming intrinsic to postcolonial practice but is hardly synonymous with it, as my own place and position of enunciation should suggest if not make clear. The logic of the latter is not interested in "giving voice" to Glissant's polemic in the Euramerican academy (instead of such appropriation, Glissant has been doing the voicing himself for years) nor in expressing solidarity for the cause of Caribbeanness (the generosity of bourgeois liberal coalitionism is matched only by the paucity of social change it has engendered) but in gauging the extent to

which a specific instance of theorizing identity disrupts the homogenizing tendency of postcoloniality as it posits itself as an object of study. Caribbean discourse is a form of cultural transnationalism not because Glissant mouths the
pietistic calls for diversity characteristic of the crisis-management mentality of
Western academies but because the knowledge at issue is not assimilable to the
Self that seeks such diversity. It is a transnationalism that will work, if at all, only
within the space and place of its enunciation, the crisis of identity to which *it*
refers, not the crisis of culture that might now, perhaps in desperation, grant it
perspicacity. Since this is a lesson about positionality, I want to note the problem of privilege and cosmopolitanism in the moment of métissage.

Glissant has never been reticent about his privileges as a Sorbonne-educated
intellectual: "The official language, French, is not the people's language. This is
why we the elite speak it so correctly" (CD 249). He also knows that when he
acts on the promise "We demand the right to obscurity" (CD 2) he not only blurs
the Western eye but ensures a relatively small Martinican readership. In addition,
apart from the moment of Algerian independence, Glissant has been free to live
and work where he pleases, a realm of choice not accorded most Martinicans.
Thus, while he is an active proponent of social transformation in Martinique,
Glissant's class position is sufficiently mobile to avoid a good deal of the oppres-
sive practices that must be met by such change. This raises an interesting question about the postcolonial intellectual's concomitant relationships to the subal-
ternity he (in this case) might explore and to the complex (and sometimes
"phantom") international public sphere in which he may be interpellated as a
"native informant." I am not going to rehearse the argument behind this question (which has been adequately elaborated elsewhere) but want to note something of Glissant's "pause" in what Bruce Robbins has termed "comparative cosmopolitanism."[58]

Cosmopolitan is a contentious term in cultural theory today because it both
heralds the significance of a new intellectual worldliness (often in the figure of
the postcolonial artist) and at the same time cannot seem to escape the sedimentation of meanings that it has amassed in intellectual history. The sedimentation
contains strong evidence of elitism and privilege, a know-no-border attitude that
skips from global culture to global culture with nary a care for the messy specificity
of any particular culture. It is easy to see why, whether in the soundbite environment of international telecommunications or in the corporate, instant "retooling" mindset of the Euramerican academy, the cosmopolitan has emerged as a
fetish of going global: why get bogged down in details when the cosmopolitan
celebrity can provide instant "insider" information in a turn of phrase or in a
conference address? At its most negative, rootlessness of this kind appears little

more than stark opportunism with its ideology suspiciously close to the very free-floating barbarism artfully deployed by imperialism. But of course everything depends on who is worldly and where they are when they are doing it.

Robbins argues forcefully for a form of cosmopolitanism that eschews the false universalism of the free-floating intellectual for a responsive (and one hopes, responsible) process of "trans-local connecting." This, it seems to me, usefully links a necessary localism to the production of knowledge and its circulation on a world scale. The "discrepant cosmopolitanism" advocated would, by its very methodology, challenge the flattening out of content or the woeful homogenizing of dominant cosmopolitanism by emphasizing the sharing of culture between observer and observee and the productivity of relation itself. This will not stop cosmopolitanism from being associated with the observer who takes knowledge and gets back on the airplane, but it might encourage a more nuanced rather than knee-jerk reaction to knowledge production within and between cultures.

Is Édouard Glissant a discrepant cosmopolitan? Yes, to the extent that he embodies some of the sedimentation and creative qualifications introduced in Robbins's argument. Here is a theorist who cannot conceive of a localism that does not connect; indeed, Caribbeanness (not simply Martinican localness) is the means to become Martinican. The problem, however, rests in the realm of the political. Robbins claims that cosmopolitanism "cannot deliver an explicitly and directly political program" but instead is "a step towards this sort of internationalist political education."[59] But the idea of a political program being an "internationalist political education" reminds us once more of the location from which this cosmopolitanism emerges: That is, surely the luxury of Euramerican academe reduces cosmopolitanism to the question of education. While Glissant is an educator himself, he does not believe that the transformation of Martinican Being rests on the imprimatur of education alone. Education must inflect cosmopolitanism, but its privilege reflects the relative absence of traditions of radical discourse in the public sphere. The form of cosmopolitanism that Robbins advocates has not retreated to the academy but "progressively" disappeared almost everywhere else. This is simply not true of other "trans-local connecting."

To push the point a little further, it is highly characteristic of recent Euramerican academic discourse to downplay or even disparage the role of agency and specificity in cultural critique (the marginality of our own agency and specificity having reached an alarming magnitude). Robbins himself gently reprimands Chandra Talpade Mohanty for finding agency among women of India rather than passivity and obedience, and likewise questions the logic "which values and rewards this insistence on ('eastern') specificity."[60] Robbins knows the scandal he courts here but usefully makes the point that academics must, as a professional principle, reserve the right to "difficult" generalization, which means not putting agency at such a premium (so that one can, for instance, explain why it might even be absent) or assuming that by finding it in one's textual analysis one is therefore reproducing it in another specific sphere of influence—the academy. Again, my point would be that it is one thing to question the fetishizing of agency in an institutional framework where such acts are less a red badge of courage than a candle in the wind, but it is something quite different to make this suspicion intrinsic to multicultural analysis. While it might signify the laudable ejection of principles associated with narratives of social transformation (the revolutionary agent is a pariah, empiricism is the plague—we have all awakened from that nightmare, etc.) it might also reconstitute critique as theoretical narcissism. The reason we should investigate cultural agency (even to the exclusion of quiescence) is because agency is not only the process that alters the conditions of emergence of a specific culture, but it also alters the mode of relationship between, in this case, a Euramerican academic and the world of change. True, the revolutionary writer is a special instance and comes with some if not all the intimations of elitism and privilege discussed so far. Yet, if we are serious in developing a new sense of cultural transnationalism, then we must place a particular emphasis on the knowledge production peculiar to that agency of specificity, for the métissage at issue will not occur initially in the mode of our apprehension but in the space that is its priority. In this respect, Glissant's opacity, for instance, might seem to lure the critic into untangling meanings that are irreducible or nonassimilable, but ultimately this is besides the point. As Caribbeanness makes clear, the first realm of agency is the periphery itself or, as Glissant opines, the relationship of the periphery and the periphery. Postcolonial by other means, means the poetics of *that* relation which, should it be realized, will forever change the knowledge of our relation, cosmopolitan or otherwise.

History is indeed fissured by histories, just as I have suggested that Glissant's Antillanité is fissured by the complex manifestations of gender, race, and nation in the Caribbean. But here let me reiterate the importance of Glissant for contemporary knowledge of what Barbara Harlow in another context has called "resistance literature."[61] Just as the maroons in Caribbean history were remarkable for their strategies of resistance and escape, so Glissant maintains a detailed and articulate provocation to disrupt and repel the logics of the colonial machine. In this sense, he is an escape writer ("un écrivain du marronnage"), a Martinican intellectual who slips every ruse of assimilation.[62] *Marronnage* in Glissant's work is not some nostalgic impulse of revolutionary desire (his activism within Franc-Jeu and the Front Antillo-Guyanais are less textual examples of his commitment), but a poignant *de*-scription of the (neo)colonial condition. His writing is not "es-

capist," but his formal experimentation traces lines of escape from ruling, or official, discourses, whether ideologies of departmentalization or those of the Martinican bourgeoisie. *Marronnage,* then, is an aesthetic/political strategy of promot-
ing critical evaluation of the state of Martinique, its insertion into history, and its
narrative methodology—its speculative Being. The model of *marronnage* for Glissant is the Caribbean tale (the sense of the collective), that which attacks, as Glissant notes, the sacredness of the written sign ("le sacré du signe écrit") and Western mythologies. Thus, while the history of *marronnage* records slave resistance
to the plantation system (including, most notably, the Haitian rebellion) Glissant
has given it an aesthetic provenance so that the act of writing itself destabilizes
acceptable procedures of writing: It is writing as antiwriting, and it is in that act
that an insurgent epistemology of Martinique becomes possible.

2

Brathwaite, Crossing, Voicing

There are many parallels between Glissant's ardent delinking of Martinique from its colonial inscriptions and the work of Kamau Brathwaite, the Barbadian poet, historian, critic, theorist, and teacher. Certainly Brathwaite shares Glissant's commitment to an aesthetic and social *marronnage*. Brathwaite knows Maroon history very well and, like Glissant, has explored its inspiration for Caribbean identity. But the specificity of Glissant's vision is formed through a different relationship to the cartography of colonial occupation and exile that also carves a division between the islands. Perhaps this makes Glissant justifiably more pessimistic, but I would like to elaborate another arc in the trajectory of the art of resistance: the *langage* may well be the same, as we have already noted, but Brathwaite comes to his transgressive notion of Nation, and Nation language, through and from lines of flight that link him much more concretely with an ancestral Africa. Indeed, in Brathwaite's imaginary state, the Nation is a constant revoicing of Africa in the Caribbean, of the Caribbean in Africa (Barbados itself is therefore always a "greater" Barbados as Nation). The to and fro between the two is like the vast Atlantic itself and is an imaginative expression of what Brathwaite calls "tidalectics"—a cyclical and circular process of connection and identification. This is "crossing" as catharsis and critique: it is certainly a creolization of national form. But most of all it is about voice, about the spirit and place of articulation, a performative mapping. Time after time in his poetry and essays, Brathwaite infuses English with voice as spatiality, a psychic repossession of the distance between past and present, Africa and the Caribbean, root and rhizome. It is not just the sound of English that is rearticulated, but its visuality, so that lines are fractured by punctuation, by line splits and sudden capitalization, by trickster punning, and especially by font changes. Language is reterritorialized in the process of its representation as if to confirm that a poetics of place is also literally, whatever else it is, a taking up of space.

Obviously, Brathwaite's active embrace of an African heritage puts him at odds with the rootedness in the Caribbean landscape that Glissant favors, or C. L. R. James's argument to create opposition from the immediacy of the experience of Westernization rather than rely primarily on a cultural esteem built on ancestry brutally broken by slavery (a difference that can also be seen between Brathwaite and Derek Walcott or V. S. Naipaul).[1] But it seems to me that the force of political engagement that derives from Caribbeanness needs that African linkage as much as it needs James's own brilliant reaccentuation of cricket in the Caribbean critical imaginary. (It is noteworthy that the first part of James's opus on cricket, *Beyond a Boundary,* is called "A Window to the World." Needless to say, the title of the volume itself urges a transnational dialogic[2].) Brathwaite's sense of Caribbean cultural specificity argues for a historically embedded internal distancing of colonial lore at the level of language, music, and memory. Brathwaite attends to the elaboration of that connection/disjunction by voicing a history, polemically and poetically. His Caribbean cartography attends to spatial identity through the voice, through a nation language, as he calls it, that invokes an affirmative ground for community. In the rhythms and cadences of his poems, Brathwaite eschews a narrative history of victimhood for the energy that a history of struggle creates. In his most effervescent and experimental works, the video-style poems for instance, Brathwaite invokes not Caliban, he rewritten under the sign of hegemony, but Sycorax, a mother of invention and a wild spirit beholden to no White memory, no slave mentality.

> not fe dem/not fe dem
> de way caliban
> done
>
> but fe we
> fe a-we
>
> for nat one a we shd response if prospero get curse
> wid im own
>
> curser[3]

The Middle Passages (a term that also forms the title of one of his collections) are about movement, a restlessness that gives Brathwaite's elaboration of roots a dynamic connectedness. For Brathwaite, the Middle Passages do not simply mean slavery and colonization (although when he subtitles *Barabajan Poems* "1492–

1992" it is clear that connection must remain indelible); they refer to a state of commonality and cultural contact. The geographic distance between West Africa and Barbados may be vast, but even natural phenomena, like hurricanes and the harmattan winds, connect one to the other. Like Glissant, Brathwaite's sense of place is an intensely dialogic vision, but one inscribed and overdetermined by the subversive potential of language as creative memory. I want to consider this insurgent promise in Brathwaite's fiercely idiosyncratic nation language and the poetry that forms at least some of its most profound evidence. The "creative chaos" that Benítez-Rojo sees in Caribbean identity is given "sound" evidence in Brathwaite's poems. That nation language does not describe the borders of a national entity is not some failure of political imagination but is rather its triumph—a very precise blow to the Nation idea that built the Caribbean on colonial expansion and oppression, and also a riposte to those who measure progress by whether nations are developing—whether, indeed, they can "see" developing nations. Brathwaite's "Sycorax video-style" sees differently (fig. 1).

Figure 1 is a page from *Barabajan Poems*. The "too many hundred years" lead from 1492. The process of deculturation refers to the deracination of self intrinsic to colonization and the production or "imposure" of "slave mentality." For Antonio Gramsci, this would be a version of hegemony in which the dominated become complicit with domination or convinced of the ruse of domination that says that the dominated have no viable cultural identity. The use of *our* here is appropriate not just because Brathwaite often appeals to collective identity, but because of the occasion of his poetry or "not lecture" as he calls it, his delivery of the twelfth annual Sir Winston Scott Memorial lecture on 2 December 1987. Given the establishment context of his lecture (Brathwaite spoke at the Central Bank of Barbados and was introduced by the prime minister, Erskine Sandtford), one should not be surprised by the double-voicing in the presentation, which points out the collusion of Government House in the self-abasement of Bajan identity only to suggest that present company (never an innocent word) is 𝒳cepted. The crux of Brathwaite's argument at this point is that the state of Bajan culture itself is being left to outside forces to define. To reverse such deculturation, the self, as Brathwaite perceives it, must come to terms with the conditions of its own expression, hence the mention of Dr. Allsopp's Caribbean dictionary as a resource of, quite literally, self-reference. The size of type and line breaks reassert this selfhood, claiming the page with the bold voice of "Caribbean speak."[4] Is this ego compensation, that large fonts counteract the deleterious effects of colonial history and its episteme? The imaginary state acknowledges the importance of space for the imagination. Just as Charles Olson spells space large in writing of America, so Brathwaite imagines the text of Caribbeanness as so much

**Too many hundred years you see
of insult of neglect deculturation
apparent deculturation**

have so corrupted us that we are

**ashamed to face our face admit
our
selves even unto our very selves**

**esp since these 'things' have not
been accepted by Government Ho-
use** (present Company of course Xcepted!) **&**

*The Times Literary Supplement &
The Oxford English Dictionary &
The Washington Post & the Nikki
Index -* **which is why we need Dr
Allsopp's Dictionary of Caribb-
ean Language** - not *English,* Dr Allsopp,

Figure 1. From Kamau Brathwaite, *Barabajan Poems* (New York: Savacou North, 1993), 168. Used by permission of the author.

more than specks of islands in a sea. A culture that is simultaneously Caribbean and African is big and requires its own dictionary and more.

If Glissant argues for resistance through opacity, then Brathwaite offers a complementary counterhegemonic discursive strategy in his explorations of the deep structures of Caribbean experience. The constituent features of this approach are emphases on process, place, and speech. Like Glissant, Brathwaite draws on the actual physical environment of Caribbean island culture for his poetic expression. This does not mean including descriptions of rain forests, coral outgrowths, or hurricane seasons as a backdrop to island experience; it means, more precisely, working the immediacy of environment into the very texture of the poetry:

The ancient watercourse of my island
echo of river, trickle, worn stone,
the sunken voice of glitter inching its pattern to the sea,
memory of foam, fossil, erased beaches high above the eaten boulders of st
philip

my mother is a pool[5]

Nation language is in part a way to build identity through the environment. This "landscaping" is Brathwaite's architectonic of archipelago aesthetics. It is a language of "time/place/self"[6] with place as the central coordinate.[7] And yet it is always place as process, as movement, even when Brathwaite clearly evokes the actual details of *a* place, Barbados (or Jamaica, as in *Trench Town Rock*).

> All of us, I know, have X perienced Bathsheba in a very deep & significant even re-ligious way & from we are very young, growing up green, thirsty for knowledge & image, amazed (since most of us live in the West) at the strange transformation in our consciousness as we make the crossing over the heights of the island at say Joes River Station (via Horse Hill) or St Elizabeth's or Lamming's or Spring Field And then that sudden precipitous, vertiginous vision of the coastline in sunlight or cloud-shade cloudshadow below us with the dark blue & purple-coloured wall of water rolling from Africa all white at its edges & without sound at that distance but as we get nearer, the influence of that mass, that munificence, that glassy magnificence, the tons of boulders rolling in and crashing down white wild & spuming up like forever & the black rocks standing up also forever like 'thunder made visible', our eastern warriors of sound.[8]

It is tempting to suggest that it is the element of speech itself that catalyzes the invocation of place as movement, just as the sound of the sea for Brathwaite indicates its shifting plenitude. Yet even this would have to be qualified to ac-count for Brathwaite's deep interest in music, the music of speech in all its meters, itself determined to a great degree by the tonality and totality of the sea-again, what Brathwaite refers to as "tidalectics."[9] Nation language, then, is a place formed by the interrelationship of speech and music, both natural and human compositions. Brathwaite's poems evoke a strong sense of orality, but a sound system dependent on a consciousness of space. In part this is an outgrowth of Brathwaite's sustained research on the Caribbean's cultural past, something reflected in the titles of his many works: *The Development of Creole Society in Jamaica, 1770–1820* (1971), *Folk Culture of the Slaves in Jamaica* (1972), *Caribbe-an Man in Space and Time* (1974), *Contradictory Omens: Cultural Diversity and Integration in the Caribbean* (1974), *Our Ancestral Heritage: A Bibliography of the English Speaking Caribbean Designed to Record and Celebrate the Several Origins of Our Structural, Material, and Creative Culture, and to Indicate How This Is Being Used by Us to Mek Ah-we* (1976).

But this identity research extends into the texture and place of language itself. Usually, this geographical node is symbolized by *dialect* but Brathwaite uses *nation language* to distance his oraliture from *dialect*'s pejorative implications. The new term simultaneously connotes a historical and geographical trajectory: "Nation language . . . is the *submerged* area of that dialect which is much more closely allied to the African aspect of experience in the Caribbean."[10] The challenge of tidalectics, like dialectics, is to think simultaneously its time/space coordinates without sacrificing the specific nuance of either. This, of course, is something of Paul Gilroy's approach to the Black Atlantic, which is a heuristic device in the "inner dialectics of diaspora identification."[11] Indeed, one could argue that Brathwaite's tidalectics is a poetic elaboration of the main tenets of the Black Atlantic, a conceptual space of identification that links blacks across the Atlantic by culture, politics, and history (although one of the reasons Brathwaite uses tidalectics is to separate his spatial imagination from the colonizing and racist consciousness of European dialectics, particularly, of course, Georg Wilhelm Friedrich Hegel). In this respect, nation language challenges the prescriptions of the Nation idea within modernity: it is a "counterculture of modernity" that redraws the "belonging" of nation according to the spatial logic of diaspora and displacement. As Ngũgĩ wa Thiong'o comments on Brathwaite as a teacher: "He saw no barriers between geography, history, and literature. What formed the African and Caribbean sensibility could not be divorced from the landscape and the historical experience."[12] This constitutes the seedbed of Brathwaite's conception of nation language.

If nation language is a rhythmic invocation of a shared African heritage, then what sense of Nation does this imply? Brathwaite lived in Ghana for ten years, and this taught him an immense amount about history, culture, and the function of memory between African and Caribbean identification (since this follows his period of studying at Cambridge University, he also pithily refers to it as his "de-education"). In *Barabajan Poems* he recalls his arrival in Ghana:

> smooth voices like pebbles/moved by the sea of their language/**akwaaba**/they smiled/ meaning/**welcome/akwaaba** they called/**aye kooo**/well have you walked/have you journeyed/**welcome**/you who have come/back a stranger/after three hundred years/ **welcome**/here is a stool for/you: **sit:** do/you remember?" (71)

This is not some postmodern nostalgia for the present (of a past he never lived). Indeed, Brathwaite also confounds any romantic identification with Ghana by almost immediately registering the existential crisis his arrival confers: "whose ancestor am I?" (73). This is the dilemma of the diasporic Subject. One can "return," but even welcome recognition does not undo the difference that time and space have wrought. Brathwaite's arrival is announced as a trauma not because of the memory it conjures, but because the return itself cannot possibly confirm the original violence that made it possible. Again, the sense of Nation is ambivalent. It is a means to unlearn colonial lore (which makes even everyday slogans suspect, e.g., that "Goldie Flake cornflakes makes the Best Breakfast" [68]) but it also signifies the impasse of Nation on its own terms. The real reason Brathwaite uses the term *nation language* is not to forge a nation where there is none but is to suggest that if the notion of Nation depends upon the shared culture and language of a community, then the force of modernity has also forced a community that is not simply dependent on a bordered location for its national identity (and thus requires a "forced poetics" that is a mark of Glissant's intervention).

Yet this stands in a complex relationship to the constitutive features of the Nation idea. Ernest Renan in his famous essay "What Is a Nation?" develops his position from the idea that the nation is precisely not determined by geographical contours, religions, race, or language.[13] For Renan "a nation is a soul, a spiritual principle" (19). It is always already willed into existence beyond other putative levels of correspondence. The paradox of the Nation form is that it materializes a substance that has none. And, as Benedict Anderson notes in his revision to *Imagined Communities,* this paradox is enabled by active forgetting, a need that requires a genealogy to remind the Subject of the Nation what she or he has already forgotten,[14] the barbarism that made this "soul" a logical consequence. Nation language, a "submerged language," interrupts the order of this genealogy because it bears in its very expressive modes an alternative logic of memory as an active presence—in Brathwaite's case, "in an English which is like a howl."[15] When Ngũgĩ wa Thiong'o describes Brathwaite as "the voice of African presence," he has this logic of connection in mind:

> He explores the African presence in Africa, the Caribbean, and the world, not in its staticness but in its movement, in its changingness, in its interactions. In these interactions the African presence is not a passive element. Whether across the Sahara deserts, through the savannas and tropical forests, across the Atlantic, say, in all its continental and diasporic dimensions, it is a resisting spirit, refusing to succumb, ready to build anew from the ashes of natural disasters and human degradation.[16]

If, as Ngũgĩ suggests, "acknowledgment of the past becomes the basis of strengthening the present and opening out to the future,"[17] is not this part and parcel of the same will-to-nation that Renan elaborates? Again, the discrepancy lies in the vectors of power implied. There is a great deal of difference between a "resisting spirit" and one that forgets on the basis of active suppression. Indeed, it is the difference between the two that necessitates a national consciousness (in the Fanonian sense) as the will for decolonization.[18] The wily deconstructor might here intervene to suggest that what blocks successful resistance is a reliance on presencing itself as the linchpin of the national imaginary. The fact that such presencing is voiced would only compound the view that the Being of nation language is compromised by the medium of selfhood privileged.

Yet another approach would clarify the issue. The "submerged" or suppressed subjectivity of nation language is that which cannot be taken up within normative notions of the Nation as narration. A "nation is a soul," but one that is inscribed, one that bears in its identity an attempt to write out its existence as a documented ground. This can take the form of an actual written document, yet this does not exhaust the principles of its inscription as, to borrow from Homi Bhabha, an accumulation of signs.[19] Bhabha points out that this scene of writing, the place of writing the Nation, is caught between a pedagogical and performative imperative—itself an integer of a ruptured temporality. The pedagogical concerns the inculcation of a national past, and the performative connotes the necessity of acting out that pastness as a condition of an "enunciatory present."[20] What Bhabha provocatively suggests is that the selfhood implied in the presencing of the present cannot but mark a difference (as a signifying process) with the claims of its pedagogy. The present performance not only dissembles, but disseminates, and the sign of Nation is therefore cleverly written out as dissemiNation. What I would urge is a greater understanding of the performative as a performance, not just as the significant play of the signifier that threatens the conceptual integrity of the Nation as sign. For one thing, this would have the advantage of including Brathwaite's own performances as a poet and a teacher (always extraordinary events) as instances of the Nation otherwise, as nation language in process.

At a very basic level we know that the Nation is played: it is sutured from moment to moment by countless acts of repetition as (apparent) confirmation of its presence. A plethora of rituals and ceremonies assume this role in the active negotiation of national longing and belonging. I think that it would be a mistake to view the voicing of nation language as the simple expression of that performativity. Rather, the eventness of nation language accentuates the logic of the Nation as form, without being self-present with that identity. By voicing, it mimes the Nation form, and this is also a dissimulation, or a dissemiNation in Bhabha's parlance. Part of the supersyncretism that Benítez-Rojo identifies in the Caribbean text is achieved through performativity, and not just novelistic performativity, but the voice and the body themselves as instruments of both asserting and miming identity. Just as Benítez-Rojo associates this with dance and poly-rhythm, with rumba and carnival, so Brathwaite will emphasize the words and music of calypso, jazz, and blues. The language of this performance is unofficial discourse, that submerged inflection Brathwaite associates with the specificities of Caribbean history usually written off as "dialect." Indeed, cast against the stul-tifying imposition of English in the anglophone Caribbean, nation language functions as its ardent and critical image. It offers something of Anderson's sense of a vernacular language of state without conferring statehood as a Nation idea.[21] The mimicry, then, is not copying but is instead a creative displacement, as Bhab-ha puts it, "a recognizable Other, as a subject of difference that is almost the same, but not quite."[22] That orality is its strongest feature is not the reimposition of a dire Western presence but is actually a decentering of the Same. The spoken word to which Brathwaite refers is a product of colonialism but also its excess, its su-peradequation, just as the figure of the mimic in Bhabha's formulation is the "effect of a flawed colonial mimesis, in which to be Anglicized is most emphat-ically not to be English."[23] Indeed, for Brathwaite this mime or shade of English takes nation language not to Europe, of course, but to Africa, the main source of creative tension in the nation his language signifies.

> Out
> of this
> bright
> sun, this
> white plaque,
> of heaven,
> this heaven-
> ing heat
> of the seven
> kingdoms:
> Songhai, Mali,
> Chad, Ghana,
> Tim-
> buctu, Volta,
> and the bitter
> waste
> that was
> Ben-
> in, comes this shout
> comes
> this song.[24]

That this displacement differs from Glissant's approach to Antillanité should not surprise anyone (Glissant offers no connection as return in Césaire's or Brathwaite's sense), but that is not to say that these writers do not share a similar political episteme. As I have noted earlier, Glissant's notion of the detour and diversion might also be used to characterize his opacity, a miming of colonial depth, but also its *écrasement,* its effacement. Brathwaite's *detour* as *retour* is to pull effectively both the Caribbean and Africa into the conceptual space of the Middle Passage that is common to both but reducible to neither. In this respect, his nation language is the language not of a nation, but of an ocean: it is the discourse of the Black Atlantic.

Yet Brathwaite does mark a subjective presence in the strongly drawn characters that feature in his poems (say Bob'ob, his great uncle, or his mother) and these are crisscrossed and overdetermined by that transatlantic sensibility. Indeed, his most powerful identification is with the real inhabitants of Barbados, or Jamaica (both writers, family, and fellow workers), but rather than sentimentalize them, in the main Brathwaite problematizes the Being they collectively represent. This is most evident in his use of χ, which does not cross out the self of the Caribbean, but modifies it according to a consciousness of history (which, of course, is also its meaning for Malcolm X). The χ/self is not simply the obliteration of selfhood according to a colonial idea but a border self that troubles the projection of the self Same itself. Brathwaite describes himself as an χ/ile, which cleverly captures his own sense of being physically outside the islands of the archipelago and also signifies a Being beside itself, a Being that repeats without being self-identical, just like Benítez-Rojo's repeating islands. While some may put this down to Brathwaite's extravagant enthusiasm for the keyboard (from which Sycorax video style emerges—see again his "Letter Sycora χ"), the χ deftly marks an identity in process, a Caribbean border identity that is never finished off but is itself performative, voiced by the eventness of the Middle Passage.[25] Nation language is a way of staging this process, naming it as it were, without succumbing to an ideology of place in nationhood that excludes contingency. Brathwaite thus writes the Nation very much in the way he writes his poetry, as a draft that is repositioned, reaccentuated according to narratives that χceed its putative cartography. This is also a recognition of the contingent status of the Nation as archive, as well as an acknowledgment of the tenuous nature of Brathwaite's own literary production. In lectures, for instance, Brathwaite recalls the mudslide caused by Hurricane Gilbert (September 1988) that claimed a massive portion of his manuscripts, books, and audio collection in Irish Town, Jamaica (an irony not lost on him, for what may come from Africa can take away). He also recounts the harrowing and terrifying experience of the raid on his home in Marley Man-

or, Kingston, when he himself was attacked (1990). As the tragedy of the dub
poet Mikey Smith underlines (he was stoned to death in Kingston in 1983), a
history of the voice can be as fragile as he who speaks it.

Perhaps, given the delicate nature of nation language, we should not be surprised that spirituality attends it and in that, at least, it remains connected to
Renan's formulation. I would argue, however, that we seriously underestimate the
imagination if we believe that it exists merely to reinscribe the integrity of the
Nation form as Renan conceives it. Brathwaite, as χ/ile, does construct *a* Barbados as nation, but primarily as an indication of its absolute dependence on a
history that will not secure it. The history of the voice undoes the local through
the vocal, just as *mabrak,* or black lightning (both Bongo Jerry and Roger Mais
are inspirations in this regard[26]), shatters the quiescence and silence of the Caribbean as a white playground. Both *mabrak* and *shango* (thunder) are of African
derivation and, as Benítez-Rojo among others has pointed out, they are part of a
complex culture of African religions and spirituality refracted throughout the
Caribbean. Voodoo spirits like Legba, Ogoun, Ananse, and Damballa(h) feature
prominently in Brathwaite's poetry: gods "who came over—who arrive—walking on the water of our conscience as they say in Gulla—rising from the silvers
of our souls in Haiti—as they say from Guinea."[27] They are spirits of sound, of
inspiration, and also of rebellion. Brathwaite continues: "Shango & the others
of PanAfrica are here too, were already always here from since we listened since
we sang & clapped & drummed & danced & dreamed—transformed & thun-
derous as a train, the loco-motive engine."[28] When Brathwaite writes of his great
uncle Bob'ob, the carpenter, he is both Legba, the "cripple" god of the doorway
or crossroads, and Ogoun, the ironmaker. The gods are in everyman, and the
everyday man or woman (most notably, Brathwaite's mother as Sycorax) bears
the mark of ancestry. Brathwaite writes of the "African Presence in Caribbean
Literature" and he roots this in African religion, "the kernel or core of the culture in the New World."[29] The point is not the mere existence of this lineage
(which is well established) but its fragmentary, explosive, or chaotic nature (again,
that Benítez-Rojo uses Chaos Theory as a literary model for the Caribbean is a
reflection not just on poststructuralism but on the material conditions of Caribbean history). It is true that Brathwaite often seeks a unity from this plurality,
which for many will invoke a fairly conventional image of Nation, but I think
in general he sees the sounds and cultures of the Caribbean as radically χcen-
tric, opposed, that is, to a Western rationality that renders Caribbean communities merely in a Western frame of reference. In this sense, Brathwaite's spirituality is a kind of spatiality, for spirit possession is a riposte to space possession in
the colonial imaginary:

So on this ground,
write;
within the sound
of this white limestone vèvè,

talk
of the empty roads,
vessels of your head,
clayposts, shards, ruins,

And on this sailing ground,
sprinkled with rum, bitten
with the tenor of your open wound,
walk

. . . .

For on this ground
trampled with the bull's swathe of whips
where the slaves at the crossroads was a red anthill
eaten by moonbeams, by the holy ghosts
of his wounds

the Word becomes
again a god and walks among us;
look, here are his rags,
here is his crutch and his satchel
of dreams; here is his hoe and his rude implements

on this ground
on this broken ground.[30]

The vèvè is the space of conjuring, of invocation. In the synaesthesia of these verses, Brathwaite denatures the word of the master and offers instead Legba, the "alter/native of the doorway,"[31] who reinscribes that space with ancestral sound and inspiration. The ground, like the culture, remains broken, but it is nevertheless a vital imaginary space where one can write, talk, and walk. And in Brathwaite's poetry this is always a crossing, a moving to and fro, as if the coastline of the Atlantic traced a single, vibrant vèvè to and from the Caribbean and Africa. But this imaginary space of cultural enunciation is also announced in the very form of Brathwaite's poetry, which, particularly in his video style (the experimental typefacing and spacing that Brathwaite develops by composing on a computer) is nothing less than the "broken ground" of Caribbean space. Brathwaite skillfully uses the space between words to indicate breaths and pauses (as any good poet should) but also visualizes the rhythms and beats that accompany recitation by varying the typefaces in size and style (see figs. 2 and 3). Some pages feature only a word or two (usually in gigantic proportions), others are packed full of detail in mixtures of prose/poetry/quotation/citation and background material. *Barabajan Poems* itself, in its wild size and chaotic visual surfaces, is a form of possession, spiritual and spatial. In the dramatic shifts in pacing and intensity, the contents underline its creative restlessness; indeed, as Brathwaite reworks and repositions poems from his past, he enacts a form of *marronnage* that both reclaims a cultural history and opens it out as an agonistic aesthetic. Just as Walcott proffers history as sea, so Brathwaite ponders the poetry of Nation in the same way.

There are many writers who have thought deeply about how the sea connects those of African descent with Africa itself, and if that were Brathwaite's only contribution to Caribbean culture and Black consciousness he would not strike one as so singularly engaged. Eschewing pat or pietistic claims for roots and rootedness, Brathwaite yet develops an innovative and recondite aesthetic on the vital and submerged components of Caribbeanness. Even here, where his use of the Ironwood font evokes the picket fence he remembers separating the family yard from the sea in his youth, the effect is not undermined by the forced approximation. Instead, the space of the text betrays what is and is not signified by

Figure 2. From Kamau Brathwaite, *Barabajan Poems* (New York: Savacou North, 1993), 283. Used by permission of the author.

*A*nd then there is the great small-ilann

saying

sea

d oan have no

BACKDOOR

Figure 3. From Kamau Brathwaite, *Barabajan Poems* (New York: Savacou North, 1993), 282. Used by permission of the author.

physical borders. The difficulty of nation language is its struggle to name a process of identification that has been butchered in the name of civilization. This is what Brathwaite calls the "nam" of naming, a resource of hope, "where the heart of culture resides in its uttarness where it cannot any longer be destroyed."[32] Brathwaite, as in so much of his work, runs together English with West African languages, and thus describes "nam" as "soul, secret name, soul-source, connected with *nyam* (eat), yam (root food), *nyame* (name of god)."[33] Indeed, one lesson for imaginary states is the significance of naming otherwise (from Edward to Kamau included) when so much has been calcified by the routine nomenclature of the geopolitical powers that be. In this sense, Brathwaite even gives new meaning to dub poetry because, although he favors calypso and blues over reggae as a musical source, he nevertheless dubs (names) a lyricism that is in beat both sides of the sea (crossing from the backdoor of Barbados to the frontdoor of Ghana). While there are other Caribbean poets who have embodied this spirit, as living voices or vessels of history (one thinks of Louise Bennett or Mikey Smith), Brathwaite has used it to complicate one's sense of poetic space so that the nation might reside within it and not simply as an identitarian decree. If *nam* is, as Brathwaite terms it, "an alteration of consciousness,"[34] then his poetry visualizes its material force by understanding the name of Nation as more than that.

3

Condé, Crossing, Errantry of Place

When one writes about imaginary space, that cultural aura of yearning and rearticulation, one is troping on another sordid history than that conspiratorial nexus between Nation and colonization in Western ontology. Here is not the place to recount the depth of that history in the Caribbean where space is engendered under the sign of social hierarchy, but by reading Maryse Condé's intervention on that terrain I do hope to indicate at least some of the parameters of insurgent crossing that delinks in an ardent and articulate manner the conditions of reimagining or imagining otherwise from the white male panoptic eye that surveys it. The nature of my own subjectivity traces one level of impossibility here (even what is crossed out remains a pertinent palimpsest that no amount of solidarity can eclipse), but, just as importantly, the question of crossing itself troubles summary notions of navigation. Condé has described herself as a "wanderer," and critics are usually quick to shuffle such statements into Caribbean cosmopolitanism rather than think of this difference in terms of the problem of Nation for the archipelago. While Guadeloupean literary history is not epitomized by the "crossing" Condé invokes, she nevertheless grapples with a sense of how a woman writer can "belong" (to that history or to that territory) when the process of identity, the *ing* in crossing, seems to deny that very affiliation. This is one way, at least, to understand the provocation in Condé's suggestion: "Je suis vraiment à l'autre bout du monde" ("I am truly at the other end of the world").[1]

Like Glissant, Condé understands wandering and outsideness as historical conditions with stronger links to traditions of *marronnage*[2] than modernist conceptions of Odysseus. As Bernabé, Chamoiseau, and Confiant say of *créolité, marronnage* shares that "interactional or transactional substance of Caribbean cultural elements"[3] that constitute a poetics in situ. But, and also in the manner of Glissant, Condé reads the interactional as a specific mode of communication marked by opacity as much as explication (with the subsequent and subtle qualification that gender deconstructs normative *marronnage*). The maroon escapes the voyeur not just by hiding in the hills, as it were, but by coding and overcoding languages of mutual recognition. Obviously, as I have hinted with Glissant, this strategy contains an aesthetic and social risk for opacity itself may be read as obtuse complexity, and culture complex enough to be the subject of someone else's cultural study, while the reading publics of Martinique and Guadeloupe might view such verbal skill itself as highbrow or elitist—hardly the kernel of solidarity that Caribbeanness attempts to nurture. (Condé, like Glissant, bemoans the lack of readership of her work in the country of her birth.[4]) Again, there is no simple solution to this dilemma: It is an active component of the agon I have been attempting to elaborate.

To some degree, the aesthetic articulation of this dilemma is precisely the linchpin of the imaginary state, for it struggles to name a desire that the realities of the Caribbean basin confound or displace. Most literary criticism of Condé, for instance, tends to focus on a symptomatic exegesis of the literary "journey" where aspects of Condé's biographical "search for identity" in France, the Ivory Coast, Guinea, Ghana, Senegal, France again, the United States, Guadeloupe, then back to the United States, stand in for how this postcolonial condition of errantry is written from within by the changed circumstances of the Caribbean itself.[5] This is not to diminish Condé's profound literary accomplishments but to acknowledge how her transnational credentials might get sutured to a desire from elsewhere for the elsewhere of multicultural élan.

To clarify an alternative approach (or an alterNative approach as my introduction indicated), let us remind ourselves of Glissant's opening to *Poetics of Relation:* "La culture est la précaution de ceux qui prétendent à penser la pensée mais se tiennent à l'écart de son chaotique parcours. Les cultures en évolution infèrent la Relation, le dépassement qui fonde leur unité-diversité"[6] (Culture is the precaution of those who claim to think thought but maintain a distance from its chaotic route. Evolving cultures infer Relation, the overstepping that grounds their unity-diversity [1; my translation]). This is part of what Glissant means by *imaginary,* and I think it connotes ways of seeing that are not cosmopolitan in the normative sense (that worldliness bequeathed by a primarily modernist conception of the wandering being). Instead of viewing Condé's journey as an extended preamble to a "return to a native land" (and we should not forget Condé's specific reading of Césaire[7]), perhaps it is itself a condition of thinking through forms of Caribbeanness, the very texture of difference in belonging.

Certainly it is not my intention to slot Condé unproblematically into Glissant's contradictory system of anarchic errantry (since for one thing the word *iconoclast* comes too readily to hand in terms of Glissant's poetics). But if, as I believe, Caribbean cultures have exploded certain mythologies of the modern (as Césaire puts it, "colonization and civilization?"[8]), it is partly because the natures of specific islands have been connected in particular ways. Antillanité, créolité, Caribbeanness, métissage—all are means of sensing these connections even if they do not chart the archipelago in any unified way (that mapping, of course, was part of the problem). Like Glissant, and to some extent Brathwaite, Condé's concern is for an understanding of the logic of connection itself. To what extent can she "belong" to the Caribbean in general and Guadeloupe in particular? How does her exploration of the pitfalls of identity (especially in terms of the engendering of space) simultaneously defamiliarize concepts of Nation *and* of Caribbeanness? What follows is only the beginning of an answer that, like the crossing that Condé's work articulates, invokes a process much greater than the critical apparatus deployed.

It is tempting to organize Condé's oeuvre so far into periods or stages of development: her ardent education in Paris, the cynicism she feels after her firsthand experience of African nationalism in Guinea (although there were certainly other factors that contributed to a more general air of despondency beyond the excesses of Sékou Touré), a more circumspect approach to the independence movements that characterized her time in Ghana (having come from Guinea, she was assumed to be a spy for Sékou Touré and so was arrested, but eventually released only to be deported a short time later), a stabler but no less difficult existence in Senegal, a period of intense political and intellectual activity in Paris where she worked for *Présence Africaine* and wrote a study of oral literature in Martinique and Guadeloupe, the fame that accompanied her Ségou novels that also precipitated her return to Guadeloupe, and the most recent period that includes living in the United States for much of the year and teaching at Columbia University.[9] Condé's extensive literary production, from *Hérémakhonon* to *La migration des coeurs* (Migration of hearts—available in English as *Windward Heights*) can be worked into this biographical grid in fairly precise ways, but I want to argue for a thematic approach to her work not because it represents the essence of her imagination but because that imagination itself interrogates the status of the writer in Caribbean identity. The latter presses the issue of Nation in interesting ways: For one, it augurs a métissage in method that invokes a "being Caribbean" without necessarily assuming the self-presence of that state. Again, the slippage between state of mind and a troubling political correlative is not some theoretical sleight of hand. Thinking difference transnationally requires the art if not the artifice of Caribbeanness precisely because of its cognitive challenge to the protocols of the Nation State.

That the biographical details alluded to above partake of that supersyncretic possibility outlined by Antonio Benítez-Rojo is both fortuitous and dangerous, given the long history of metaphorizing woman within a discourse of Nation State formation (the errantry of the author is not the equivalent of the ambivalence of postcolonial statehood).[10] Yet Condé's self-consciousness about the frustrations built into the Nation narrative do provide an alternative perspective on the borders, territories, and origins of the Caribbean nation that seems to have none.[11] Guadeloupe, as a *département d'outre-mer* (DOM; overseas administrative district), does not stand in for this problematic absence/presence but certainly is Condé's touchstone in rethinking an aesthetics of identification. In this regard, I want to outline the logic of identity that Condé elaborates in her book *Guadeloupe* and then link this to the dissembling self in *Traversée de la mangrove* (*Crossing the Mangrove*). If modernist wandering seemed eerily in step with the emerging transnational abstractions of monopoly capitalism (a universal that, as Terry Eagleton has noted, offers the Hegelian discomfort of everywhere being like everywhere else[12]), then the postcolonial writer wrestles with an equally pernicious aura; that her displacement plays out the wish fulfillment of global/local strategies of late capitalism. But this ideological endgame is not quite the trap faced by Condé's modernist forebears.

Guadeloupe is at once a fascinating and disturbing work. Produced with the support of the tourist office of Guadeloupe and filled with the lavish photography of Jean Du Boisberranger, the book looks and feels like a tourist memento.[13] This, of course, is part of Condé's point—that which enacts an exotic lure is also a contestatory field through which a counterdiscourse can be voiced. What she introduces, quite literally, into the field of vision of the touristic gaze is the question of cultural difference. A tourist may "see" difference only to confirm the logic of the Same (this is a standard psychological and colonial critique of the politics of vision), but under what conditions might this logic of collusion (in "I"/eye) be rewritten by a process of creolity itself? Condé's transnationalism does not elide the socioeconomic determinants that structure, to a degree, the nature of her intervention; rather, she builds this conscience of a space into the traditional forms of its annulment. Thus, opposite a standard exotic image of a young black island boy smiling brightly behind a cluster of dangling fruit, Condé writes "In the twentieth century, to discover Guadeloupe, in spite of the everyday roar of French or American Boeings and tourists of different nationalities filling Raizet airport, to my mind seems a task more perilous than that of the time of Christopher Columbus. Because it urges one to rid oneself of a good number of received ideas. Let us sweep away the first, the least original idea, that of a paradise for lovers of exoticism" (10).

In just a few sentences, Condé conveys the complexity of the Caribbean condition. She alludes, immediately and ironically, to that original and originary engagement of the Other constructed by Columbus (who alighted on the island in 1493) and problematizes "discovery" in the same moment. For if the nature of Columbus's mission has now been reconceptualized under the sign of a more general interrogation of the terms of European "history," the ideological baggage of "discovery" continues to accompany the adventuresome tourist on the journeys that she or he makes. Recognizing the perils of the persistence of such vision, Condé yet invites the reader to shed the detritus of their own psychic overinvestment in discourses of the Other. This is far from a welcome to paradise.

Condé continues to play on the tourist brochure genre's realms of expectation. What do you expect to see and where do you want to be taken? She cajoles the reader by invoking a tourist mapping out their itinerary: so much to see, so little time to do it. This is less cynicism and more an intricate carnivalizing of convention. This is precisely the way she approaches literary conventions or genres like the family history (*La vie scélérate* [Wicked life—available in English as *Tree of Life*]), or dynastic epic (*Ségou*), by confronting their prescriptions head on.[14] Here, whatever joy one might derive from the descriptive powers of a "native informant" is bracketed both by Condé's sense of marginality (vis-à-vis Guadeloupean everyday life) and by her nonidentification with Western desire. Guadeloupe is drawn in the interstices of memory and the trace of history. And at every moment when the tourist might gush before the tropical plenitude that confronts the eye, Condé punctuates the pictorial with something other than the infamous eternal present cast before the inquisitive postmodernist: "Continuing this quest to remember times gone by, find once more the highway ("la route nationale") and go back by the town of Capesterre. It is, don't forget, the place of discovery of Guadeloupe by Christopher Columbus" (20). Condé continues: "Take the road from the Carbet waterfalls, quickly leave it behind, and we are lost among banana trees with smooth shiny leaves." Club Med? Not quite: "The names of places which rise from this verdant mix speak for themselves. Ace of spades. Lost Zombie. Guadeloupe and its traditions welcome you" (20). This is extraordinary narration for most tourist guides, but just in case this air of menace might also be reabsorbed into a discourse of "thrilling" discovery (zombies!), Condé underlines that what is at stake is a different way to think the present through the pastness of the place. The delirium of a confrontation with "exotic" spirits (something akin to the patriarchal and colonial vision of hysteria painted in E. M. Forster's *Passage to India*) is quickly displaced by a more material ground of historical possibility: "All the characters of the collective imaginary come to life. It is in this pond, a dead eye three quarters covered with a blanket of duckweed and lilies, that Ti-Marie, sister of Ti-Jean, the hero in many fables, jumped to her feet to escape the devil ('guiab')." It is while touring around this veritable rampart of green that mothers sing:

Up there in the woods
There is a small hut
Nobody knows
Who lives there
It's a kalanda zombie. (23)

But why is this any more "material" than the revery that precedes it? Condé adds that this same region was a secret place of refuge for maroons, those "intrepid fighters" who challenged colonial domination and the requirements of the plantation machine. The myths and the substance of Guadeloupean history begin to mingle there, in the tangle of trees and pondweed. As Condé remarks, it represents "a certain history, a human history, of the woods and forests of Guadeloupe [that] remains to be written" (23). And then, beneath a striking photograph of "Mme Hyppolite Douat des Abymes," her face "etched by life," Condé explains her authorial sense of (the) place: "You have already understood as you have followed me that I don't like the sun simply pouring down on the sea and Club Med style group activities. My Guadeloupe is a little more rainy and more than that, a little sullen, not a bit modern, not laughing with all its teeth showing at the first thing that comes along" (26). Between this statement, beneath the pursed lips of a woman with the experience of life, and the opening page of Condé's narration, alongside the white teeth of a youth yet to live that experience, lies a call to cross or traverse Guadeloupe differently. It is a gamble of course, to use the form of tourism for a narrative that deconstructs the exotic imaginary, yet it is to Condé's credit that this approach is no rhetorical gesture but is born of a deep artistic commitment to what Guadeloupe could possibly represent beyond the facile fabrications either of a regulative history courtesy of "the Hexagon," or of the tourist who wants a tan and trinkets with as little of what makes history hurt as possible. But there is another twist here that needs elaborating before considering Condé's "Nation narration" in her fiction.

Condé does not just take the ardent explorer on an idiosyncratic tour of Guadeloupe; she also punctuates the text with more or less forthright political and economic critique. One reads standard historical detail like the creation of Guadeloupe's DOM status by France in 1946 and that this colonial structure encouraged emigration to the Metropole in search of work at the rate of 4,400 a year (about 1 percent per annum of the total population). More interesting is her sketch of the political scene, including the growth of independence parties like the UPLG

(Union Populaire pour la Libération de la Guadeloupe) and MPGI (Mouvement Populaire pour une Guadeloupe Indépendante) and the adoption of the PCG (Parti Communiste Guadeloupéen) of a broadly independence agenda. Traditional French parties remain a powerful force in Guadeloupe not because the majority of Guadeloupeans believe themselves to be French, but because the aura of assimilation is based on harsh economic realities; for one, the amount of cultivatable land cannot by itself sustain the population, even with traditional cash crops like bananas and sugarcane (with the highly prized strain of malavois) as central commodities. Condé is not supporting dependency theory, but she does understand that delinking from the French is not simply an ideological battle. When she ran for political office in 1992 she did not think that she would win, but nevertheless her involvement underlines Condé's commitment to the independence movement as an ongoing war of position.[15] Cognizant of the "imperatives of global production," Condé comments, "This country is not a vast consumer market, a big mouth that one can cram full. We don't produce anything" (34). It is at this point that Condé introduces the question of culture and of language in particular.

The twist, then, is not that cultural concerns might compensate for a nationalist agenda thwarted by the brute realities of economies of space, but that independence also requires a cultural knowledge, the combinatory potential of métissage. Lurking within this tourist guide, therefore, is something of Condé's cultural manifesto for Guadeloupe. She notes, for instance, that Creole is wrongly assigned the status of picturesque folklore, whereas it foregrounds a more significant cultural arena in which literature and oraliture wrestle to free themselves from the literary shadow of French. This, of course, is Condé's own struggle for, like Glissant, her French is creolized by her conscience of Caribbean space (one does not, therefore, have to write only in Creole to be a Creole writer). When she writes of "doudouism" in her guide (a derogatory Creole term for that process of exoticizing, in this case, Guadeloupe within a Western discourse of the Other), Condé is elaborating how cultural struggle is manifested linguistically. It is easy to romanticize this kind of intervention, but her point is that if "créolité" is a reality of Guadeloupean culture, then even a postcolonial Guadeloupe retains its force: The one is a provision of the other. There is much more to *Guadeloupe* than this: detailed observations on cooking, dress, music, architecture, and religion accompany and interrogate a pictorial that might otherwise confirm the powers of surveillance of the béké, the "negropolitan," or the all-seeing eyes of the tourist set. Let me summarize its provocation within a project of writing the Nation otherwise.

First, Condé is realistic about what is and is not possible within contemporary Guadeloupe vis-à-vis Caribbean nationhood. The imaginary state is here not a confirmation of Anderson's crucial invocation of the arbitrary sign, that which grants the temporal incursion of the "meanwhile" and the subsequent narrative of national time, but is instead an acknowledgment of the difference written into the "transactional" specificity of the Caribbean itself.[16] All cultures are syncretic, says Condé (78), but Antillanité is a measure of how those combinations are defined in specific ways. The model nation in the Caribbean is not one that asserts its autonomy through the "meanwhile" of identity, but one that emerges through an understanding of its shared history that then undoes any formula that would render its presence metaphysical. Thus, Condé reads Guadeloupe's predicament of identity as a question about the logic of separation as much as it is the form in which Guadeloupe takes up a position in a larger Caribbean community. As Étienne Balibar among others has pointed out, this conception of Nation does not oppose the imaginary to the real, since the "instant" of the nation, that which links the institution to the people, cannot but be imaginary.[17] Yet conventions of Nation certainly develop, ossifying either under prescriptions of power or codifying their existence through less obvious deferrals of the difference that denatures their legitimacy. It is not singularity itself that demands Guadeloupean nationhood (there is no single island, no single language, race, or ethnicity); it is this less than holistic métissage that allows it to repeat (Benítez-Rojo) or double (Jacques Derrida) the identity that would fix it.

This is not meant to provide theoretical solace for a land under colonial control (and one could see how such theory might provide a sophisticated crutch for doudouism), a point that might be underlined by extending a second provocation in *Guadeloupe*. Condé wanders the land of her birth to displace a fiction of identity, not the principle of fiction in identity itself. As she disables summary notions of the tropical paradise, she also journeys through the nature of her own fatalism (or, as she puts it in an interview, "the awareness of failure [in independence] must not prevent or retard action. Quite the contrary!"[18]). But Condé remains a writer, and her commitment to Guadeloupean independence is simultaneously an artistic mission (which is why her Guadeloupe is closer to her character Uncle Jean's book, "Unknown Guadeloupe," in *Tree of Life*). To say she imagines a nation that is not one is too easy. It was at some cost to Condé emotionally and aesthetically that she came to comprehend her own stereotypical projections in her younger encounter with Africa and the African nation (or perhaps still further back with her assumptions of French identity). And this is why, I believe, that she tends to cancel, in advance, any teleological imperative in Guadeloupean identity. Neither prescriptive nor simply descriptive, Condé's *Guadeloupe* is a commentary on processes of identification in which the commentator herself is questioned as a living witness to what Guadeloupe is or might be. The lesson here is perhaps Condé's epigraph from Pascal that begins her novel *Hérémakhonon:* "Je crois volontiers les histoires dont les témoins se font égorger" (I willingly believe stories whose witnesses get their throats cut).[19]

Creolity has been characterized as some masculinist conspiracy[20] and, although the evidence for this is quite strong (particularly among its most prominent practitioners, like Confiant or Chamoiseau), Condé remains generally sanguine about its possibilities for the Caribbean woman writer. Both her work and that of Simone Schwarz-Bart destabilize the patriarchal tradition of the *marron* or *quimboiseur* by writing matrilineal fictions of desire and memory. But feminism itself is creolized in this confrontation, which means it may dissemble even from the ardent categories of critique that may be applied. When Condé claims not to know what feminism means, she is not only remarking upon a certain inscrutability in the feminism she has encountered (which is chiefly French and American) but is reserving her right to be as "unknowable" as the Guadeloupe she articulates. The danger in this gambit is familiar, for harmful projections of the Other seek precisely this unknown as a precondition of phallic law. This, of course, is where the strategic use of opacity discussed earlier recommends itself, but it also calls attention to the need to clarify how Condé might appropriate a narrative technique while simultaneously altering the terms of its logic. This is how I would like to elaborate the "crossing" in *Crossing the Mangrove.*

On the surface, *Crossing the Mangrove* is a modernist exercise in style. Like Faulkner's *As I Lay Dying,* it is an open-ended tale oscillating to and from the central fact of death (and might also usefully be compared to *Finnegans Wake* in this regard).[21] The action is the process of narration itself, which, as in most modernist novels, is never far from the narration of Nation. But the perquisites of such discourse are almost literally dis-located, a critical geography that we have already registered in Condé's *Guadeloupe.* The dead heart of the story is the character of Francis Sancher, a mulatto exile either from Guadeloupe or Columbia (or Cuba, if you believe his assertion that this was the place of his "rebirth") whose cosmopolitan errantry has brought him to Guadeloupe to write a novel of place called *Crossing the Mangrove.* He cannot complete this book, just as he cannot write the multiple narratives by island inhabitants that mark the brute reality of his death. Nobody can provide a comprehensive picture of Sancher, just as he demonstrably fails to articulate a vision of Guadeloupe. Two mysteries meet one another, and this fateful collocation undermines the very wandering that precipitates the encounter. Cloaked in modernist technique, Condé's novel yet creolizes its technicist pretensions and, just as Faulkner challenges a certain metaphysics of American place in his writing (for his Yoknapatawpha is a border zone of what is and has not been "America"), so Condé's imaginary state of Guadeloupe distances both exilic exoticism and the inclusionary fantasy of Creole authenticity.[22]

As each character in the book draws an image of Sancher, the enigma Sancher faces in Guadeloupe is intensified, as if rumor and his rapidly expanding folkloric status on the island texture from within his inability to read and rationalize the landscape before him. It is for this reason that Condé portrays Sancher as "the European vis-à-vis the West Indian world."[23] She suggests that Sancher belongs to Europe, and thus he carries the sin of slavery and colonization that Europe brought to the Caribbean. It is a sin he cannot escape and in part it is this legacy that kills him. But of course, this is no more the essence of Sancher than Xantippe's masculine revery that Guadeloupe was formed from a jet of his sperm! Like many of the judgments that derive from the nineteen (or twenty, if you include the omniscient narrator) testimonials that form Sancher's wake, it is not the truth of such symbolic value that is at stake but its associative effects. The mode of narration is a way to understand that, in the manner of a mangrove itself, identity on the island is a tangle, not a checklist of easily definable attributes. On this level, Sancher's failure to come to terms with Guadeloupe is of similar mettle to Spero Jules-Juliette's unsuccessful painting career in Condé's *Last of the African Kings*.[24] There, Spero's doubts and constant questioning of his cognitive ability to represent Guadeloupe and its people is tied to a complex triangulation of the Caribbean, Africa, and America. Whereas his African American wife Debbie has no trouble imagining a unified black diasporic culture, Spero's ancestral lineage seems to pick away at his powers of articulation in the face of what Guadeloupe has become and what he remembers of it:

> What can you really say about Guadeloupe? OK! The island is no longer the hell it once was. The békés from the Great Houses no longer grow fat from the sweat of the niggers. Yet over there in his Élysée palace the great white president still lays down the law. In his predicament Spero resolved to get a book that would provide an answer to his sudden soul-searching and went to Marcus's. Alas! The section on the Caribbean had only a few rather yellowed translations of *Notebook of a Return to My Native Land* and *The Wretched of the Earth,* whose opening lines he found singularly discouraging. (139)

Similarly, Sancher is compelled to pen a tale that demonstrates the nature of the impasse in his relationship as a writer to his subject: "You see, I'm writing. Don't ask me what's the point of it. Besides, I'll never finish this book because before I've even written the first line and known what I'm going to put in the way of blood, laughter, tears, fears and hope, well, everything that makes a book a book and not a boring dissertation by a half-cracked individual, I've already found the title: 'Crossing the Mangrove'" (158). When Vilma tells him that "you don't cross a mangrove. You'd spike yourself on the roots of the mangrove trees. You'd be sucked down and suffocated by the brackish mud," he replies, "Yes, that's it, that's precisely it" (158). Although Spero does not appear to share this avid self-consciousness of failure, it too marks his artistic acumen. Yet this question of representation also links Sancher and Spero in their gender politics (for which the mangrove functions as an abyss, a more literal "no-man's land," to recall Benítez-Rojo's argument once more).

Spero is known as a "notorious womanizer" who does not begin to understand the sensibility of the "modern black woman." Throughout the book he is gently chided for his weakness, his misjudgments, and generally masculinist obliviousness. While Debbie is obviously not beyond reproach either (for Condé is never an absolutist about gender or race), Spero's confusion is often linked to a form of male delusion in which a general lack of control is compensated by flights of fancy that ultimately end in frustration or cynicism. Sancher's artistic vision is insistently compromised in this way, but to this is added the weight of guilt that stems from the inglorious exploits of his forebears (who may or may not have been rich landowners on Guadeloupe). Like Spero, Sancher finds solace in womanizing, but his various sexual exploits (which include Dinah, Mira, and Vilma) do not bring him any closer to Guadeloupe or its people; indeed, many despise him precisely because he seems bent on repossessing the land through its women. I am not suggesting that these men fail to render an adequate artistic vision of Guadeloupe merely on the basis of their highly dubious sexual outlook; I would, however, press the case that reimagining Caribbean identity beyond its colonial constellations is not unconnected to limiting mutations of masculine selfhood (this is most egregious in the incidence of men raping women, a masculinist violence that Condé explicitly addresses in *I, Tituba, Black Witch of Salem*, *La colonie du nouveau monde* (The colony of the new world), and *La migration des coeurs* [*Windward Heights*]). Part of the difficulty in reading *Crossing the Mangrove* is separating this impasse from Condé's genuine sympathy with Sancher as an artist and exile (one could argue, for instance, that she writes the book that Sancher cannot as a counterbalance to the fact that the inhabitants of Rivière au Sel tell us more about island identity in their ruminations on Sancher's death than he can in his studied approach to their lives). Condé's tactical ambivalence on such issues has a strong political edge which questions who has the power to represent and in what medium. Her use of Creole in this novel is not a stylistic embellishment but a stand on the multivalence of a creolized writing for Caribbean expression (again, a "movement" that has itself been accused of racial and sexual essentialism). Creole also functions to dialogize the narrative as if each testimonial were a transcription of internal and external monologues. So, while not necessarily subscribing to the central precepts of créolité, Condé creatively extends its aesthetic and political possibilities. Indeed, this is the plane upon which so much of what is held to be "normative" in Caribbean life is fractured and recomposed along different community vectors. While Condé is forthright in denying "militancy" in her writing, it is rare that forms of patriarchy are not challenged in her work linguistically or simply by twists of plot. But what does this mean to Caribbeanness and the art of crossing to which this imaginary is dedicated?

The "crossing" in Condé's title is an important way of understanding the emergence of Caribbeanness in the archipelago. Crossing, "traversée," invokes a history and a present predicament. The French verb and its cognates describe both the process of passing through *and* the possibility of a barrier to precisely that journey, something that crosses or traverses one's path. A *traversée* is also, of course, a sea crossing, and no one should underestimate the force of the Middle Passage in defining what the Caribbean can become. Similarly, crossing evokes the realm of error, a mistaken path, as well as the process through which a journey is thwarted. The mangrove ensures that the path will be difficult (as in *de travers,* crooked or awry) or indeed impossible. The story of Francis Sancher, then, is itself a narrative of crossing. An assortment of hearsay, insight, misrepresentation, and mystery, it fails to offer an individual as Subject that might stand in for the Being of Guadeloupe as a DOM. It is tempting to mark this circumspection purely as a function of Condé's considerable stylistic tenacity, one with its roots firmly in modernist experimentation of the *Rashomon* variety. Yet the fate of Sancher is bound to a history in which it is precipitate, that his culpability for the sins of his ancestors is simultaneously a remark on the state of Guadeloupe and a question about the limits of art in demonstrating this historical block. The mangrove is literally a wild feature of Guadeloupe, but the true narrative of its future is demonstrably tied to the fortunes of the banana, sugar, rum, and tourist industries whose own stories remain inextricably linked under the sign of dependence. Condé is well aware of this predicament. Thus, although *Crossing the Mangrove* can indeed be read as an exotic mélange of subtropical delight (which is what the artwork on the Anchor Books edition suggests), like Condé's *Guadeloupe,* its aesthetic effect is tempered by an opacity redolent in Caribbeanness in general. As Sancher demonstrates, every assumption of possession from the outside is answered by mystery or a need for a more perspicuous understanding of the nature of the mangrove itself. And even heartfelt identification (like Sancher's earlier alignment with the oppressed of Cuba) falls short of providing simultaneously a key to Guadeloupe's culture or the exact form of its decolonization. Sancher, the artist, hopes to "fixer la vie avec des mots" (capture life in words) but the struggle of Caribbeanness is to make a life that is not simply deracinated in advance by the experience and reality of colonial Being.

It is for this reason that Condé, like Glissant and to some extent Brathwaite, favors a form of errantry, for "fixing a life" inhibits a process much more vibrant than the inevitable blueprints made for it (the alternative, as noted above, is "to live the world"—"vivre le monde"). Individual writers do not constitute a rule for errantry, nor indeed Caribbeanness, but one lesson from their aesthetic provenance is that the imaginary relations of Nation (for every nation must hypostatize an illusory origin) do not exhaust the possible relations of island identity. "Il faut errer. L'errance est salutaire" (one must wander, wandering is salutary), suggests Condé, and there is no doubt that some privilege attaches itself to that possibility. Yet if one keeps in mind the notion that the islands repeat (they "wander" in place with a cultural complexity specific to that momentum), then the errantry at issue is not just a modernist agon or bygone: It is a struggle over the terms of identification, a struggle that must—always already—take place on the plane of the imaginary. Just like "sly civility," errantry has some valence in the process, the "crossing" that is decolonization. Here, Glissant seems to be speaking of a political formation, a sense of being in process, that Condé (or George Lamming and Caryl Phillips from anglophone perspectives) would appreciate:

> The thought of errantry is not apolitical nor is it inconsistent with the will to identity, which is, after all, nothing other than the search for a freedom within particular surroundings. If it is at variance with territorial intolerance, or the predatory effects of the unique root (which makes processes of identification so difficult today), this is because, in the poetics of Relation, one who is errant (who is no longer a traveler, discoverer, or conqueror) strives to know the totality of the world yet already knows he will never accomplish this—and knows that is precisely where the threatened beauty of the world resides.
>
> Errant, he or she challenges and discards the universal—this generalizing edict that summarized the world as something obvious and transparent, claiming for it one presupposed sense and one destiny. He or she plunges into the opacities of that part of the world to which he or she has access. Generalization is totalitarian: from the world it chooses one side of the reports, one set of ideas, which it sets apart from others and tries to impose by exporting as a model. The thinking of errantry conceives of totality but willingly renounces any claims to sum it up or to possess it.[25]

The circularity in the form of Condé's novel evokes this sense of errantry even though it must have a final line. Just as Sancher (or Spero, for that matter) cannot sum up Guadeloupe, no one can claim this task about Sancher himself. But the narrative plays a cruel trick on Sancher: His end is in the beginning. This also explains why Condé's writing on Guadeloupe does not offer an imaginary resolution for the real contradiction of her country as a DOM. Crossing takes time, which is to say that the contradiction that Caribbeanness addresses is, whatever else it is, historical and inscribed.

4

The White of Algeria; or, The Paroxysms of the Postcolony

> Today, at the end of a year of somber death, dirty death, in the darkness of a fratricidal struggle. . . . What do you want to be called, Algeria!
>
> —Assia Djebar

Cultural transnationalism, if it is to have any significant bearing on the protocols of cultural studies, must come to terms with the vexed geopolitics of the Nation in the current era. Some of the tasks involved remain as necessary as they are obvious. One could analyze the historical trajectories of the Nation idea by, for instance, tracking how it is challenged and redefined under the terms of decolonization. Concomitantly, one could specify the persistence of the Nation as cornerstone within "independence" movements and how the laudable and appreciable efforts to carve a space beyond colonialism yet get sutured to geopolitical agendas that acknowledge the postcolony only to find its subjects ripe for subjection once more. Each example of postcolonial statehood qualifies and extends the conditions of Nation, and it would be unwise to derive a formula from this, if only to register that the formulae for Nation are also at stake in postcolonial delinking. Of course, the other matter at issue in this example is postcolonial theory itself, which is also pinned to the question of the geopolitical, however minor its role must be. In the argument that follows the tension in these problems form something of the background to the space of writing Nation that is Assia Djebar's feminist intervention. Yet this is just as much the texture of Djebar's writing as the *parergon* is the frame for a painting's understanding.[1] By this I do not mean simply context: In the otherwise unimaginable violence unleashed in Algeria in recent years, Djebar picks away at the frames of reference available to show how these too are the subject of critique and judgment. This is important both in dispelling the myths of postcolonial nationhood, and also in maintaining the voice of woman as agent in what the nation becomes, issues that Djebar has negotiated in artful and inspiring ways. It is easy at this moment in history to see Algerian women, in all their differences, as once more the victims of patriarchal logic, as if they were simply duped by the ruse of anticolonial exigency so that now, despite their pivotal role in the war of independence, they are but a cipher in the discourse of men. But this fails to register, as Djebar most certainly does, the active contribution of women to the real of Algeria, as well as its imaginary scope. Such efforts are not simply "outside" Algerian statehood or its contemporary geopolitical significance; rather they work against the dilemmas of postcolonial subjecthood and the Western illusion that all a crisis in a postcolony needs is a good dose of Western machination (since, for one, the machinery of Western intervention has already been written into what a postcolony can and cannot become, at least in those states formed in the wake of European imperialism).

What is the "white of Algeria"? In 1995, Djebar published a *mémoire*—or a "rememory" as Toni Morrison would put it—a reflection on the current crisis in Algeria written through a communion with the dead—in particular, close friends, intellectuals, writers who have been assassinated. (The book is dedicated to three of them: Mahfoud Boucebci, M'hamed Boukhobza, and Abdelkader Alloula.) *Le blanc de l'Algérie* (translated as *Algerian White*) is in many ways typical of Djebar's oeuvre: Part history, part autobiography, part elegy, part fiction, it registers in a profound manner Djebar's forceful connection to the fate of Algeria.[2] White cannot be innocent in the passage from colonialism to postcolonial subjecthood. But Djebar's book, like her writing in general, is not a study in "whiteness" in the conventional sense, the whiteness of those who lorded in the name of civilization. On one level, the white of Algeria is the whiteness of a target or the space of being targeted, the space in which one meets death. Yet the whiteness of death is not an absolute nor a means for absolution. For Djebar, it may well be a zone of death, but it remains a space of engagement. She is well aware of the history of "le blanc" in colonialism, just as she understands its meaning for art (she quotes the abstract expressionist Vasili Kandinsky, "white on our soul works like absolute silence"); Djebar's deployment of white, by contrast (and the connection in the contrast, as I've mentioned, remains at issue) takes up the symbolic aura of whiteness (the white shroud, the white veil, the white of desert expanse) and reads this into the imaginative capacity of writing itself. Writing may literally be marked by white (the white background, the space between letters) but it can also be the medium of whiteness, the absence of that which differentiates that simultaneously takes up the *différance* that is its very possibility. What Jacques Derrida terms a "white mythology" is not just about the binaries and metaphysics that gird a Western view of the world but is about the myth in whiteness as that which marks itself off from a plenitude of difference.[3] The nonwhite becomes the invisible, the nonmaster, or as Hélène Cixous remarks of her upbringing in Algeria, "women."[4] Djebar writes in the white ("écriver dans le blanc," but the phrase she borrows is "donner dans le blanc" [264]) in the language of the Other, in the language of the Same. Djebar writes in French as a stranger, as a foreigner (l'étranger), yet this strange writing is precisely what defamiliarizes the white, just as to historicize the Algerian civil war makes strange the largely Western projection that it is North African madness. In this sense, the "white of Algeria" is, in a Fanonian spirit, an imaginative disturbance in the field of the Other. Algeria becomes the space *of* writing, not the space *off* writing.[5] It is not the void or blank (the pun on white in French) to be written in by colonial desire once more (although this remains persistent threat under the sign of neocolonialist "global" strategies), but a state of imaginary urgency compelled by an all-too-real emergency: the implosion of a postcolony.[6]

But surely, Djebar's philosophical and aesthetic disposition regarding *white* is not the hard kernel of geopolitics or even the somewhat softer shell of cultural transnationalism? What Djebar's work often speaks to is the question of writing difference when difference itself has the imminence of disaster.[7] The call, most often, is for an understanding of that difference precisely to guard against a kind of geopolitical displacement that elides the specificity of space that is Algeria. This is, once more, a conscience of space, but one that has evolved out of a writing as urgency. There is a danger, of course, of romanticizing the act of writing itself, as if writing might save Algeria from its brutal implosion, but I think Djebar is more interested in the centrifugal meanings of Algeria, in its complex history and current impasse, that make her own exotopic relation to the country of her birth (she is in Paris, "in" French, or New York, in French and English) a provocative source of understanding, despite its fragility and contradictions. Can one write a nation from the position of transnational subject?

A fiction on a fiction, perhaps. Just as poststructuralism "begins" with the Algerian war of independence (as Robert Young points out, Sartre, Althusser, Derrida, Lyotard, Foucault, Cixous, and others were either born in Algeria or involved in the war in some way[8]), so one could argue that postcolonial feminism is structured by the difference that Algeria represents. The trouble of the postcolonial subject is further troubled by woman's relationship to its history. Marie-Aimée Helie-Lucas, also an Algerian feminist, has drawn attention to the exclusion of woman, in her own name, from the narrative of Nation except as a mythological symbol of revolt and solidarity.[9] Yes, women were a vital component of the struggle against the French, yet she underlines, using Djamila Amrane's study of Algerian women in the war of independence, how the terms of liberation themselves are gendered and discriminatory. The image of the veiled freedom fighter is a strong one (and appears in Fanon's works as well as the films *The Battle of Algiers* and *Frantz Fanon: Black Skin, White Mask*), but official veteran registration data lists a grand total of one woman armed fighter and no women at all in decision-making positions. As Helie-Lucas points out, the fact that women were raped, tortured, and killed by the French during the war suggests a different story, not one in which we should extol the virtues of violent martyrdom in the cause of liberation, but one in which the question of woman destabilizes the terms of freedom drawn by both sides. "This is the real harm [that] comes with liberation struggles. The overall task of women during liberation is seen as symbolic. Faced with colonization the people have to build a national identity based on their own values, traditions, religion, language and culture. Women bear the heavy burden of safeguarding this threatened identity. And this burden exacts its price" (107). The price is being paid in the Algerian civil war, which, for all the pieties about brutalized women at the hands of fanatical Muslim males, continues to inscribe the dilemmas of liberation redolent in the anticolonial struggle some forty years earlier. The paroxysm of the postcolony is not the product of its failure to approximate the democratic ideals of the former colonial masters but that it replicates the coding of woman as symbol in the nation's logical integrity. On the cover of *Le blanc de l'Algérie,* two women are whited out by their veils, their full-length *haïks:* Djebar's task has been to write out the white-out of Algerian history. And this by all means imagines a different space of Nation formation.

Rather than summarize all Djebar's long and distinguished career in writing (and to an important extent in film) I want to focus in particular on her engagement with Algeria as Nation, not because she unlocks the secret of its current crisis, but because she picks away at the logical integrity of its current constellation.[10] Djebar is a trained historian of the Maghreb, and she has insistently brought this knowledge to bear on the imaginary state that energizes her fiction. While often hesitant in articulating a political foundation for her vision, Djebar has increasingly elaborated a creative sense of how "things fall apart" in the Algerian postcolony. It is a complex vision, and one that is cast against and directly influenced by the extreme situation to which she bears witness. Again, one must say that her relationship to Algeria is profoundly exotopic in the Bakhtinian sense.[11] This outsideness is not just a function of her literal exile, the fact that she lives and works outside Algeria, in France and more recently in the United States (like Glissant before her, she had a position at Louisiana State University —a francophonic vantage point over the Caribbean and beyond—both are now in New York), nor is it purely a perception of her writing in French—although this clearly is vital to any understanding of how writers de-scribe the postcolony as part of a cultural evisceration of the logic of colonial domination. No. The force of her exotopy is Djebar's identification with, yet separation from, the Other *as* Algeria and *in* Algeria. The "white" again is the ground of contrast, but it is also a medium of profound inspiration. Such exotopy has been greatly intensified by the Algerian civil war, which has not only taken the lives of several of her close friends and relatives (thus *Le blanc de l'Algérie* is both re-memoration and memorial) but represents a significant threat to Djebar's own existence.

For Mikhail Bakhtin, exotopy is an aesthetic relationship, and I do not mean to undermine Djebar's social consciousness by invoking it. The Other that is Algeria, however, has increasingly become the object and the cause of much of Djebar's writing. It is that which defies writing, by its voice, by its blood (in *Vaste est la prison* [translated as *So Vast the Prison*] and *Le blanc de l'Algérie* Djebar will often refer to the blood of writing), but is nevertheless that which must be written for its Being to be apprehended. What defies the logic of description is not the horror of the civil war (which is often the tack taken in the Western media) but the grounds of the Nation as aesthetic object. The familiar retort is that to render the object in this way is precisely to aestheticize rather than politicize its reality. That is certainly a risk in this and other readings of *Imaginary States,* but the point is to come to terms with the imaginary schema of the Nation, the better to understand its possibilities and contradictions. In exotopy, as Bakhtin presents it, the "I" of the author is aesthetically unreal; it cannot be the object of its own aesthetic production (even when the solipsist believes this to be the case). But what of the postcolonial subject—is this not always already constituted as an Other, as that which, according to the very terms of its alterity as subaltern, is less "outside" the Other as object that may be its chief concern? The white of writing from this point of view is the danger of silence it represents, for in the face of a colonial legacy and a postcolonial crisis, writing is condemned not to speak the horrors of its identification. The problem is not whether Djebar, as a middle-class feminist francophone Algerian living in France and America, has a right to speak about the nature of Algeria, but whether anything can be said at all (whether, indeed, the right to speak is operative). Djebar's response has proceeded at at least two levels, both to intervene in the narration of Algerian history and to question assumptions of identitarian formulae through the act of writing itself.

Much of the critical work on Djebar refers to her ability to "give voice" to the women of Algeria, and clearly her fiction is a sustained attempt at such articulation.[12] But this inscription of the voice remains a vexing problem for politics and philosophy, indeed a politics of philosophy, since it offers a conundrum about subjectivity, presence, and ontology. Derridean critique has attempted to undo the privileging of the spoken through the *différance* of writing, but this too comes with a significant pause, for the interpretive mode applied to the sentence (appropriately, death sentence or *l'arrêt de mort* in Derrida's approach—which, for interpretation, is both an order for death and a stay of execution) might also seem to elide the violence within speech, the power relations that trace the curve between the word and silence. Since such philosophy has emerged in the shadow of North African decolonization, what then to make of Djebar's postcolonial critical consciousness based, in part, on the insurgent voice?[13] The disabling of the Master's Voice should not imply the displacement of voice *tout court,* for this would seem to conspire with an ideology that insistently confers a panoply of silence on those whose voices would otherwise transform the conditions for dialogism. And what of silence, does it not speak back to a force of silence that would render it merely soundlessness? The rhetorical ploy that might accompany the question "Who speaks for Algeria?" is an empty gesture if a consideration of silence is not written into the response, for this too interrogates the boundaries of the utterance in Algeria as Nation. Bakhtin, for instance, understands the logic of such boundaries as context-specific and as historically informed. What he calls the "distant and barely audible echoes of changes of speech subjects and dialogic overtones" (93) determine and texture the very possibility of Algeria *as* Nation in the present.[14] Thus, even amid the murderous shouts in Algeria's ongoing civil war, the silence of words on the page can become a scriptible intervention against a mode of production that would render silence only an empty voice.

How vast is the space of silence for Djebar? Greater than most attempts to speak or write it. Theory continues to struggle with this space as much as it does with the inscription of the voice: to acknowledge it, to think it, to trace its logic of affective answerability (its inward state of Being) without merely speaking, writing, thinking in its place. There is no single strategy for positioning oneself with respect to silence, partly because that place is beyond voluntarism and volition (formed therefore by more than this or that individual consciousness or praxis) and partly because even in the moment of apprehension, the apprehension of silence, the eventness of the event is possible only in the field of the Other—the complex processes of identification that do not resolve themselves in the steady self-incriminating voice of the "I" (to say, "I hear silence," is to erase the Other). Like intersubjective relations themselves, the space of silence is a plethora of positions in the realm of the "possible answer," or the dialogic. This very multiplicity is not necessarily its virtue, for the ability to take up various positions may confirm a certain tenacity in the production of silence. Ideologies, for instance, can achieve longevity through such flexibility.

Historically specific matrices of power *produce* silence, enact its aura of absent subjectivity (one should add that strategic silence can oppose such matrices). The hegemonic mode of production of silence is extremely underestimated, but in various forms it has come to betray the logic of oppression in colonialism, racism, nationalism, patriarchy, and capitalism—to name but five of its most egregious manifestations. The difficulty remains whether the critic or writer as subject can speak to this position, the Other under the subjection of silence, without merely reproducing the insidious desire of modes of domination themselves. This is what must be risked, however, for to absolve oneself from this scene of silence, from the space of its production, is to oil its mode of *écrasement* (effacement). To understand the mode of production of silence is not to describe its vastness, but is to answer it, to come to terms with the way it might be made answerable in the field of the Other's silence perceived otherwise.

How can one provide detail of the crisis of Algeria, a "beyond" of the mediatization of civil war as event? The problem of media "eventness" is a vexing one—as Djebar explains in *Algerian White:* During the war of national liberation, the French government and the media referred to the struggle as "events."[15] Of course, the war that is closer to the black heart of the Age of Europe, the nationalist delirium played out in that presumptive phrase "the former Yugoslavia" in the 1990s, is the one that is dear to the transnational media machine, that still depends on an ideology of Eurocentrism (in this case, Europe literally at the center of the world). I would, however, like to indicate at least some of the components of the Algerian crisis (the "not event" rather than nonevent) before Djebar's disarticulation, an interruptive and interrogative gasp, "Je ne crie pas, je suis le cri" ("I don't cry, I am the cry"[16]). I do not believe that Djebar's de-scription of masculinist hegemony through the scriptible voice is the only or the best way to oppose the bloody frenzy unleashed in contemporary Algeria, but neither do I think that Djebar's eloquence, academic or otherwise, is "another way of silencing women, this time by a woman."[17]

First, the hegemonic mode of production of silence in postcolonial Algeria is primarily economic. The austerity program introduced in 1994, for instance, was clearly an attempt to appease the International Monetary Fund (IMF), with whom the government was seeking to reschedule Algeria's more than $26 billion in foreign debt. The interest on this debt alone was the equivalent of Algeria's entire export earnings that year. Inflation remains high, and unemployment hovers around 30 percent. Ninety-five percent of Algeria's export earnings come from the sale of oil and gas (one pipeline alone provides Spain with 40 percent of its natural gas), yet much of this money disappears in the white haze of corruption and graft. In recent years these "facts" appear to define the postcolony as Nation, as further examples like Nigeria and Liberia would demonstrate. Second, the mode of production of silence seeks a guarantee in and through violence. A violent pathology is not postcolonial (if anyone, the colonizer in history has exercised that compulsion), but it is produced in postcolonies where global economic forces ignore the value that independence confers. The violent will to silence of mono-logism is not innate: It is the product of a state's desire to harbor power in the face of an economic duress that cannot but fail to provide it with a mandate. In this respect, we can say that monologism is a mark of absent authorization—the authorization for power—if not authority. The "Security Council" or "High Council" in Algeria provides neither security, counsel, nor height and has accepted military hardware from the French, against whom its generals had once waged war. The influx of weaponry only exacerbates the thralldom of violence that has already killed some 100,000 Algerians (the official government figure is about a quarter of that) since the annulment of the election that took place on 26 De-cember 1991. The annulment and the emergence of military rule were spurred by the FIS (the Islamic Salvation Front), winning 188 of the 231 seats contested in the first round of elections. Third, the mode of production of silence is gendered. This is highly controversial, and so let me be precise: It matters little to a mascu-linist hegemony whether a critic or a writer uses Algerian women as a metaphor for an abstract feminine condition. The gendering of silence depends upon a brute concretization of oppression in the form and structure of power relations. To be sure, the discourse of man is still in the metaphor of woman (as Gayatri Chakra-vorty Spivak says of the use of *woman* within a patriarchal symbolic order), but this should not obscure the fact that women in Algeria are primarily objectified within a discourse of oppression because they are women, not because they might stand for something else. Here the question of silence becomes tangible, not ab-stract. The Algerian women who were stabbed to death or had their throats cut in 1994 first for not wearing the veil and then second for wearing the veil are in neither case a metaphor for masculinism: They are its very instantiation. In Oc-tober 1997 near Bentalha a dry well was found stuffed with girls aged 13–19, their throats cut, which in some cases was the least of the atrocities performed upon them. And all this becomes a page, black on white.[18]

There is no single strategy for an understanding of silence across the space of Algeria. Nevertheless, just as the Algerian civil war has intensified the mode of production of silence, so Djebar's work now overflows in a multiplicity of oppo-sitional writing—a kind of *écriture désaccordée* (discordant writing) that writes out silence just as it inscribes the voice. Certainly this has been a constitutive feature of Djebar's writing, which artfully *de*-scribes or deconstructs French co-lonial discourse while not sacrificing the scriptible voice of Algerian women that

informs such delinking. Gender is the central fact of Djebar's oppositional critique because (1) gender differentiation drives the colonial episteme, the desire
for the Other constructs the Other as woman, that which must be possessed and
assimilated to the Self of masculine certitude; (2) the Law of the Father preexists
the colonial adventure—it is inscribed in the social discourses of the Maghreb,
sometimes reduced to patriarchal interpretations of Islam, but also functioning
within a more general code assumed to sanction gender hierarchy (this includes
interpretations of tribal and class-inflected economies of difference); and (3)
gender riddles the language of difference, not just between the alternative and
alternating registers of colonizer and colonized discourses, but also within the languages of state, which have often produced a celebratory masculinism in articulating the "imagined community" of Nation, however important the concept of
Nation has been in delegitimating colonial subjugation. In this light, Djebar
addresses a central problem in the languages of liberation: How can one enunci-
ate a new sense of Being (the postcolonial subject, for instance) when the very
process of delinking is grounded in ontologies of the Male whose power seems
to give to that design its logical integrity?

Several cultural strategies recommend themselves, including *écriture féminine*
(women writing) and *parler-femme* (speaking [as] woman), which both suggest
a deterritorialization of masculine space in language. Again, Djebar is aware of
such theoretical approaches—her cosmopolitanism, for instance, includes debates
with and within Paris over precisely such issues. Yet the point is that her writing
the voice of Algerian women is a politics in situ, a discursive scheme that differs
not only from the perquisites of the Parisian scene, but also within itself, for the
Maghreb is plural and contradictory. The space of enunciation locates the ad-
dresser in a specific way. In the case of Algeria, the polyphony of the Maghreb
continually contradicts Algeria's ideology of Nation and Nationhood. This,
against a backdrop of an increasingly conservative vision of Islam, intensifies a
crisis of identity (for this vision itself questions what form an Islamic republic
might take). Djebar reads this agonistic function in postcolonial subjectivity as
irrevocably engendered (that is, before women can be more than women they
must be themselves) and therefore she articulates a "scriptive discontinuity"[19]—
a break from a certain history of identity as a prelude for what might become. In
the interanimation of these diverse counterhegemonic voices, a heteroglossary
begins to emerge, one whose philosophy of language is always already a politics
of language in contemporary Maghrebi aesthetics.

Djebar's *Femmes d'Alger dans leur appartement* (translated as *Women of Algiers
in Their Apartment*) begins with a scene of torture from the past; a woman is being
electrocuted by minions of the French regime, scarred for her work in the Alge-

rian war of independence. Both Sarah and Leila carry these scars because they carried fire (in the war there were women who attacked the occupying army with grenades—Djebar calls them the "fire carriers," *porteuses de feu*): Their scars are born of insurrection. For Djebar, scars and scarring are a touchstone of memory, something that must be voiced. But this is not just a question of artistic creativity but one of access to language, to the arena of the *Le Verbe*, an arena of class struggle as Bakhtin puts it, and more besides (that is why in Djebar's quartet, as Mildred Mortimer has pointed out, French *écriture* is opposed by Arabic *kalaam*, and thus the colonizing male is disarticulated by the indigenous peasant woman, *l'écrit* by *les cris*[20]). In the torture scene male violence is written onto the body of the woman: For Djebar, that inscription cannot or should not be silenced, secluded, or veiled. But this is but one cadence in a discourse of postcoloniality.

The colonizer has memories, too, as Djebar evokes in her extraordinary "Postface" to *Women of Algiers* by reference to the "intoxicated gaze" of Eugène Delacroix, whose brief encounter with a harem in Algiers in 1832 produces the famous painting whose title Djebar borrows for her collection of stories. The final essay, "Forbidden Gaze, Severed Sound," dramatizes why a philosophy of language must also write out the cognitive and corporeal space of sight and sound specific to women's Being. This bears comparison to the way that Bakhtin begins to sketch the complex coordinates of I/Other through the body and affect in *Art and Answerability;* in this case, however, Djebar writes the body through the scriptability of an unraveling discourse of domination. Djebar argues that within Delacroix's "stolen glance" (which is also the viewer's who sees this painting) "Elles demeurent absentes à elles—même, à leur corps, à leur sensualité, à leur bonheur" (*Femmes* 173) ("They—the women—remain absent to themselves, to their body, to their sensuality, to their happiness" [*Women* 137]). In a sense, they are looking nowhere, because, in a cunning reversal and unlike the spectator who mischievously pores over this phantasm, they do not have the right to look. Yet it is not just the voyeurism of the colonial gaze that marshals this figurative absence: It is also the surveillance by the women's own culture that, a century and a half later, and despite a "progressive" relaxation of social codes in between, continues to situate or condition an affective absence (a felt and persistent marginalization—which is Djebar's way of accentuating that postcoloniality does not imply postpatriarchy). The struggle over the Family Code of 1984, for instance, is about the stark contrast between the promise of equality and institutionalized patriarchy.

Djebar knows that in highlighting the woman question, merely by having women speak (that is, in recording their oral expressions), she runs a gamut of oppositional critique. First, to oppose the marginalization of women in the new society is seen to detract from the integrity of Algerian nationhood (feminism itself can be attacked as colonial baggage). Second, feminism, while certainly not anathema to Islam, is regarded as an affront to conservative interpretations of the Koran and *Hadith* (the sayings of the Prophet) and as a profane symptom of non-Arab modernization (given the violence of 1988, when a student protest against bread prices was crushed by the military leaving 600 dead, and the continued instability of Algerian politics since December 1991, this makes Djebar's interventions all the more remarkable). Third, the use of French, even when it attempts to tongue-tie His Master's Voice, can be read as complicitous, a cosmopolitanism that again allows the woman question to be read as an antinationalist agenda (of course, that Djebar has attacked the policy of "Arabization" because "Official Arabic is an authoritarian language that is simultaneously a language of men" [*Women* 176] has only fanned those particular flames).[21] Fourth, and most crucial given my own position vis-à-vis Maghrebi writers, there is a strong tradition of criticism in Maghrebi postcoloniality (the *Souffles* group for instance) that is highly suspicious of works that (intentionally or not) feed the ethnographic desire of the West. As M'hamed Alaoui Abdalaoui has commented on the situation of Moroccan novels in French, "in France (and elsewhere in the West), [such] novels are still universally read as sociological documents (the most highly prized being those that deal with the condition of Muslim women)."[22] This is not just a knee-jerk masculinism but is a position shared among some Maghrebi feminists (Marnia Lazreg for one has pointed out that narratives focusing on the veil, seclusion, or clitoridectomy play into the obsessive interests of the Western colonial unconscious—a fetishism inexorably inclined to ingest images of the oppressed woman *elsewhere*).[23] Here I will say only that the position of adjudication (or what Foucault describes as the place and subjectivity taken up by a subject in order to make a statement) cannot be produced by simply displacing the woman question into categories of ethnography, sociology, or indeed neocolonialism (which seems to unite the other two). If Djebar's fiction has a material correspondence with specific inequalities within Algerian society, it is not out of a desire for Western readers (*Women of Algiers in Their Apartment,* for instance, was first published in Algeria), and even if it is, would this constitute an adequate grounds for dismissal from *within* the very texture of that lived inequality? There is too much at stake for Djebar to allow the decentering of Euramerican colonial desire to detour or defer women's enunciation—a condition that requires even more than a war of independence, but social transformation more broadly construed.

In the first two novels of her quartet (*L'amour, la fantasia* and *Ombre sultane,* translated as *Fantasia* and *A Sister to Scheherazade,* respectively), Djebar suggests that the first priority must be the woman's story (*l'histoire femme*) that artfully links the scriptible voice to memory and so to history.[24] Both books depend upon a canny oscillation not just in the space between languages, but in that which marks the field of intersubjective exchange and diachronic "eventness" as Bakhtin puts it. These are indeed the weave of a dialogic, itself a significant mark of Djebar's novelistic discourse, but here the point is that Djebar's biculturalism is specifically dialogized by the woman's voice. This utterance is the product of an arduous collocation of historical research and a painstaking attention to oral traditions that denature the "established" borders of Algeria (those established by colonial fiat—one could argue that even in its name Algeria is literally beside itself, since the word comes from Arabic and originally described the islets off the coast of Algiers, not the mainland—the name was provided during the Arab invasion of the seventh century). Thus, even as *Fantasia* proceeds by a clever juxtaposition of the French invasion of 1830 with the events leading to the liberation of 1962, the central *histoire* is writing the voice, a question of women's performativity directly linked to aspects of Djebar's upbringing, her acculturation. At one point the narrator comments on the differences among the veiled women of her community, especially that which refuses the realm of silence: for instance, women shouting between their patios.

> To refuse to veil one's voice and to start "shouting," that was really indecent, real dissidence. For the silence of all the others suddenly lost its charm and revealed itself for what it was: a prison without reprieve.
>
> Writing in a foreign language, not in either of the tongues of my native country— the Berber of the Dahra mountains or the Arabic of the town where I was born— writing has brought me to the cries of the women silently rebelling in my youth, to my own true origins.
>
> Writing does not silence the voice, but awakens it, above all to resurrect so many vanished sisters. (*Fantasia* 204)

Voice does not confirm presence, at least not in the philosophical sense of ontology, but it does imply a relation, one that links, sometimes imperceptibly, a historical chain of dissidence in dissonance. The voice is interventionist not just because it textualizes the testimonials of those who have often been confined to the realm of silence or the unheard (and therefore the *inconnue*), but also because it is an agonistic archive, a restless register of what *can* be said, and differently. Even when the "chronicles of defeat," the defeat of 1830, are the reminiscences of men in the narrative, the presence of women begins to seep through: "Ces lettres parlent, dans le fond, d'une Algérie femme impossible à apprivoiser" (*L'amour* 69) (between the lines these letters speak of Algeria as a woman impossible to tame). H. Adlai Murdoch has suggested that Djebar feminizes the figure of invaded Algeria, but in a sense this has always been there in what Jenny Sharpe calls "an allegory of empire."[25] The greater strategy is that, while she does not falsify the records, Djebar scrupulously marks the gender trouble that conditions their very possibility, so that the invasion "reverberates with the sound of an obscene copulation" (*Fantasia* 19), one that attempts to objectify and possess in the same instant.

Djebar recognizes that the colonial episteme requires a fantastic overinvestment in the colonized as Other. For her part, she presents this delirium fantastically; specifically, in *la fantasia,* in which we see something of the contradictory logic of the grotesque. *Fantasia* refers to both the warlike display of Arab horse-riding skills in which the riders charge the spectators only to stop just before they overrun them and also the musical style (common in Europe from the sixteenth century) in which the form of composition is made subservient to "fancy" (the link between a fantasia and quartet in musicology is obviously also relevant). Commenting on Algiers in 1818, Blaquière described the fantasia as a "paroxysm of passion," which for me connects the violence of one interpretation to the creative reverie of the Other.[26] (During a fantasia in Djebar's novel, Haoua, a young Algerian woman, is [accidentally!] kicked to death by a horse ridden by a lover she had rejected. The historical incident that Djebar reimagines is recorded by Eugene Fromentin in 1852 during the French occupation.) Today, the Maghrebi fantasia is not just a measure of tribal masculinism but also a bizarre, carnivalized mirror of orientalist desire (and can include "flying carpets," belly dancers, snake charmers, and any number of generalizations worthy of the tourists' gaze). The fact remains that Djebar tracks fantastic projections of desire through every level of culture she articulates (one could also connect this theme to the letter-writing campaign of the adolescent girls in the first part of this novel). But she also focuses on the oppression of women as women rather than simply revel in the description of such fantasy, which by itself would only replicate the desire she wants to challenge.

Like *Fantasia, Loin de Médine*[27] (translated as *Far from Medina*) uses a close reading of history to speak to Algeria's present, in this case to offer a narrative of Islam's comparative flexibility in the final days of the Prophet's life and the immediate aftermath of his death. Djebar supports her tactical contextualization of this moment through respected sources like Ibn Sa'd and al-Tabari, an essential although still a dangerous move in the current political climate. Djebar attempts to round the characters and their everyday interactions by accentuating what is latent in the classical histories; that is, that the wives of the Prophet and other women in their environs were "women of the verb" and women of action and were respected as such even if part of their power derived from patriarchal genealogies (for a nonfictional account of this period, the work of Leila Ahmed is highly recommended[28]). The lesson is consistent with Djebar's other works; her double words or dual words are an exhortation to remember, and in that memory to conjure a subjectivity deferred or confined: "Ah, far from Medina, to rediscover the wind, the exhilaration, the incorruptible youth of rebellion" (*Far* 275). This is not idealism but an utterance contracted to the specificity of a historical context. In October 1988 in Algiers Djebar saw "blood flowing in the streets." *Far from Medina* becomes her book of blood—not a call to bloody uprising but a meticulous reconstruction of the spaces through which the voice is engaged in an otherwise bloody and violent situation. As the singer of satires, the poetess says to Muhajir before he has her teeth pulled out and her hands severed, "My eloquence, my voice will remain when you are dust" (*Far* 106). While hardly a philosophy of language in the accepted sense, it inspires a dissonant sense of writing that now claims greater urgency.

The third novel in Assia Djebar's projected "Algerian quartet" is further evidence of her complex sense of Maghrebi women's "rise to the word." *Vaste est la prison* develops many of the critical tools of enunciation that Djebar has deployed in her other works, including a nuanced approach to the problem of the scriptible voice (here most critics favor the term *polyphony*—although the consciousness that these voices connote is not always "independent" according to the terms of Bakhtin's model: The independence of consciousness is here circumscribed, for specific historical reasons); blood as a cultural sign (of violence, violation, initiation, and resistance); and memory as palimpsest and imbrication (a process of conflicting historemes through which an ancestral woman is collocated—*Far from Medina* is probably the most salient other example here). Let us focus, however, on the construction of narrative space, a narrative from silence that I invoked earlier. While critics have remarked in the past on Djebar's articulation of a women's space in Algerian culture (that which resists the confinement of women, or their separation from the public sphere, except as veiled), there is less understanding of what grounds the abstract space of resistance that informs Djebar's construction of a counter-public *énoncé*. Part, at least, of the "vastness" of Algeria's contemporary hegemony over women, is answered and indeed confounded in Djebar's prose by a perspicuous privacy that throws into relief the privations of a masculinist Algerian public sphere that leaves out or denies an actual public presence for women. What Djebar terms the "silence of writing" is an implosion of this inhibiting interpretation of public space. True to the fictions of Algeria as Nation, woman as metaphor "exists" as the space of Algeria, yet real women are denied access to this space as women (this reflects back on the Family Code of 1984 once more, and also on the acute housing crisis for independent or divorced women).

This is relatively easy to gainsay in Djebar's otherwise highly stylized and pa-
tiently but insistently formal quartet so far—the critical and metaphorical space
of Algeria as woman in the language of the colonizer artfully deconstructed in
L'amour, la fantasia; or, "the world outdoors" without the *haïk* (veil) and the open
secrets of the *hammam* (public baths) as a nonmale refuge in *Ombre sultane* (translated as *A Sister to Scheherazade*). But the recoding of space in *Vaste est la prison* is
itself repositioned by the crisis since December 1991, just as the October riots of
1988 structure (or texture) the very language of *Loin de Médine* (translated as *Far
from Medina*), the *langue vive* of a distant past in the service of an alternative rebellion or *Itjihad.* The third novel of the quartet, then, responds to an utterance
context, as Bakhtin would have it, that forces Djebar to rethink the logic of history's power and, of course, history's erasure. For critics, all that narrative on blood,
silence, writing, and voice in Djebar's previous books may have been the stuff of
abstract play, but now it assumes the condition of real slit throats, real charred
bodies, real butchered vessels of the word. This is the prison that history makes.

There are three strategies that I believe Djebar attempts to weave between the
bars that words alone cannot break. To begin with, *Vaste est la prison,* like much
of her other fiction, refuses the subject statement of a unitary self. But this stock-
in-trade of postmodern "schizophrenia" (in Deleuze and Guattari's sense) is giv-
en a further interpretation in the novel by the silence of writing itself. What noise
can invade this silence, which is not a last resort but words that live unvoiced?
In the first part of the book ("L'Aimé en silence"), this silence is a scene of battle
in the heart and mind of the narrator as she remembers a love affair with L'Aimé,
a younger man with whom she experiences the passion of youth she had never
had (105). The intense privacy of this affair is not just a traditional refuge but an
opening out into questions of inscription—how can this love affair get told, and
in what language, the medium of narration? And this is a feminization of space,
a reclaiming (and sometimes an invention or a dream) of a language of desire,
but one that is answered in a familiar way: The narrator is beaten up by her husband and admonished that she deserves to be stoned. Whatever the moral judgment of the affair and its consequences, Djebar links the narrator's experience to
the status of man in the unconscious of the Algerian woman. Beyond "La bru-
talité et le désordre conjugal" (marital brutality and dysfunction) Djebar seeks a
reason for the imposition of silence in an economy of death, one that is marked
as masculine in the organization of space in Islamic Algeria (or more specifically
an Islamic fundamentalism that has emerged in Algeria). This is a mask, both as
a disguise and as a death mask, worn by the husband as a right, as a tradition, as
a law of history. The mask of authority is what allows the patriarch to beat, and
to speak.

What, then, can be read as melodrama (and the narrator says as much) is also "une translation de la vision de l'autre" (a translation—and an anglicism of *traduction* that underlines it—of the vision of the Other): a critique of the logic that interpellates the narrator in silence. Such a logic is worse than death (here silence does not equal death) for it takes a woman's heart in her mode of expressivity and effaces it: It erases not just its emotional content but also the language it creates. The vastness of this silence might seem to be the lot of an individual woman, the narrator, but the second part of the novel suggests that this narrative of erasure is precipitate in Algerian culture and history, in the narrative of Nation itself. Thus, Djebar will develop a counterstrategy of identification through a double-voiced discourse of history.

"L'effacement sur la pierre" (Erasure on the stone) refers to a complicated story of imperial and colonial erasure in the face of "native" inscrutability. Briefly, this section relates the discovery and effacement of a key "texte bilingue" of North African history—the stele of Dougga Jugurtha, the king of Numidia who fought long and hard against Roman expansionism (and subsequently would be an inspiration to the FLN in their war with France). The stele makes a declaration of defiance in two languages—the first, a Punic or Phoenician script, and the second a sign of hybridity and alternative identification. This language is at the heart of Djebar's polemic about the silence of writing (writing's silence and the imposition of silence on writing). The secret language on the stele is related to *Tamahaq,* and the alphabet is *Tifinagh* (preserved in Berber, a language of the Hoggar Mountains, the language of the Touareg, the nomad). We are jumping across this fascinating and detailed history, but Djebar's point is vital to our understanding of the novel. The Touaregs themselves have practiced a specific mode of cultural assimilation and autonomy that has not been averse to rejecting those aspects of a patriarchal interpretation of Islam that threaten the active roles that women occupy in their cultural practices. When wave after wave of foreign invaders supplanted the indigenous languages of the region (for instance, with Arabic, Turkish, and French), it was the women who preserved the ancestral writing: They were the scribes who gave the language its historical integrity when every other mode of archeology (which, in this history at least, means colonialism) tried to burn it, steal it, or scratch it out. Djebar is forcing the issue as a scribe herself, and one who is bound by the living contradiction of French, the mark, if not the guarantee, of "les pieds-noirs" (the popular term for the French colonizers and/or their sympathizers). The narrator identifies with the ancestral lineage even as she knows she cannot be synonymous with it. Instead, "C'est dans la langue dite 'étrangère' que je deviens de plus en plus transfuge" (It's in the language called "foreign" that I become more and more a renegade—a defector to the other side).

Obviously this could be read as compensation, but this is not the point. The spirit of Jugurtha's resistance, an answerability to the land and not just a shadow of male warriorhood, lives on in every mode of writing that refuses erasure by the dominant, and in particular resists the prescriptions that deny the history of women that writes Algeria. This, then, is the second strategy.

In the third section, "A Silent Desire," Djebar works out this renegade spirit in the form of a polyphony, a disjunctive series of women of the land (Lila, Isma, Lla Fatima, Bahia, etc.) whose narratives, "fleeting" but forthright, do not so much recover the *écriture illisible* of Jugurtha but put it to work in a matrilineal memory that is the other side of history (the other side of that which erases, crushes, or silences). It is a generational memory to be sure, and one that measures a potential that has not been completely obliterated by the course of history before and after the war of independence. Just as the narrator recalls the valuable knowledge that her mother learned not from books but from the liberation struggle itself, so she attempts to teach her daughter the submerged "tenor" of silent desire. But her daughter learns too, in the moment of history (she is, for instance, in Algiers when the October 1988 riots occur) when it is enough to want a breath of free air in the stifling vastness of state repression. Within this polyphony the narrators do not ask for absolute separation from men; indeed, the "shadow of that separation" itself is seen as traumatic (as in the death of Uncle Sidi). But separation among the women is certainly more deeply felt, and it is the death of one of them, young Cherifa, from typhoid that forms a fulcrum within the text. As the women lament the loss of Cherifa, they reflect too on a history of misfortunes all the way back to the inscription on the stele. A cousin sings in Berber, the language of the mountains: "From the first day of the year, we have not had a day of rest/vast is the prison that crushes me, where will you come from, deliverance?" (237). Vast is the prison ("meqqwer lhebs" in the Berber), but this is no ordinary lament: It is a voice of defiance. For Jugurtha, the prison would be *his* trap, so that, even when captured and taken to Rome, there would be a part of him that could not be inscribed or taken up within the narrative of Roman domination. This existence, as a hole, as a void of the unassimilable, would be, according to the narrator, literally a hole in the heart of Rome. And it is this spirit of the nonrecuperable, the unassimilable, that is a catalyzing strategy for the women's community against the myriad hardships they may face.

There is much more to Djebar's novel than this, but let me press the point on its relevance to Algeria's war within a narrative of Nation. The spirit of Jugurtha remains not in the form of an idealistic national purity, but as the sign (like language) of a discordant but vibrant multiplicity, a *bilangue* of historical integrity, that which must return (as Bakhtin notes, "Every meaning will have its homecoming festival"[29]). The dead Cherifa herself comes back. As the narrator comments: "On the earth of Algeria, so much later, the dead return. The women, the forgotten, because they are without writing, form a funeral procession, the new Bacchantes" (338). On the one hand, there is a masculine death, one that is explicitly linked to a specific interpretation of Islam in the present, a promise of monologism. On the other hand, Djebar offers another version of this narrative; one that recognizes a Muslim reality but in a discrepant double language of history—one made possible by, for instance, the Touareg women's other language. It is this cry that infiltrates the mode of production of silence. Fleetingly (*fugitivement*), perhaps, it collapses the embrace of that silence. It writes it out.

> You live as far as possible from Algeria. From now on you want to turn your back on it once and for all, and then suddenly you feel, growing on your own back, new eyes, deep, open eyes with an immobile gaze, eyes that open and grow wider watching your past. Yes, and these eyes are there to look once again at this country, at its drama, at its blood, to contemplate its treachery, its martyrdom, and . . . its malediction.
>
> Eyes? These are the eyes of language, the eyes of lost memory. . . . The language that rustles, having taken its words from you, the mute underground language that no longer has the power to move your hand. . . . Language without signs, with only the sound itself that disfigures, that destabilizes the second language, this language called sacred, that made you falter before your mother and her woman-poet friends who would read their work, who would improvise, but always in this other language, Arabic, the language of the Sacred book, when they wept for the dead through their lacerating verses. During all this time, the first, secret, pagan language that became deafening, that clamored for speech, that stuck at the back of your throat, its monologues strangling you, during all this time, the primitive language often dismissed as barbarous wanted to dance within you, to make you dance, but now it is too late. (785)

The intensity of this personal testimony is reason enough to study Djebar's artful negotiation of vision, voice, and script. Her dilemma is clear: She may challenge the orientalizing eye of Delacroix, but from her privileged position outside the immediate strictures of the local, how does she face her Arab and Berber countrywomen? Similarly, while she tears at the language of a colonial education and malevolent forms of Arabization, what can she do with the language that sticks at the back of her throat, Berber, the other side of her heritage, historically preserved and internalized by the women of her community? In *Le blanc de l'Algérie*, Djebar's constant struggle with what the Nation gives in its contradictory multiplicity is compounded by the deep sense of loss she feels for her murdered friends. Fatima Ahnouch has suggested that *Vaste est la prison* is "a hymn to the feminine imaginary" (795) and to some extent *Le blanc de l'Algérie* extends that song. But it is also a dirge, a requiem to a national imaginary written through death up close—the necessity of language in the face of violence and brutal murder. What can words say, the text asks, what resource of hope can they provide where blood is the medium and the message? *Vaste est la prison* had ended with

> writing to stave off the unflagging hunt
> At every step the open circle closes
> Death ahead, the trapped antelope
> the Algerian huntress in me is swallowed up. (348)

The first chapter of *Le blanc de l'Algérie* is titled "The Language of the Dead" and explains poetically and painfully why Djebar must now commune with the dead. Death here becomes a kind of white noise, it saturates the air and makes the possibility of erasure and silence tangible in Djebar's articulation. The "blood of writing" gives way to the white, the shroud that seems to cancel all before it. There are places in this elegiac narrative where Djebar herself appears close to succumbing to the thrall of violent death itself: "An Algeria of blood, of streams of blood, of bodies decapitated and mutilated, of the looks of stupefied children. Desire takes hold of me, in the middle of this funeral gallery, to drop my pen or my brush and to join them, to dip my face in their blood (the blood of the assassinated)" (162). This is a disturbance not just in the field of writing, but in principles of textuality that construct Algeria. Here, dipping one's face in blood is a ghastly echo of another initiation, the newborn Arab Muslim sipping water infused with Koranic scripture (Gafaiti). The promise of purity has become the precipice of death. And yet *Le blanc de l'Algérie* is not a book of death, despite the long line of departed writers and intellectuals Djebar considers (including Frantz Fanon, Albert Camus, Mouloud Feraoun, Jean Amrouche, Mouloud Mammeri, Kateb Yacine, Youssef Sebti, and others). Djebar calls it a "liturgy" (12), a rite of public worship, which in this case does not appear beholden to a particular god or religion but to the power of writing itself, however diminished or exhausted expression might be.

The *mémoire immédiate* that informs Djebar's book is a stark contrast to the immediacy of events that litter the international press. I should say, however, that Djebar's focus on Algeria's history of targeting intellectuals and writers, while historically valid, may also be read to detract from the far-reaching social cataclysm of the civil war and may require further contextualization. Think, for instance, of how the public outcry against the *fatwa* hanging over Salman Rushdie is often deployed to elide in fairly precise ways the history that led to the Iranian revolution, or the stark differentiation in various forms of Islamicism. Yes, it is wrong to murder or threaten to murder writers on the basis of their political or religious beliefs, but this is only a part of the horrible vendetta that structures the crisis. Initially, then, the violence was directed principally against leading government sympathizers and prominent secular figures. Key journalists and writers were murdered who not only criticized the Armed Islamic Group but *also* the military-backed government of Zeroual. The international community was flummoxed by these events—it wanted to ostracize the Islamic militants but did not want to seem like this endorsed the government that, after all, had basically usurped the democratic process. Nevertheless, the military regime received a lot of assistance that allowed it to protect not only its officials and key secular or moderate supporters, but also the oil and gas fields in the Sahara that provide, as mentioned, the bulk of Algeria's export earnings and where such staunch defenders of democracy, BP, Arco, and Total have their drilling operations. The effect of economic austerity measures comes with a crass economic formula that says that social turmoil is acceptable unless it interferes with the price of gasoline (the people of Iraq were extended the largesse of this principle in 1991).

In 1996–97, however, the nature of violence in Algeria took a different turn (and this is why Djebar's intervention itself is a historical document). Now the poor and working class were visited by marauding gangs armed with guns, knives, swords, and on one occasion a portable guillotine. Some of these attacks, in Blida or Rais, for instance, went on for hours within earshot of military barracks. Yet despite the screams of the wounded, the witnesses, and those who had been set alight, no help was forthcoming. Up to 300 people died in a single incident (the government massacre of 1988, of course, far exceeded that). My point is simply that the intensity of Djebar's vision itself has its own specificity in the archive, a value that here I extol for its imaginative grasp and historicity but not as an act of finalizability or consummation, to borrow from Bakhtin once more, in the texture of Algerian identity.

Conversely, just as *Vaste est la prison* reveals the cultural vitality of women in North African history, in the preservation of *Tifinagh,* for instance, so *Le blanc de l'Algérie* suggests that the violence of the present is intimately connected to bloodletting that has characterized the modern emergence of Algeria in another suppressed history. As Gafaiti comments: "Djebar reopens the scars of her people and offers them a vision of themselves that they do not want to face. The mythical foundations of the Algerian nation collapse in a dissection that unfolds the revolutionary past as partly rotten and impure because of systematic and internecine struggles, numerous betrayals, shameful sacrifices, and successive killings."[30] Gafaiti has in mind Djebar's prodding about the bizarre vision of Abane Ramdane being reburied as a hero in 1984 next to Krim Belkacem and near Houari Boumediene in El-Alia Cemetery in Algiers. Boumediene had "murdered" Krim Belkacem (assassinated by Algerian agents in Frankfurt) who had "murdered" Abane Ramdane (Krim sided with the military after disagreements at the Soummam Conference—Abane was assassinated the following year). And how many times has this cycle of violence occurred in national formation? Of course, Boumediene (Mohammed Ben Brahim Boukharouba-Boumediene was a nom de guerre) is a somewhat obvious target, since he became Algeria's second president by ousting Ben Bella in a military coup in 1965. Whether or not Boumediene should be considered a Stalinist or state capitalist (and the difference remains important), there is no doubt that his nationalization of the petrochemical industry through SONATRARCH (a state firm) was a vital blow against French neocolonial interests in the 1960s. His brand of nationalism, however, remains crucial to the concept of paroxysm in the postcolony, of which more below.

Djebar's text is on dangerous ground, not just because she deftly reveals the lies propagated in the name of Algerian Nationhood, but because she risks reproducing that phantasm of Western modernity, the inevitable atrophy of the newly independent postcolonial state into barbarism and self-destruction (of course, there is a related but different risk in the reaccentuation I give it here because of my own subject position). Clearly, however, there is a cultural and political advantage in addressing the demons of history, particularly when, for feminism, a state's newly minted self-representation elides the violence (including violence against women) built into its esteem. This is what Djebar means by the "unsaid" of Algeria and it is precisely this "unsaid" (the "severed sound") that stands between Algeria and more egalitarian social relations. For Djebar, the dilemma of writing against this will to silence is poignant and acute:

> The white of silence and that of the page waiting in vain for an original text and its translated double, at the risk of being somewhat betrayed.
>
> The white of writing, in an untranslated Algeria? For the time being, Algeria, writingless, despite all the actions of writing, despite its angers and groans; alas, for the time being, a bloody but writing-less country.
>
> How can we mourn our friends, our colleagues, without beforehand saying out loud why yesterday's funeral took place, the funeral of the Algerian dream? The white of dawn—between the colonial night and the rising day? "White square on a white background," like a Malevich painting, exclaiming, at the turn of the century: "But this desert is brimming with an objective sensitivity that pervades everything!"
>
> In the brilliance of that desert, in the retreat of writing in search of a language outside languages, endeavoring to scrub out, in ourselves, all the furies of collective self-devouring [auto-dévoration], to find that place "from within among words" that remains our one and only fertile homeland.[31]

Like Djebar, Marie-Aimée Helie-Lucas knows of that silence kept by women after "liberation." The exigencies of the new state-prescribed silence while the busy work of national consolidation and legitimation took the fore (a surprise border war with Morocco following independence underscored the necessity—a vigilant silence while nationalism shored up the state in the face of its clear fragility). For Helie-Lucas, this precluded or constrained international feminist identification, as if solidarity itself was a foreign import intent upon blasting social cohesion. What both feminists have witnessed is the danger of strategic silence in the name of the state. The difference in their positions, however, is instructive. For Helie-Lucas, the cost of Algerian identity "in the name of the Father" was too heavy a price to pay even before the current crisis. She therefore urges feminist opposition that is "truly internationalist."[32] Helie-Lucas also characterizes another imaginary state: "Let us dream of secular states. Let us dream of the separation of religion and state. Let us dream of the end of using nationalism to further oppress the already oppressed."[33] For Djebar, by contrast, the trajectory of this dream folds back into the question of language itself. In 1993 in Strasbourg, she notes: "Algeria . . . has increasingly become culturally fragmented (and where the traditional sexual segregation has tightened all the screws), words have, of necessity, lost their edge even before they could sharpen themselves by their own flickering light. And yet, I am moved only by that need for words with which to confront this imminent disaster. Writing and its urgency."[34] For some, this remains the texture of that permanent split between activism and aestheticism, but both, it seems to me, constitute a challenge to the structural logic of the Algerian state. When the FLN declared its own existence (1 November Proclamation, 1954) it also asserted "the preservation of all fundamental freedoms" and the "internationalization" of the revolution. At a time when fundamentalist freedoms and internalization have shifted the terrain of the State and its signifiers, activism like Helie-Lucas's is well complemented by Djebar's engagement in the "war of languages" (which she lists as Arabic, French, Berber, and the most crucial all, the language of "power"). Against the anestheticizing vocabulary of state power that describes the civil war as "events," what is "white"? Djebar asks, the white of dust, light without sun, the white of dilution?[35] Djebar describes it as the vanity of saying or statement (*la vanité du dire*) but also asserts its necessity. If we can say that Djebar has attended to the submerged or erased speech and writing that girds Algerian identity in history, a concern that has meant writing out history, then whiteness is the most intense expression of this urgency, it burns like acetylene in the crucible of her imagination.

This scene of writing is complicated and contradictory from both political and philosophical standpoints. White is a metaphor that comes with its own ideological baggage in the colonial episteme. For Derrida, for instance, a "white mythology" is precisely the metaphysics of the white European male—he who takes a very specific philosophical history of metaphor and tropology and casts it as a universal, Reason. "White mythology—the metaphysical has effaced within itself the fabulous scene that produced it, and which remains active, restless, inscribed in white ink, invisibly sketched and recovered in the palimpsest."[36] What is true of the colonial episteme is also true of Nation. As Bhabha reminds us: "Nations, like narratives, lose their origins in the myths of time and only fully realize their horizons in the mind's eye."[37] I am not suggesting, however, that Djebar merely repeats the ruse of Western metaphysics in metaphorizing the "white" for Algeria. On the contrary, her reinscription on Algerian identity, like another layer on the stele of Jugurtha, displaces the aura of white in imagining beyond the moment of colonization. Yet it is easy to see how such a creative rewriting might succumb to romantic inclinations, hypostatizing the act of inscription in a move that conveniently grants the diasporic writer herself perspicacity. The Nation fills in the white to stabilize the metaphor against the rootlessness and displacement that is its cause. But the white remains as metaphor, and Djebar returns to it to ponder the logic of its instability, just as the voice in her fiction troubles the formality and formalism of the word as law. As a subjective state of Being, Djebar's identification with Algeria questions the Reason in its community. (Is it merely Arab, is it Berber, what of French, and how can it be a hybrid of all three and more?) Yet, as Gafaiti's comments indicate, this is not without its compensatory implications: "It is because there is an absence of expression that violence erupts. In these circumstances, since expression is forbidden ["forbidden sound"] in the public sphere, it must inhabit writing. Writing becomes the way to escape one's exile from one's own society and culture; it becomes the site of memory and survival."[38] Yes, but this personalizes the white in a way that the identification itself appears to challenge. Perhaps Djebar has fallen into what Benedict Anderson describes as "long-distance nationalism"; one could just as easily argue, however, that "the funeral of the Algerian utopia" that Djebar invokes, "the whiteness of a dawn that was soiled" (*White* 275), clears a space for writing only to acknowledge that white itself is overcoded, palimpsestic, and therefore always already "written." Here then is a path to paroxysm in the postcolony. It is not an illness or attribution of a violent pathology; it is, rather, a critical ambivalence in the narration of Nation that, caught between the joy of independence, and the pain of Nation formation, struggles to name (and write) an alternative means of community identification.

This alternative includes but is not limited to the emergence of woman as a national subject in Algerian life. Clarisse Zimra, one of Djebar's most attentive

critics, has noted that in popular Algerian political discourse women are often
excluded from what counts as an Algerian.[39] Clearly, Djebar interrupts and interrogates this inevitability in state formations that wear their patriarchy as a badge
of faith (legitimized in Algeria in documents like the Family Code of 1984). Yet
whatever is illogical in such discourse (a state must always claim to represent its
constituency even when its practice indicates a systemic failure in that regard),
this does not fully describe the paroxysm of the Algerian nation. Several competing discourses are at play that determine and overdetermine the exclusion and/
or suppression of woman as Algerian subject. Interpellated within an anticolonial and socialist agenda, the valorization of woman's active social status seemed
assured, but, as we have already noted, a historical exigency does not make a
political guarantee. Today, the barrier between woman and Algerian identification is typically characterized as Islam, yet this not only misreads the diversity of
Algerian women's community identity but also the complexity of competing
political and economic forces within the state itself. For instance, a secular solution to the current crisis (along the lines of Helie-Lucas's powerful invocation)
would not in itself remove the military machinery behind the High Council, nor
would it terminate the agreements among men to marshal economic resources
(Algeria's vast oil and gas reserves) in their own interests. It would be quite possible to bracket patriarchal versions of Islam in Algeria without displacing conditions of women's oppression in general. The paroxysm of the postcolony in this
sense is that for feminism real social change is much more than the political process named "democratic" or secular.

Djebar understands this, not just because she has the power to imagine Algeria differently, but because she has studied its history long enough to see beyond
the violent events of the present. White in this instance is not resignation but a
signature of the possible within what is otherwise a demonstrably acute impasse.
"For my part, I am haunted . . . by a long and abiding state of morbidity"[40] declares Djebar in Strasbourg, yet she refuses to succumb to it. Her problem, as a
writer, is the means to combat this morbidity in Algerian culture without writing itself becoming an imaginary resolution to a real contradiction, which again
would reduce the crisis to a function of the word and not necessarily accentuate
its responsible speakers, writers, and activists of many persuasions. The fix of
women's victimhood in Algeria is answered by a belief in the multiplicity of subjectivity—something that allows Djebar to identify with male writers of the tradition but in general acknowledges the fundamentally plural basis of Algerian
constituencies. What the crisis wants to white out in the intensity of violence and
internal strife is what Djebar is compelled to write into Algerian history and creativity. When Djebar states that Algeria is untranslated, she is not simply erring

on the side of an infinitely writerly metaphor (a metonymic substitution for the metaphor of Nation itself), she is acknowledging both what Algerian writing (particularly francophonic) is literally untranslated into the national language, Arabic, and also what is in essence untranslatable in the discourse of Nation that is Algeria. In the international mediatization of the "events" of Algeria, the desire for translation is also a desire for transparency, a logic that would render the madness of Arabs, the madness of Africans, the norm of coverage. Yet this is also a reminder about the difficulties of multiculturalism in Djebar's conception, for, whatever she does to French to make it a stranger to itself within its colonial legacy, there will always be legitimate reasons for questioning its role in liberating Algerian women.

How, then, to characterize the crucial intervention of Djebar in reimagining Algeria? Certainly this cannot be done purely on the grounds of writing, even as that remains the primary focus of my comments here. Critics have already explored several alternative means of understanding Djebar's oeuvre—in particular, the question of the gaze (a visual economy that extends well beyond her significant film efforts) and the use of musical motifs and structures—all of which provide an expansive sense of one of Algeria's greatest authors. But I want to conclude by pushing why Djebar's Algeria is exorbitant to what Algeria represents. In a book of photography that is rarely discussed in criticism of Djebar, *Chronique d'un été algérien: Ici et là-bas* (Chronicle of an Algerian summer: Here and there), Djebar writes a commentary on the work of four photographers who explore everyday life in Algeria in 1992. The idea behind the book was to focus on the work of Claude Bricage, who died of AIDS before the project was completed. Bricage is honored in a short afterword, "L'Algérie de l'auteur absent" (The Algeria of the absent author) by Christian Caujolle, and there are many ways in which this is an apt description for Djebar herself. She is the absent author both literally and figuratively in the white she ascribes to Algeria. But more than this, Djebar's words outside the frame (in which each image has its own language) underline both the prescience and the dilemma of her white writing. The text is full of observations, but remarks charged with Djebar's sensitivity to the very question of observation, both as an exile "looking in" and as a distancing of the project of "looking in" itself. Once again, the spirit of the gaze of Delacroix is refused and displaced. She concludes: "Because death knocks at Algiers. In its wake of blood, of fears and of tears, Algeria, 'my' Algeria, staggers" (36). This shaking, wavering, or vacillating (*vaciller*) does not make Algeria an undecidable in lieu of Nationhood or national identity (although, to some extent, the "imagined community" of Nation is always that); rather, Djebar's marginal notes here (the parerga of the frame) accentuate the difficulty in writing Algeria, in coming to terms with its history and predicament, when the shorthand of "events" can stand in for the depth of struggle in identity and identification. If distance provides Djebar with perspective, she continually doubts the truth of "seeing" Algeria. And, just as Derrida knows that much can be made of white (mythology) for philosophic sense, the white of Algeria exists as a French supplement to its language of Being ("in the white"). Djebar does not answer blood with blood, but elaborates instead the texture of the crisis that would otherwise leave her and the living and the dead of Algeria a blank space in a global imaginary.

5

Chronotope of the Shoe (Two)

The fulcrum in a greater understanding of globalization is the life of a commodity. Certainly this is a very different life from the imaginary scope of literature considered so far, but the schisms between the two are highly instructive for methods of cultural transnationalism. The idea is not to transpose the theoretical framework in the analysis of the literary to the calculus of profit and loss in trade but is to come to terms with the imaginary conditions of both as mutually determining. This requires thinking of production and cognitive reach in a time/space, or chronotope, heavily influenced by the nature of the commodity form itself. The following project on athletic shoes is continually being rewritten, not just because its key elements are alive in public consciousness (Nike, Indonesia, capital), but because the otherwise innocent logic of the commodity interrupts and displaces the will to historicize what makes it a linchpin in the way the world is imagined. We would like to believe that the imaginary effect and affect of the commodity is a world removed from the literary or the aesthetic, a belief that has attained the status of a classic bourgeois antinomy. Yet it is not enough to identify simply the superseparation that carves out the sublime for the culturati while leaving popular or mass-produced items for the less discerning. Neither is it adequate to advance the notion that commodity aesthetics are just aesthetics that, bereft of a premodern aura, weigh on the living like the Mona Lisa's smile or Edvard Munch's "Scream," as mechanically produced caricatures of a lost origin. To investigate the commodity at this time is neither to venerate nor to equate the commodity with the aesthetic but is to fathom the extent to which what undoes the aesthetic in the commodity is also what unhinges the imagined community of nation. Thus, if the chronotope of the shoe mutates according to what Bakhtin ponders as the eventness of events, it also changes because that process itself is linked to a key phenomenon for transnational inquiry: the deepening contradictions of the commodity for Nation formation but also corporate desire.

Karl Marx once suggested that a commodity "is a very strange thing, abounding in metaphysical subtleties and theological niceties."[1] A social history of the shoe would show as much, for there is no commodity in modern history with a greater capacity to confound thingness and spirit, use value and exchange, desire and displacement, and production with consumption.[2] The commodity stands in for Being where Being itself threatens the logic of the commodity form. The shoes (pairs, hence the "two" of my title) deconstruct the binaries that bind while yet confirming the convenience of their duality (the commodity status of shoes makes their use and their function as objects of desire both separable or collapsible within a marketing machine). Rather than elaborate the social history implied above, I want to examine in more detail the contemporary chronotope that links culture and capital in the aura of the shoe. In the manner of Gilles Deleuze and Felix Guattari, one could state that the aura of the shoe spreads, rhizomelike, across the globe as an (almost) metaphysical index of desire in capital (indeed, to be "over the shoes" is an expression of desire). But while this allows an understanding of the theological and theoretical inside/outside of the shoe it does not coordinate the affective points of responsibility that historically have left the trace of a Jakarta woman shoe worker in a rubber sole and, as we will see, a working-class African American male dead in the streets of Chicago with his shoes removed.

To chart this chronotope I will elaborate the *pointure* (as Derrida describes it) or pricking of the shoe in theory, and the rise of a particular commodity, the athletic shoe. The aim throughout will be to map the "metaphysical subtleties and theological niceties" of commodity culture as it currently confers aphanisis on the workers of the world (even when, or precisely because, the workers are positioned between the earth and the people who use them[3]). I have three claims that are central to commodity critique: first, a materialist understanding of transnational capitalist commodification is not simply a problem of totality, but one of imagination;[4] second (but a point that is, in essence, inextricable from the first), time/space compression in transnational commodity culture offers an abstruse simultaneity that necessitates a reevaluation of the fetish and fetishism;[5] third, commodity desire is no more inevitable than responsibility—both desire and responsibility are produced within regimes of truth that are irreconcilable—their contradictions are themselves an index of the world system.

The chronotope of the shoe invokes a Bakhtinian framework of affective responsibility—a means to fathom the logic of the commodity.[6] In Bakhtin's interpretation, the chronotope was multivalent, a complex constituent feature of his developing "historical poetics" that could link recurring literary devices across cultural history.[7] Yet this immediately marks Bakhtin's chronotope as a contradictory concept. If, as Bakhtin argues, literary chronotopes develop from and respond to specific extraliterary contexts, then how can these chronotopes be manifest transhistorically? Michael Holquist suggests that we distinguish between chronotope as a device or category of narrative and the principle of chronotopicity itself. The latter refers to time/space relations that structure the always already mediated condition of art and life.[8] As Bakhtin notes, "Out of the actual chronotopes of our world (which serve as the source of representation) emerge the reflected and *created* chronotopes of the world represented in the work."[9] While chronotopicity is not a stable bridge between art and life, it nevertheless draws attention to the mediatory functions of time and space in their interrelation. Beside its transhistorical inclinations, however, there are other obvious weaknesses in Bakhtin's articulation of the concept. For instance, the concrete forms of everyday life that Bakhtin summons draws attention to the situatedness of *his* critique from which one must ask what it would mean to specify "the actual chronotopes of our world." Would one not be forced, by the very terms of Bakhtin's exegesis, to particularize quite radically what is "ours" in that phrase? And what are the processes by which "our" world gets generalized so that in a chronotopic economy "our" world might stand in for others? Again, one must distinguish quite carefully the "worldliness" that Bakhtin advocates, despite and because of its correlations with the transnationalism of the commodity form. My point is this: If, as Katerina Clark and Michael Holquist contend, the chronotope is "a concept for engaging reality,"[10] then we would do well to examine the chronotopes of that world and not just their artistic or literary correlatives *in isolation* that are the hallmarks, for better or worse, of the "world" about which Bakhtin wrote in "Forms of Time."

When we are in life we are not in art and vice versa, as Bakhtin muses. But of course, chronotope, like dialogism and exotopy, is a Bakhtinian bridging concept that links these autonomous yet interdependent worlds: "However forcefully the real and represented world resist fusion . . . they are nevertheless indissolubly tied up with each other and find themselves in continual mutual interaction; uninterrupted exchange goes on between them, similar to the uninterrupted exchange of matter between living organisms and the environment that surrounds them."[11] Bakhtin is recalling the thought of Alexander Ukhtomsky from whom he first heard and used the word *chronotope* in 1925. There is little use in substituting directly these comments on uninterrupted exchange with the production of value in exchange represented by the commodity form. Can they be coordinated or tied up within cultural critique, however, without losing the specificity of either? And, if the aura of the shoe, the athletic shoe in particular, is enabled by what Fredric Jameson calls the cultural logic of late capitalism[12]—indeed, is symptomatic of its transnationalism—can these terms be interrelated without inexorably reproducing the inclusionary fantasy of worldliness that most transnational corporations (TNCs) tout as the very integer of their success?

Here, the chronotope is a story of a shoe and the worker to which it refers. The invocation of the shoe, however, does not build a world picture of culture and capital at the present time (for representation itself will remain the problem and not the provider) yet it can implicate cultural critique in the fate of the increasingly absent or disappearing worker whose labor "disappears" in the commodity form but now also vanishes in the commodification of theory itself. The strategy I recommend is not only to inscribe the shoe within a metonymic chain of affective being, but also to elaborate the shoe within a code of affective answerability. The shifting registers of the symbolic of the shoe are less about the capabilities of the cultural researcher than about the abject culpability of the Same. The aim is not the production of guilt (however some may revel in the discourse of victimhood); rather, I seek the production of a counterlogic, one which challenges the tidy knowledge that the trail of the shoe might leave. Cultural critique cannot (following Gayatri Spivak's powerfully argued notion)[13] make the subaltern (Indonesian shoe worker) speak, but it can attend to a geopolitical imagination that challenges the production of that "existence" on a world scale.

The shoe is magical, both within the history of the commodity and the psychological compulsions of modern "man." The shoe is *the* emblem of the fetishism that links the commodity to desire. And the most magical shoe of all is currently the athletic shoe because it is simultaneously a symbol of cultural capital, physical prowess, self-esteem, economic and psychic overinvestment, and crass economic exploitation; in fact, it epitomizes late capitalist flexible accumulation *and* continuing masculinist regimes of desire and disavowal.[14] Although Donald Katz has a different argument in mind, he stated the case quite nicely in 1994: "The name-brand athletic shoe might seem an unlikely seminal artifact of these last years of the twentieth century, but that is clearly what the shoes have become."[15] One brand in particular demonstrates the aura of the shoe for Katz, and that is Nike—named after the Greek goddess of victory, and a company that marks the triumphalism of transnational corporate élan.[16] This "seminal artifact" conjures the chronotope that is our chief concern and runs from the culture of consumption to the international division of labor and the critical methods that must be answerable to both.

What is the magic of capital for late capitalism? In 1962 Phil Knight "faked out" a Japanese athletic shoe company and became their distributor in the United States under the name Blue Ribbon Sports. Ten years later Jeff Johnson, an employee of Blue Ribbon Sports, sat bolt upright in his bed one morning and blurted the word, "Nike." Phil Knight was looking for a new moniker for the company and its sports shoes. Within thirty years the name of the winged goddess of victory became synonymous with the success of American transnationalism in recreational footwear, enough, for instance, to produce nearly $10 billion of annual sales and profits of $800 million in 1997 alone (a year in which Nike sold more than three hundred pairs of shoes a minute).[17] But Nike has also faced severe problems in its form of globalization. With the economic downturn in Asia in 1997–98, changes in fashion demand, classic overproduction caused by its contract futures, financial and social instability in its main production hubs like Indonesia, and burgeoning opposition in Asia and in Nike's "homeland" to transnational sweatshop practices, Nike saw its profits drop by 35 percent in the first quarter of 1998; indeed, in the second quarter of that year it reported a net loss of $67.6 million—a disaster quickly followed by layoffs and public-relations campaigns. It has since recovered, but it is clearly subject to intense competition/opposition at home and abroad. Despite these shifting fortunes and the emergence of a formidable antiglobalist and anti–World Trade Organization network, the story of Nike has become a legend in American capitalist history, a lesson in tremendous company growth and a benchmark for savvy marketing tactics.[18] To underline the latter, one should note that Nike is not really in the business of making shoes: What it does is market shoes. The shoes themselves are made through contracting and subcontracting in twelve- to eighteen-month production cycles outside its major market, the United States. Currently, Nike uses more than 700 factories worldwide that employ more than 500,000 people (110,000 in Indonesia).[19] It is the metaphysical subtleties of the shoe that Nike has harnessed with a godlike touch that few have matched. Yet who is vanquished in Nike's "victory," and what other rendezvous of victory is possible in the nexus of culture and capital?

For some time now cultural theory has been concerned to integrate levels of economic and aesthetic interpretation within what we may broadly term "cultural logic." (Fredric Jameson's analysis of postmodernism or Arif Dirlik's interrogation of the postcolonial resonate, albeit in different ways, with this possibility.)[20] Among other requisites, this has meant developing an increasingly sophisticated and complicated theoretical apparatus to unfathom the apparently unfathomable or nontotalizable: global economic and cultural difference. The problem is not just that "going global" can mimic the neocolonial urge of contemporary transnational capitalism, which wears, as its badge of honor, all the flexible positional superiority that Edward Said once attributed to the cultural logic of orientalism,[21] the problem is that the power of imagination required is very close to fantasy, an illusion that masks the authority of comprehension. The desire to map cognitively is compromised by imaginary maps that exceed or deconstruct cognitive intelligibility. We understand quite well the power of position in the production of knowledge (who is the "we" of this sentence, who speaks for whom, from where, at what time?), but much less the logic of imagination that emanates and returns to it. If cultural theory is to avoid the apparently endless reproduction of the inclusionary fantasy ("We are the world" slogans, Benetton multiculturalism, etc.), it must do more to rearticulate or reconceptualize the time/space coordinates of imagination that are intrinsic to its operations. The cultural logic of late capitalism depends upon a simultaneous suppression of critical imagination coupled with an overinvestment in the fantastic metaphoricity of the commodity form (typified by advertising). The danger is that a critical imagination can collapse back into the fantasy that the commodity itself enacts. Given the compulsory conspiracy of inclusion, can the world not just be imagined, but imagined otherwise?

In *The Geopolitical Aesthetic* Jameson attempts to extend the critique of postmodernity provided in his 1984 essay and subsequently revised for his book on postmodernity in 1991. While his interest in the more recent volume is primarily the techniques and technologies of contemporary cinema as a representational quandary, the subtext is an extended critique of culture in the world system. The geopolitical aesthetic is not the geopolitical chronotope of the present discussion, but it shares several significant features that require elaboration. Jameson underlines that attempts to "map" the world system often end up as caricatures because they fail to engage the "non-visual systemic causes"[22] that, together with their figurative representations, are constitutive of social totality. Obviously, the "cartography of the absolute" that Jameson offers does not carry the risk of responsibility that, I would argue, prescribes and destabilizes the imaginative power adequate to that task. Yet Jameson is aware that world system analysis at the cultural level does not resolve itself into the "Third World" national allegories he initially proposed. Now, by invoking a geopolitical unconscious, Jameson hopes to "refashion national allegory into a conceptual instrument for grasping our new being-in-the-world." (GA 3) But, if the idea of national allegory was too narrowly defined, the geopolitical unconscious comes with an indemnity of equally alarming sweep; namely, "that all thinking today is *also,* whatever else it is, an attempt to think the world system as such" (GA 4).

As with every overstatement in Jameson's oeuvre, however, this one comes with a cogent insight. If capitalist relations permeate dominant culture to the core and its everyday "reality" is sutured, however imperfectly, by ideologies that rationalize its nature, then awareness, or what Jameson fondly recalls as "self consciousness about the social totality," is going to be harder to find or trace than its unconscious correlative—that which cannot be simply matched and marked by the representational compulsions that lie beyond it. The trick, as it were, is that this unconscious is indeed manifest in everyday life but not in the form that one would expect it (if it were, it could be commodified and colonized by capitalist social relations much more readily). It comes as no surprise that in Jameson's model allegory reemerges as the unconscious mode of articulation, yet seemingly stripped of the parochialism (and essentialism) of its earlier "national" configuration: "On the global scale, allegory allows the most random, minute, or isolated landscapes to function as a figurative machinery in which questions about the system and its control over the local ceaselessly rise or fall, with a fluidity that has no equivalent in those older national allegories" (GA 5). The allegory is "beyond the landscape" of conventional representations of the world system, yet strives to stand in for its unmappable integration.

Jameson's formulation about absent causes as no less causes for all that bears crucially on his overall argument; the worldliness of seeing within media technology in fact plays out the shortfalls of its desire to represent. The problem remains the line of fantasy between this desire and the alternative globality of the unconscious which apparently does not have a form in which to express itself. The political consequence is that the former is taken for the latter and history marks time rather than makes it. It is as if historical depth is on pause while allegory, as a spatial concept, measures the evacuation of the temporal. This paradox is shared by Bakhtin's articulation of the chronotope, which ostensibly represents the time/space connectedness in certain literary expressions but often elides the history that informs it. The modernist moment of Bakhtin's creativity, however, does not exhaust the richness of his authorial point of view. Yet the paradox of the universal in the particular remains, since one could fairly easily recode the micrological aspects of the forms of time Bakhtin elucidates for the exceptionalism now called "postmodernity."[23] This returns us to Jameson because a literary formulation, allegory, is itself performing a double function in Jameson's theory: first, within an analysis of the artistic processes of contemporary culture; and second, as a touchstone for a geopolitical critique of capital. But the allegorical mode extends to the very process of critique itself so that capital provides a surface meaning under which one can find the nitty-gritty cultural correlatives that are the heart of the matter. The story of capital appears almost incidental or arbitrary alongside the artistic playing out of the allegorical mode. Like Bakhtin, therefore, Jameson displays a tendency to prioritize an aesthetic universal in the face of an inscrutable reality. And for literary criticism this has always been an entirely natural reflex.

Jameson realizes, however, in a way that Bakhtin did not (except, perhaps, in *Marxism and the Philosophy of Language*) that the universality of aesthetic categories like allegory does not inexorably entail the aestheticization of the political. Nevertheless, the danger remains, just like fantasy's relationship to imagination. This is not just the inherent risk in deploying the terms of classical aesthetics: It is also the ineluctable hazard of tracking the way capital structures commodity desire on a world scale, since consumption must begin with the subject who perceives—the commodity must be sensed to be consumed as a function of desire. The chronotope of the shoe, then, is interlaced by desire and the claims of answerability (an ethical dimension to the mode of commodity desire). Like Jameson, I will eschew the easier representational labor of the "landscape" this might offer; unlike Jameson, however, I will focus on the commodity *as* the scene of capitalist culture and not the symptom of the commodification *of* culture. This will emphasize the actual process of commodity production (which still seems to require labor) rather than its realist representation or the critical process used to describe it.

The time/space coordinates of capital and culture today present themselves in dizzying plenitude: a multiplicity that is at once both concrete and abstract. The concreteness is often only seen to lie in the tactile presence of the commodity form in all its manifestations (even the image is "touched"), yet of course its abstraction lies in this very same thingness: the object that is an expression of being. There is no definitive outside to this commodity form: There is no space or place where the commodity itself empties out the content of being. Why this is the case is not a product of capital's nefarious saturation of global economic relations, despite the earnestness and compulsion of its embrace, but because the process of capital consistently denies or disavows any and all logics that attempt to disconnect the naturalized sublation of Being in the commodity and its "possession." Delinking from capitalist logic is nothing new—it has often formed the constituent desire in a number of sociopolitical movements, from Marxist and socialist revolutions to those of postcolonial nationhood and the more recent challenge of the "Greens." But the problem has taken on an increased urgency in light of the collapse of "actually existing" socialism around the globe and the end of the cold war. The inevitability of capitalist social relations seems all the more "naturalized" even as its dysfunctional operations are still more apparent. The tendency is to aestheticize this moment, this bizarre interregnum in which various forms of capitalism compete not just with each other for accumulation on a world scale but with real and imaginary agents who might spell their collective demise. There are, however, significant lessons to be learned from reading the processes of the commodity against the grain of aesthetic formalism.

The chronotope of the shoe immediately invites questions of desire (the projection of the fetish and its disavowal) that are more than a subtheme: They describe both the limits of a geopolitical cultural transnationalism and the geopolitical in general at this historical juncture. Thus, the worker "exists" at the nexus of economic integration, spatial differentiation, cultural globalization, *and* masculinist disavowal. While the notion of existence as aphanisis follows Marx's analysis of the commodity to a certain degree, it also links the fate of the worker in contemporary forms of engendered power. The financialization and transnationalization of the globe is partial (despite the triumphalism that its proponents proclaim) but significant enough to throw into relief the patriarchal and capitalist ideologies that inform its mode of accumulation. These must insistently be made answerable to the being of the worker, however decentered that self has become. The task is not to make visible that which has been transmogrified beyond recognition (for that visibility is also often at man's behest): The point is to understand the contemporary processes (psychic, social, economic, political) by which workers must be rendered a convenient abstraction—the shoe for the flesh.[24]

Nike makes shoes in Indonesia.[25] Indonesia is a country that needs no "national allegory" to understand its integration into global capitalist and cultural relations. (Here I agree with Aijaz Ahmad's cogent critique that Jameson's characterization of the "Third World" text is an exercise in "positivist reductionism."[26]) Indonesia's contemporary ties to the world system begin in 1965, first with a military coup, then with the overthrow of Sukarno and his populist regime, and the subsequent crushing of the Communist Party (PKI) by the Western-backed forces of Suharto.[27] Suharto's "New Order" meant several things: a political system that continually steamrollered any and all forms of opposition to its "beneficence" (what was left of the PKI was outlawed in 1966, and periodic social unrest, like the riots of 1984 were quickly "remedied"); a foreign policy that has not been beyond a little old-style colonialism to maintain hegemony in the Indonesian archipelago (the process of incorporating East Timor cost several hundred thousand lives, but in the aftermath of Suharto's "withdrawal" from the political scene and an East Timorese independence movement sanctioned first by Suharto's "interim" successor, B. J. Habibie, then Wahid, and most recently Megawati Sukarnoputri, that bloody annexation is being remedied to some degree[28]); an enforcement of constitutional rule that often meant a narrow interpretation of the *Pancasila* (the Five Principles originally devised by Sukarno as a basis for the modern Indonesian state[29]); and an opening to foreign investment that undoubtedly raised living standards in many sections of the population but did not fundamentally address the root causes of systemic inequalities that attract transnational corporations in the first place. Development in Indonesia has meant this and more.

The periodic World Bank country reports on Indonesia make for dry and clinical reading.[30] The studies appear to have been prodded by the typical traumatic stress associated with massive foreign investment and the exploitation of Indonesia's natural resources (including large oil reserves, a factor that has clearly spurred growth but, because of the geopolitical significance of oil prices, has often meant internationally produced austerity programs—and strategic silence on state-sponsored atrocities). The piles of statistics on poverty rates in Indonesia are a measure of the World Bank's own hesitation about investment strategies.[31] Not surprisingly, poverty rates are highest in the agricultural sector. Families are generally bigger, wages lower, and living conditions substandard compared to their urban counterparts, especially those in Jakarta. In several reports the concern is about the social and political consequences of fostering a large and generally poor underemployed population (Indonesia's population is now the world's fourth-largest). And, of course, the economics of development strategy are closely tied to this. The Suharto regime, mindful of any IMF or World Bank attempted to influence the internal politics of the state, generally followed the advice of these reports and the examples of other Asian "miracle" economies like Taiwan, Malaysia, and South Korea by drawing surplus labor into other segments of production. But industrialization has raised not only real wages but the specters of class division on the one hand, and environmental disaster on the other (the latter has included the deliberate setting of massive forest fires but also an explosion of urban blight). Both now threaten to drive transnationals away, but in the early years of the New Order these considerations were distant, to say the least.

Indeed, it is tempting to say that Indonesia garners importance not because it makes shoes, but because it was made for shoes, which is of course merely to underline that transnational capitalism is not that interested in what Indonesia might otherwise "represent."[32] The political, social, and economic circumstances of Indonesia after 1965 increasingly made it ripe for exactly the mode of light industry, low-tech, labor-intensive "development" symbolized by shoe production. Yet this capitalist desire is simultaneously a masculinist desire, both a product of the search for higher profit margins in the process from production to consumption *and* a symptom of global fetishistic disavowal. The shoe stands in both for the desire that compels it and the actual conditions that inform it. This means not only the feminization of the developing world through the rubric of transnational market "penetration" (such language is not marginal but part of the very texture of the socioeconomic relations that accompany it); it also means that the internationalization of markets has attempted to efface the psychic inscriptions on the commodity form by exporting the nonrepresentation of the worker to the farthest corners of the globe (farthest, that is, from the object of the commodity's production—the consumer).

What starts out, then, as a conventional narrative about the onward march of late capitalist "development" in the Newly Industrialized Countries (NICs) in the thrall of TNCs becomes a web of complex synergy that the commodity presents as its natural apotheosis. To be sure, the roots of this process of commodification of relations on a world scale can be found in Marx's reading of industrialization, but there it was seen as the rallying point of a unifying labor movement conscious of the world that left it underfoot; now, however, it is the mark of amnesia and aphanisis—the great complexity of commerce that precedes the arrival of the commodity is repressed (disavowed). The commodity appears in its advertisement, and not in the hands of the shoemaker or rubber molder twelve thousand miles away. Naturally, a capitalist is taciturn about using the immiseration and inequality built into the production of the commodity as a way to sell it: That is one of the meanings of capitalism. But it is only now, in the transformed time/space relations of global capital, that criticism of this process seems beyond the powers of the cognitive. Even radical approaches to knowledge like cultural studies inadvertently buttress this point of view by concentrating on the subversive meanings of the consumer—what the consumer does with the commodity. The worker is either an old shoe or has disappeared, except as an ironic integer of her or his continuing absence from the realm of social, economic, and political power.

Again, a different sense of time/space critique does not solve that absence, as if a chronotopic imagination alone might disarticulate the logical consistency of superexploitation. Yet the internationalization of cultural critique, with all its dangers, may be a necessary evil if one is to understand culture's implication in the order of things and thingness at this time. The story of Indonesia in the twentieth century was one of colonization, occupation, revolution, independence, counterrevolution, development, integration, and so forth. That it was also the disjecta membra, the refracting shards of Western capital and culture, is not a coincidence, however specific that narrative must be. That continues to be the real foundation of the chronotope of the shoe.

No shorthand version of Indonesian politics and economics will provide an adequate understanding of the tremendous changes wrought on society by the New Order's version of modern statehood.[33] The transmigration program of relocating large numbers of people to outlying islands in order to ease the burdens of population explosion in Java would itself serve as a case study of the disjunctions of Indonesian development (during and after colonization). And, of course, given the rapacious sway of transnational capital, some comparison with the business practices of the Dutch East India Company in the preceding centuries would also shed light on the differences in the extraction of surplus value from labor today.[34] From the above, three characteristics, however, have particular relevance to Indonesia's recent integration into the global economy: an excess of labor suitable for labor-intensive low-wage light-industrial production; little or no organized labor infrastructure; and an authoritarian regime that routinely disregarded the nominally democratic nature of Indonesian statehood epitomized in the five principles in order to smooth the flow of capital in and out of the country.

In terms of the Asian economic miracle since the end of World War II, this adds Indonesia to a metonymic chain that has included Taiwan, Malaysia, and South Korea. As transnationals move around Asia (and that obviously includes Asian transnationals, particularly those of Japan), competition for cost effectiveness has intensified. Interestingly, as the Asian markets seek out cheaper production costs, many of the companies who were subcontracted to boost production in places like Taiwan and South Korea are now subsubcontracting in other emerging economies. This is certainly true of Indonesia, and it appears to be the case in China, which is rapidly becoming the metonym to supplant all others in this process. Focusing on Indonesian shoe production is not meant to stand in unproblematically for developments of this kind elsewhere in the region, but rather it emphasizes what elements disrupt an otherwise tidy metonymy. In the end, it is not simply desire for cheaper labor in accordance with the appropriate prerequisites that produces these changes but also the logic of desire itself—that which does not favor mere cause and effect, but abstruse simultaneity.

The chronotope of the shoe can be schematized as a psychic compulsion linked simultaneously to gender hierarchization and commodity fetishism, a narrative that comprises the actual production of a shoe within regimes of capital, and a tale of the embodied labor of a shoe worker here interpellated in the Indonesian economy. The shoe is a particularly useful way to understand the chronotope of culture and capital because it accentuates the process of desire intrinsic to the logic of global circuits of production and consumption. The importance of the shoe relates simultaneously to its status as a commodity and to its function as fetish. In Freud's famous formulation, fetishism is a masculine prerogative—a reflex to the "horror of castration"[35] produced by the boy's belief in the woman (the mother) having a penis. The boy does not repress the contradictory evidence of this projection so much as disavow it (*Verleugnung*), a process that more properly describes the function of a fetish as an external reality. Why the shoe emerges as a fetishistic substitute for the "absent female phallus" is only hinted at in Freud's explanation: He avers that the young boy fixates on the shoe or the foot at the very moment of disavowal as the boy glimpses the woman's genitals from below. In the absence of the phallus the boy fantasizes its presence: The shoe, particularly the woman's shoe, becomes the metonym for something that it is not; namely, the belief that the Being of female is male.

More of a sketch than an essay, Freud's thoughts on fetishism have produced a plethora of interpretation. Indeed, recent discussion would seem to underline still further the importance and the controversy of this piece.[36] The psychic significance of Freud's formulation is accentuated by its ambivalent relation to its cognates in political economy, anthropology, and literary theory in which its critical function alternates between touchstone and gravestone. Marx preempts the Freudian turn to a certain extent by associating fetishism with the general aura of the object as a commodity. Behind what he refers to as the "hieroglyph" of the product lies value, which Marx explores as the social character of labor, precisely what the money-form's relationship to the commodity must erase or deny. In Freud's theory, the object arises as a presence for something that was never there; for Marx, the commodity stands in for a real absence, the social labor that produced it. In *Feminizing the Fetish,* Emily Apter explores a "curious compatibility" between these readings, a space where the commodity's "secret" and the "strangeness" of consciousness form (and here she quotes from Michel Leiris) an "affective ambivalence, that tender sphinx we nourish, more or less secretly, at our core."[37] Apter persuasively theorizes ambivalence as a "third term," as the space where fetish, fetishism, and theories of fetishism ("the fetishism of fetishism") seem to mutually deconstruct—and is thus a place where "feminizing" becomes both necessary and ineluctable, as long as one limits its function to literary narrative (the textual examples that Apter provides). Whatever the ambivalence of Marx's own tropes on fetishism,[38] the "metaphysical subtleties" of the commodity do not stand in the same relation as Freud's fetishist to the fetish. Not quite.

Within commodity fetishism the social relations in exchange between commodities stand in for the social relations of those human beings who have labored to produce them. The illusory aspect of commodity fetishism is that the value of the commodity appears inherent to it, whereas its value is not natural, but social. This is a *real relation,* not simply a representational fallacy. One can easily accept Jean Baudrillard's exegesis of simulacra on this point,[39] but not the overhasty displacement of the economic onto the signifying chain for the very same reason. Thus, commodities can simulate one another without reference to an actual original (which never existed, hence the link to psychic fetishism), but labor value does not exist as an imaginary referent to the commodity even if it is presented as such. In addition, in the rush to find equivalence between Freudian "affect" and commodity effect it is easy to overlook that commodity fetishism is specific to the relations among things (that is, their exchange value), but fetishizing the shoe or foot is a displaced relation of subject and object, not two shoes' *danse macabre.*

One could examine the possible category errors in much more detail (the pre-capitalist realities of the fetish, for instance), but here, at the risk of "fetishizing the fetish" as Apter warns, I wish to push the historical confluence rather than conflation of such phenomena in capital and culture. For instance, it is entirely prescient that the cover of Jameson's *Postmodernism; or, The Cultural Logic of Late Capitalism* features Andy Warhol's "Diamond Dust Shoes."[40] In the opening chapter, the veritable Urtext for materialist analysis of the postmodern, Jameson includes a valuable discussion of several "shoe paintings." Jameson sets up a se-ries of polemical contrasts between Vincent Van Gogh's "Peasant's Shoes" as a "Utopian gesture" and Warhol's "glacéd X-ray elegance" (PM 9). For my purposes, two orders of the shoe are operative—two chronotopes indeed. In looking at Van Gogh's painting, Jameson stresses that one should reconstruct the "initial condi-tions" of the work in order to understand its symbolic act—"as praxis, and as production" (PM 7). The raw materials he elucidates include "the whole rudi-mentary human world of backbreaking peasant toil, a world reduced to its most brutal and menaced, primitive and marginalized state" (PM 7). Jameson is wax-ing allegorical once more, for he knows that the reproduction or inert objectifi-cation of the painting about which he writes itself describes capital's commodifi-cation of culture that remains his central concern. Counterposed to this is his own reconstruction, the stunning "mental restoration" of hermeneutics:

> I will briefly suggest . . . that the willed and violent transformation of a drab peas-ant object world into the most glorious materialization of pure color in oil paint is to be seen as a Utopian gesture, an act of compensation which ends up producing a whole new Utopian realm of the senses, or at least of that supreme sense—sight, the visual, the eye—which it now reconstitutes for us as a semi-autonomous space in its own right, a part of some new division of labor in the body of capital, some new fragmentation of the emergent sensorium which replicates the specializations and divisions of capitalist life at the same time that it seeks in precisely such fragmenta-tion a desperate Utopian compensation for them. (PM 7)

This reading is every bit as effervescent as Martin Heidegger's famous inter-pretation, which Jameson paraphrases in his own argument. Heidegger imagines the world of the peasant woman who wears the shoes and the more general Be-ing that they signify but, unlike Jameson, does not fathom the materiality of the art (the paint, which is Jameson's point) in reconstituting its origins.[41] Jameson claims that high modernism can function in this way, interrupting the order of the commodity form by compensating, in a Utopian fashion, the deracination of modern life. The comparison with Warhol could not be starker. If the shoes represented by Van Gogh invoke a vaster reality of meaning and possibility, Warhol's deathly assortment of women's pumps seem to close off that hermeneutical avenue. Of Warhol's picture Jameson opines, "it doesn't really speak to us at all" (PM 8). The denial of this larger lived context naturally fascinates Jameson, all the more because of Warhol's biography (which includes the fact that he once illustrated shoes for the fashion business and designed display windows for shoes). Jameson makes several points that can be briefly summarized: In highlighting the commodity fetishism of late capitalism Warhol does not appear to provide strong political critique of it; the stridency of modernist expression is in Warhol answered with "depthlessness"; and the death of the world of appearance typified by the shoes signals the now famous "waning of affect" in contemporary culture. Art has finally succumbed to the regime of commodification that it has incessantly opposed. Where the first chronotope offered utopia in the midst of alienation, the second displays defeat through the contradictory celebration of fragmentation.

But of course, as several critics have pointed out,[42] the examples that Jameson uses do not necessarily support the sharp contrast he draws. There is no logical reason, for instance, why one could not argue for Warhol's "Diamond Dust Shoes" performing the same compensatory move as Van Gogh's, albeit on this occasion by answering the busy commodification of the world by accentuating its flatness, depthlessness, and forbidding homogeneity. Yet this suggests a further point: that the all-too-brief critique of Heidegger's view of Van Gogh's peasant shoe painting nevertheless marks an affinity with its subtext in a form that counterbalances just like Van Gogh's art through nostalgia. In Heidegger's essay the nostalgia is most pointed for the rootedness, the organicism of peasant life (which, of course, is also a foil), but although this is at some distance from Jameson's invocation of the social, the latter can also be read as a nostalgia for a utopian spirit that may, or may not, be the object or aura of Van Gogh's painting.

For Heidegger, Van Gogh's shoe painting is almost incidental to the thingness of the shoes themselves, but that "almost," that space between, is what allows him to distinguish the "product" from the "thing" and the "work" (of art). The shoes are a "thing-as-product" and not any old thing, but their being-as-product is not available to them simply because they are "equipment" in Heidegger's parlance. It is art itself that calls forth this truth in being, the *aletheia* or "unconcealment of being" that is the very mark of its origins. There is a sleight of hand (or eye) in Heidegger's argument here, since in bracketing the function of the author in the origin of art, he allows the critic much more sway on the imaginative terrain. The work can reveal the being of a product in a way that the product itself cannot, but the world, or the worlding of the world, that Heidegger invokes is not grounded by the work of art, sui generis. The cognitive map of that world also resides in a consciousness adequate to its perception. The world of the peasant woman whom Heidegger ties to the shoes in her absence in Van Gogh's painting is only available to her in the usefulness of the equipment, the shoes themselves; whereas the truth in Being of the shoes is something revealed to the critic in his perception of its representation in the work of art. This reading is no cruder than Heidegger's suggestion that the shoes in Van Gogh's painting were the peasant woman's in the first place. The metaphysical subtleties of the process of commodification begin to unravel there, in the matter-of-factness of the ownership of the thing itself.

But these are shoes, and I do not believe there is something accidental in their choice by either Van Gogh, Heidegger, Warhol, or Jameson. The point is not that the fetishism of the commodity is simply a masculine prerogative (even as this must be underlined) but that the symbolic of the shoe describes an intricate field of desire and disavowal that links the past to the present and the moment of transnational capital. Van Gogh's shoes, like Heidegger's reading of them, are avowedly modernist, the *Stoss,* or shock, of the work of art is an alienation effect about the depersonalization of the modern world. The shoes do not represent a community "in a moment of danger," to borrow from Walter Benjamin,[43] but mark their own insufficiency to the object world that is penetrating every aspect of the forms of representation available. To this extent, the shoe is a phallic presence, but one that certain artists and critics must otherwise deny.

But how can Van Gogh's shoes help us with the moment of capital today? Before returning to the affective responsibility that links the shoe worker in Indonesia with the "world" campus in Beaverton, Oregon (the "home" of Nike), we must resole the philosophical disposition of shoes. Jameson casually mentions a point by Derrida that Van Gogh's shoes are a "heterosexual pair," but perhaps he underestimates the usefulness of Derrida's 140-page essay on Van Gogh's shoe paintings, "Restitutions," to his, Jameson's, argument. One could be more severe and say that Derrida's critique deconstructs Jameson's in advance (and is therefore disavowed), but I want to maintain a complementary materialist *pointure* of the latter, despite the ingenious convolutions of the Derridean text. Certainly, the philosophical niceties, like the shoes themselves, are not just the *parerga,* or ornaments, of the chronotope; they are intrinsic to it (and therefore *parerga* in the sense that Derrida reads Immanuel Kant, in the form of mischievous margins). Derrida's reading stages the problem of Being not only for Van Gogh's shoe painting, but for the athletic footwear that now, in a fundamental way, supersedes the question of art that the painting foregrounds.

The form of Derrida's essay, a "'polylogue' (for n + 1 female voices),"[44] is not an exercise in intricate and elliptical wordplay but a measure of criticism's inadequacy to its object. One of the reasons critics often write conversations ("dialogues") when invoking Bakhtinian dialogism, for instance, is to highlight who or what is excluded in the critical act. For his part(s), Derrida deploys the polylogue to intervene in something of a pseudo exchange between Heidegger and Meyer Schapiro over the attribution of the shoes in Van Gogh's painting. As both Heidegger and Schapiro are aware, and Derrida underlines, Van Gogh painted a lot of shoes (Derrida includes black-and-white facsimiles of at least five such paintings). Once Derrida asks "why these shoes?" the text becomes an elaborate graft on "pointing" (*pointure*), which is how the truth gets stitched.

Using Derrida's essay, I want to raise the question that he does not ask in elaborating the problem of the restitution of the shoes to "their rightful owner" (RT 258). While it is certainly true that the magic of the commodity within capitalism depends in part on the psychic investment in possession (which extends even to the exchange of Heidegger and Schapiro—"the desire for attribution is a desire for appropriation" [RT 260]), it also rests on the annulment of the producer. In today's shoes the subjectivity of the worker is marked only by a geographical referent ("made in"), but for both Nike footwear and Van Gogh's painting the chronotope of the shoe depends upon the suppression of a specific question: Who made the shoes?

To the extent that Derrida examines the process of restitution in terms of attribution of ownership, he elides the material conditions of the object's possibility. Van Gogh could have imagined any kind of shoe in order to produce *a* painting, but could he have painted *those* shoes in particular had they not been made? If the point is moot it is only because the maker has been rendered mute. Derrida calls the shoe "the lowest degree, the most subjective or underlying level of culture or the institution" (RT 264), but he bases this observation on the philosophical problem of the wearer (who is absent in Van Gogh's paintings), not the maker, who is absent even when the shoes are "filled." The double subject of the painting whose truth in *pointure* Derrida untangles or unknots is the "subject-shoes" of the wearer and the shoes as subject in a painting; yet, I would argue, the economy of the fetish works to exclude precisely the double subject of the labor that makes the shoe possible. The worker is a double subject because of the specific relationship of labor to the commodity form—a relationship that, as Marx explained, does not depend upon the material properties of the object but of value in exchange. It is the disavowal of the latter as a property of labor that allows commodity fetishism to proceed. The shoe, in particular, foregrounds both the principle of the commodity and its changing form in late capitalism. That this finds or interpellates woman as a primary worker in the newly industrialized zones of the world is not a matter of convenient coincidence in the psychic aura of the shoe but is the very logic of transnational capitalism at this time. For Jameson, the paradigmatic shift from Van Gogh's shoes to Warhol's is in the waning of affect whose ideal subject is the schizophrenic (a subject who is "easy enough to please provided only an eternal present is thrust before the eyes" [PM 10]); for Derrida the will to restitution in the *pointure* of the shoe is the delirium of modern philosophy: "These shoes are hallucinogenic" (RT 273). Yet for neither critic does the subject of shoe paintings invoke the problem of the commodity form for its makers (the "thing" with "grotesque ideas" as Marx notes[45]). Here philosophy conspires with the systemic logic of elision that the commodity wears in order to circulate.

There are, however, several aspects of Derrida's essay that may help us find our feet if not the shoes that fit them. First of all, he is careful to distinguish the "paradigm of the shoe" in Heidegger's *Ursprung des Kunstwerkes.* Initially, Heidegger discusses the "being-product of the product" with reference to shoes but not, as Derrida astutely points out, in terms of art, or Van Gogh's art in particular. Yet the product occupies a position that mediates between a thing and a work (its "being-product" appears in the latter). The artwork, then, bears a relationship to the thing but is enhanced by the presence of a being-product that, in turn, allows perspective on both the thingness of the thing and the origin of art. The distinctions are valid although, by themselves, they do not clarify the symbolic of the shoe. (For instance, would not Marx's conception of the commodity cancel through all three components of Heidegger's critique?) Derrida puts Heidegger's paradigm to work in order to ponder the specter of truth that haunts presentation and representation (while undoing the attributive compulsion in both Heidegger's and Schapiro's reading of Van Gogh's shoe painting—here, truth be told, Schapiro comes off worse). The object, of course, is not the shoe as product or the being-product of the shoe in a painting, but the truth of truth, on which any theory of representation must be based in the first place. Not surprisingly for readers of Derrida, this truth gets laced up by the law of the *parergon* "which comprehends everything without comprehending" (RT 343). To fathom the shoe is also to understand the "hallucinogenic fictions" (375) that gird, or envelop, theories of truth. In this way, Derrida finds a usefulness for Heidegger that Heidegger himself does not locate in the example of the shoes. What Heidegger discovers is the reliability of the product—its *Verlässlichkeit.* The reliability of the product is a condition of its usefulness, the way it belongs to the world it invokes (the peasant world of Heidegger's example). Again, this is not the equivalent of product reliability in capitalism (or, indeed, of built-in obsolescence), but its proximity is not irrelevant. The problem is that the proximity is displaced. Neither Heidegger nor Derrida (nor, for that matter, Jameson) is overly concerned with the specificity of the shoe as a commodity form, but more as a symbol of the way the truth gets told in art. The advantage of such an approach is that it can avoid the lure of crude empiricism (the attributive mode of Schapiro's argument) and the hasty equivalence of shoe production and the production of shoes in art. The disadvantage is that art can be read less as a specific site for the revelation of truth in Being and more as the only locus for such sublimity. Kant is kept at bay but is somehow tied to those who distance him.

Derrida's polylogue reveals, despite itself, the conditions of possibility that the regime of the commodity provides. In this regard, the shoe functions as a complex metaphor that allows Derrida to turn truth inside out without simply negating it. But the *pointure* of his approach resists stitching the shoe to the context that informs Derrida's discourse "four times *around* painting" (RT 9) including that of commodity fetishism. This is the time/space or chronotope in which the shoe is precipitate. To take Derrida's use of *pointure* seriously will pitch us forward once more to the contemporary commodity form. Derrida likes the confluence and undecidability of meanings in *pointure*—the fact that it refers simultaneously to the art of pricking or pointing in printing a page as well as the punctures made in the stitching of gloves or shoes. "Pointing" is a somewhat polite and inaccurate rendering of *pointure* in English, or at best a feminization of the process invoked (in needlepoint for instance). Here, the OED betrays that the staid eloquence of *punctura* in Latin was almost always upstaged by the brute abruptness of "prick" in the history of English. The significance of prick and pricking to the subject of the shoe should not be underestimated.[46]

In the twenty-first century, the culture of pricking or stitching shoes has changed dramatically. Van Gogh's paintings feature shoes that had been stitched or nailed for the most part. Today's athletic shoes, however, would find such technology cumbersome and not cost effective. The uppers of such shoes are so thin and light (leather is sometimes used, but in the main the materials of choice are synthetic, like Durabuck—a staple of Nike shoes) that stitching can be done very easily and quickly. But the soles are not stitched at all: they are glued. Nevertheless, the culture of pricking remains in shoe manufacture as an index of the function of masculine desire in capitalist production. Here, the truth of truth is not for all time, but is the truth in a certain mode of fetishization that offers the image of an attachment (another being-product) that it must always necessarily deny. Van Gogh compensates for the deracinated world of the peasant by celebrating her or his ever-threatened absence in the "out-of-work" (as Derrida puts it) image of shoes; later, in Indonesia, the peasant woman goes to Jakarta to work in a factory making shoes that she cannot afford to wear. Between these two moments a whole regimen of production and exchange has been transformed. And this is, by the way, why Warhol's shoes give up the ghost of compensation, or a certain form of restitution.

Although Derrida's critique tends to be most effective in the way it unpicks modernist nostalgia for the function of art against the rage of technological progress (a facet that finds Van Gogh and Heidegger in the same aesthetic if not philosophical shoes), he also pricks the conscience of contemporary logic by defamiliarizing its gendered suppositions and dubious oppositions. Briefly, Derrida quotes himself in the "Double Session" talking of the points of the ballerina—that "each pair, in this circuit, will always have referred to some other, signifying too the operation of signifying" (RT 264). He remarks that "prior to all reflection you reassure yourself with the pair" (RT 265), and this, in essence, is the problem of restitution in the associative chain of Van Gogh/Heidegger/Schapiro that Derrida painstakingly deconstructs (and why the chronotope of the shoe is always problematically two). But the pairings that occur (for instance, Schapiro "will see the 'face' [*la figure*] of Van Gogh in 'his' shoes" [RT 266]) emphasize a masculine attachment, whereas the single shoe, as an abstraction, is the fetish object of that which never was, a woman's penis.[47] The inside/out of the shoe, as Derrida notes, insistently collapses the logic of opposition in this fetishistic fantasy, for while the outside form of the shoe intimates the phallus, the inside invokes the vagina (when Cinderella is shoed with the glass shoe the double economy of inside/outside becomes palpable[48]). The production and consumption of athletic shoes does not just play out this contradictory pairing and doubling, it is its contemporary apotheosis.

If one links together the processes involved in the production and consumption of athletic shoes, several familiar patterns begin to emerge. To think these simultaneously within the chronotope is itself, as I have suggested, something close to fantasy (something hallucinogenic in Derrida's parlance), but is nevertheless the first circle of affective responsibility. Within production there is primarily a woman worker. She is hired because she is cheap and because she is dexterous (she has to be able to work inside and outside the shoe with great speed).[49] She is also assumed to be noncombative in terms of labor rights and, while unmarried, "free" to work long hours. With increasing unemployment on the land, the woman worker is lured from the village to the emerging urban centers in Indonesia. Nike moves to Indonesia from the middle of the 1980s at the same time that this labor force is itself emerging in the Indonesian economy. Light industry of this kind continues to be crucial for the Indonesian government in picking up the slack in industrial development caused by the reining in of its oil business in the international market. As noted, the World Bank played a large role in this "retooling," and some $350 million of foreign aid poured into Indonesia over three years in the late 1980s for light industry development, including shoe factories (DK 185). In 1988 Indonesian athletic shoe exports stood at $4 million, but by 1993 this had risen to $1.5 billion. For Nike, the switch to production in Indonesia becomes more attractive at this time both because of almost nonexistent government oversight in their form of business and because labor costs in South Korea and Taiwan in particular were beginning to eat into profit margins. Since Indonesia was seen to lack a sufficient managerial class, Nike encouraged the importation of managers from other parts of its Asian operations—a move that often caused friction with the Indonesian workforce (including strikes and the destruction of facilities). In 1991, for instance, the *Far Eastern Economic Review* reported a woman line worker for Nike in Indonesia protesting that "They [the Korean managers] yell at us when we don't make production quotas and if we talk back they cut our wages" (DK 172)[50] While working conditions for women workers have improved, athletic shoe production is still a harmful and exploitative business. The solvents used to glue the soles of these shoes are highly toxic and, even when the extractor fans are working well, the women constantly breathe fumes. Interestingly, the cofounder of Nike, Bill Bowerman, often made shoe prototypes using similar glue solvents and was eventually crippled by them. He developed neuropathy, a degenerative nerve condition often experienced by shoe and hatmakers. Nike opens and closes factories with such speed in its search for cheap labor that its workers are probably spared most of the long-term effects of glue sniffing. But the neuropathy remains in transnational exploitation itself.

To be sure, Nike's labor practices in Asia are unremarkable for late capitalist transnationalism.[51] Subcontractors scour emerging economies for the usual characteristics mentioned above and sufficient infrastructure to get raw materials in and the finished product out within the requisite business cycles. Some of Nike's shoe lines require more skill than others. (Air Jordans, for instance, were still made in South Korea at the Tae Gurang Industrial Company's factory called "T2" long after most of the other production lines had been shifted to Indonesia and China.) In the main, however, the price of the shoe is connected fundamentally to its image much more than the cost of the skill required to make it. Where the artwork, Van Gogh's shoe paintings for instance, might evoke the product-being of a whole community, the image of the athletic shoe provides a status in excess of the performance provided by the shoe's design. Nevertheless, the truth in *pointure* shares much of the epistemological form of the truth in advertising where shoes are concerned. To maintain the responsibility at issue one must continually reconnect these elements of the shoe's aura; that is, the sheer weight of marketing mystique with the object of superexploitation in the developing world, the woman worker.

The condition of women workers in Indonesia is overdetermined by several interlocking factors that facilitate the Nike "miracle." Among those mentioned so far, the nature of the government is vital. Despite the violent resistance to the newly restrictive Pancasila from the moment it was drafted into law in 1984 (which resulted in the Tanjung Priok massacre of protestors by the New Order in September of that year), in general the fate of women in the workforce is guided by the Pancasila's democratic absolutism. Women must know their place as wives and mothers but, when interpellated by the dictates of light industrial need, they must further submit to paternalism in the workplace.[52] Although this does not completely negate the possibility of industrial action (as mentioned, there have been significant strikes against Nike in Indonesia) it minimizes the risk by making protest appear against the foundations of continuing Indonesian nationhood. This limit on worker solidarity is not the monopoly of Indonesia; it is, rather, the unimaginable of contemporary regimes of time/space in capital. The limit always appears to emerge elsewhere.

One of these highly regulated women workers in Indonesia in the 1990s was Sadisah. In 1992 Jeffrey Ballinger, a labor activist who has done much to raise serious questions about Nike's Asian business practices, displayed one of her pay slips in *Harper's Magazine* to make visible, in an obvious way, the cost of Nike's business in the Asian market.[53] In April of that year Sadisah's wage was 14 cents per hour for a total of $1.03 for a 7.5–hour day—significantly less than the government's figure for "minimum physical need." Sadisah, like the other 114 workers on her Nike line, was forced by material need to work long hours of overtime. Ballinger reports that an International Labor Organization survey found that 88 percent of women workers in Indonesia on Sadisah's wage were malnourished. Sadisah herself has come from a peasant community to make Nike's shoes and now can afford to rent a shack without electricity or running water. The cost of her labor to make one pair of Nike athletic shoes is about 12 cents. In the American market these shoes will sell for $80 to $150 a pair.

When Derrida writes of surplus value in his shoe essay he does not consider the maker, not even for a sentence, in the production of surplus value. To raise this specter (of Marx, and more besides) is not simply a question of restitution— to somehow claim or appropriate these shoes for their rightful owner, the shoemaker. Sadisah, on the contrary, remains with the shoe, in its stitching and gluing, just as the shoe stays with her, in her poverty and in her body (the effects of both the vapors, and long-term exposure to the purple lights that have often been used to illuminate the glue employed in the soling process). She exists in the shoe in a way that the capitalist cannot. Where the shoes in Van Gogh's painting leave a trace of the subject as owner, as user, the shoe itself is always already the embodied labor of its maker (yet without the laborer's body). Air Max, Nike's most successful running shoe, illustrates the presence of this Being quite succinctly. The sole is see-through, like Cinderella's shoes, but here it is so that the consumer can see and show that "air is real," as one commentator puts it,[54] that you are indeed walking on compressed air. (It is no coincidence that Air Max is Nike's most fetishized shoe: The 1995 model, for instance, remains a collector's item.) There is the Being of Sadisah, there, where she is entirely absent, see-through, invisible. Her labor is to be walked upon because she is there, in her absence. Note, this is not a realistic representation of embodied labor, which must, necessarily, remain abstract. The Being of Sadisah is an abstraction; whereas "air is real" is an imaginary resolution of this real contradiction (to borrow from Althusser on ideology). But, occasionally, the shoe worker reminds the owner as consumer of her absent presence, for her pricking can chafe the foot, or the sole can burst, leaving the owner disconsolate but aware, briefly, that the air-to-be-seen was a product-being out of sight: the shoes had been made.[55]

In April 1992, Sadisah earned $37 net for her month's labor. Ballinger, an AFL-CIO researcher, notes an alarming disparity between this figure and that of the earnings of Michael Jordan at that time. Jordan, the linchpin of Air Jordan marketing, received $20 million from Nike in 1992 for endorsing the shoe that bears his name. Ballinger calculates that it would take 44,492 years for Sadisah to earn this amount based on Nike's payments to her. The disparity lies in the power of the image, in the mystique of "branding," in the unfettered circulation of commodity culture. Yet opposition to the nefarious aspects of such circulation is not uncommon and, as it turns out, Nike has been one of the most prominent targets of transnational labor and consumer resistance. Ballinger's article represented something of a watershed in media awareness of the plight of women workers like Sadisah. Ballinger himself formed a group in 1994, Press for Change, that published a Nike Newsletter to expand public awareness in the United States of the real price of a pair of Nikes.[56] The campaign against Nike intensified both because of labor action in the workplace and a concomitant media activism where Nike least expected it. Jose Ramos Horta, an East Timorese Nobel Peace Prize winner in 1996, encouraged and emboldened American labor and human-rights organizations to get involved in protesting rights abuses in Indonesia (not just in East Timor, but on islands like Java, where Nike's interests were extensive). Global Exchange took up the challenge and, with Press for Change, brought a Nike worker to the United States in 1996 on a consciousness-raising tour. While presence does not simply reverse the logic of aphanisis I have invoked, it remains a forceful answer to the conveniently missing worker in transnational corporate discourse. Cicih Sukaesih had been fired by a Nike subcontractor in Indonesia in 1992 for organizing workers like Sadisah to press for at least Indonesia's minimum wage (about $1.30 a day at that time). In *Reclaiming America,* Randy Shaw recounts the highlights of Sukaesih's American tour. Sukaesih arrived in Washington, D.C., during a fashion industry forum (in which she was not allowed to participate).[57] She had her photograph taken with Kathie Lee Gifford, perhaps America's most famous "reformed" sweatshopper, and also visited a Footlocker store to try on the Nike shoes she made but could not afford to wear. In New York, Sukaesih joined a protest outside a Nike Town (one of the company's superstores) and in Chicago requested a meeting with Michael Jordan, who, predictably, was unavailable. Sukaesih even made a visit to Nike's corporate headquarters in Beaverton, Oregon (another example, according to Phil Knight, of labor activists' "terrorist tactics"). Nobody from management would meet with her or Medea Benjamin of Global Exchange, a PR snafu that only served to intensify media coverage of the tour. Despite a well-oiled image machine, Nike was faced with the same quandary as the philosophers: the question of Being changes dramatically once the shoemaker is acknowledged.[58]

This acknowledgment goes beyond the pious liberal reflex to wear a supportive badge and shoes with a different product label. Newer anti-sweatshop organizations and more established NGOs have built a sustainable human/worker-rights network, despite corporate attempts to buy out such entities in order to shore up their transnational image (Nike, for instance, has promised almost $8 million over a five-year period to one such organization, Global Alliance). In general, the athletic shoe industry is dominated by the empty gesture of voluntary compliance or codes of conduct that lack enforcement procedures. Workers are less isolated, however, than they were a decade ago, and consumer awareness may yet produce the affective responsibility at issue here in a global imaginary. Indeed, the prospects of a more transnational dialogism have been considerably enhanced not just by having a shoe worker testify in consumer markets, but by having NGOs and individuals work on the ground precisely in those areas disavowed in the past. In late August 2000, for instance, Jim Keady, an American former soccer pro, worked in a Nike shoe factory in the suburbs of Jakarta in order to publicize Nike's continuing reliance on paltry wages. The $1.20 he received each day for his labor was not enough to keep him nourished and he fell ill from the ordeal. Responding to Keady's personal campaign, Nike said he had "trivialized and demeaned the lives of Indonesians who work in factories. . . . Given his privileged, Western perspective, Mr. Keady does not understand . . . the value and importance of a job . . . in Indonesia."[59]

Mindful that even Keady's firsthand experience does not do justice to the complexities of corporate culture, let us focus briefly on Beaverton itself, the epicenter of Nike's "global imagery" and a "corporate Xanadu," as Katz calls it. "Nike World Campus" is a key node in the geopolitical imaginary of the chronotope. Of Nike's more than six thousand American workers, most are based in Beaverton. It is an extraordinary think tank devoted to the magic of the commodity form, to the marketing of image. For instance, in the mid-1980s Nike was big but had not yet become a transnational "player" like McDonalds or Coca-Cola. Then, in 1984, the company signed Michael Jordan to its roster and there began a marketing partnership that would give Jordan name recognition beyond belief and Nike global brand power. Consider the "Jordan Flight" television commercial developed at Beaverton in 1985. As Jordan glides toward the basketball rim the soundtrack emphasizes the roar of jet engines. The image is slowed down to enhance the fact that Jordan is in flight; indeed, he stays in the air for ten seconds. This human impossibility is precisely the point: Jordan has become the equivalent of the goddess whose name graces the ad. He can fly. Just before his retirement in 1993 (he has since made a comeback, retired again, and made another comeback), Jordan noted, "What Phil [Knight] and Nike have done is turn me into a dream." Here there is a bizarre correlation with the immiseration of Sadisah and Sukaesih somewhere offscreen in the shoe factory, as if the hyperreality of Jordan's flight is inseparable from the phantom in Air that the worker represents in Nike's sole. It is only in Beaverton, where Adam Smith's old invisible hand is still at work, that these complementary components must be kept apart, unlaced and unglued.

The Nike World Campus at Beaverton is a world removed from the factories in Indonesia. Responding to Katz's questions, Nike employees said the Campus was "like being in a playground" and that it was "a factory for fun" (DK 49). The workforce is young (but not as young as the women workers in Asia) and often display a highly motivated sports mentality.[60] The corporate identity of Nike is predominantly white and male even if the sportspeople who endorse its products are not. (Buildings are named after Nike success stories like Alberto Salazar, Bo Jackson, and Joan Benoit Samuelson.) While this is unremarkable for American capitalism it cannot be separated from the implications of Nike's global sway. The interior walls of each building are drenched with sports paraphernalia and associated imagery (Katz compares them to frat houses). This, however, goes beyond the trappings of jock culture: It is part of the very fabric of corporate life that makes up Nike's "matrix" structure. To read book-length studies of Nike like *Swoosh* and *Just Do It* is to understand that transnational corporatism itself depends on a working logic that is thoroughly masculinist. The activities at Nike management retreats (called "Buttfaces"), corporate parties ("Nike Nites"), and the annual Nike "Beer Relays" are perhaps the most obvious symptoms of the Beaverton mindset. But the dominance of testosterone in Nike activities has still more glaring "high" points: for instance, in December 1979, when the company went public (and Phil Knight became wealthy to the tune of $178 million) no women employees were offered stock in the company (even Carole Fields, one-time controller for Nike and nicknamed "Dragon Lady," got nothing from the stock options). Similarly, even after the decision to move into the emerging and lucrative market for women's aerobic shoes in 1987 (and only after Reebok had profited handsomely from this line), it was several years before women were invited to "the boys' club in Beaverton" (as Katz calls it) to take a more active role in this marketing process (incidentally, this was a financial success, and by 1992 Nike was the leader in the aerobics niche[61]). In the playground, however, the fun is mostly male and insistently so.

The matrix structure at Beaverton must acknowledge the material force of the Asian women workers even as the images it creates are the material reality that denies this link beyond the World Campus. While "exposing the technology" might allow one to "see the air," it also belies the stark contradiction and dependence between two material forces of production, the physicality in the fetishism if you will. Both aspects are integral to the time/space coordinates of the shoe. They are, in Bakhtin's terms, "the knots of narrative that are continually tied and untied" in an apparently empty continuum. Inside the World Campus, the designers, consciously or not, wrestle with the implications of this ineluctable link. Although they all have a "license to dream,"[62] the designers must work with the contractors and subcontractors to render their imagination profitable.[63] The cost of the material components is one consideration, and Nike has, over the years, developed a highly integrated system for bringing together materials made in different parts of the globe. The production of air pockets or sacs, the air that can be seen, is not trusted to the Asian market: the heart of Nike's "technology" is produced in the United States by a company called "Tetra," then shipped to Asia for assembly in the shoe itself. Lightweight leather substitutes like Durabuck are made by a Japanese affiliate. (Nike came up with Durabuck while its lab technicians were working on Michael Keaton's Batboots for *Batman*.) And the designers must also take note of regional variations in color tastes around the globe even though preferences among youth culture often change at rates that are out of sync with the production process. Of course, Nike advocates a high degree of homogenization (a mainstay of economies of scale), something facilitated by the power of the brand, but augments its "branding" with what it calls a "psychographic" view of the marketplace. When Nike designers are indulging in "free association," they are also targeting particular psychic profiles. This is one of the ways that masculinism (and other logics of Being) gets built into the shoe.

Cultural critics find the hard-edged rationalism of marketing anathema to cultural understanding, and yet it seems to me we seriously misapprehend the cultural logic of capital by suppressing the realities of corporate culture while celebrating somewhat traditional symptoms of art in the marketplace. What the Nike psychographic approach attempts is a breakdown of market segmentation in any one production cycle. This is represented as a triangle whose apex is dominated by Nike's leading profile target: the sixteen- to twenty-six-year-old "hardbody" male "sports driver." The fetishistic impulses of this group sets the standards for the rest (including the women's segments). These young males (again, the primary market is in the United States, but global sales continue to expand) will shell out the $80–$170 for "top of the line" models (even this last word is in step with the overall logic). This segment is designated "Max," although it is not reserved solely for the Air Max line. The next segment is called "Perf" (performance) and targets athletes and aspiring athletes who might actually gain from the design technologies in the shoe. Beneath this is the "Core" segment, which is also called the middle or "kill" zone where Nike makes most of its sales. The Core identify with Perf and Max yet usually lack both the body and the psychological investment to make as much use of Nike's high-profile shoes. Eighty percent of Nike's shoes are not used for their intended purpose. (Nike always contests this figure, but gradually and grudgingly "fashion" has pushed aside "athletic" in the symbolic of the shoe that Nike presents.) At the base of the Nike psychographic triangle is the "Entry" segment, those people who must be weaned onto Nikes by an incessant combination of peer-driven, price-driven, and advertising-driven campaigns. While brand loyalty is difficult in the ephemeral life of an athletic shoe (Max, for instance, may choose another line precisely because Core and Entry are choosing theirs), the psychographic approach is also beholden to the paradox of commodity fetishism in general: The consumer must be made to sustain his or her private fantasy even though he or she covets an object or image that is traded publicly. The savvy theorist has an answer to this dilemma, but then so too do Nike's marketing gurus, like Jim Riswold, who says of the psychography: "it never appeared to me as part of some grand strategy. I mean, it's not nineteenth century philosophy" (DK 151). Quite. Commodity desire gets a lot more help than Marx (or Freud for that matter) could envisage. The magic of the fetish requires the magic of money. In 1997, for example, Nike spent $975 million on promotion.

Most of Nike's shoe lines play to and reinforce conventional definitions of masculinity. Just as the Greeks used Nike to symbolize victory in war (at one point they clipped her wings to keep "victory" in Athens), so Nike laces the sports profile with the language of aggression. Featured shoe models have included Air Assault, Air Barrage, Air Force, Air Magnum Force, Air Raid, and even Air Stab. Other companies in the business have marketed shoes like "Run'N'Gun," "Predator," "Marauder," "Shooter," and "Slasher." (It is noticeable that with the increased focus on every aspect of sneaker production the politics of naming has retreated to the relatively safe havens of cliché, abstraction or technobabble—Air Pegasus, Air Current RW, or Air Accel Low.) The association of sport and violence is not surprising, but it has other repercussions along the chain of affective responsibility than the epistemic violence that produces the superexploitation of Asian women workers. Before considering that in more detail, let us consider the design process of a typical Nike shoe.

For instance, the Air Carnivore was first dreamed up by Bill Worthington in 1992 and remains in many ways an archetypal lesson in Nike's creative logic. The path from idea to actual shoe is a laborious one: out of curiosity Nike employees once sketched out the process of a shoe's development, and the resulting map, cognitive or otherwise, was sixty feet long. Even then, the designer is weighed down by doubt. Worthington muses, "The question now was whether the consumer would be able to appreciate the technology inside the shoe, or to understand its true personality" (DK 159). This is something of my own approach in stressing the chronotope of the shoe. Worthington, however, stops short in his assessment of Air Carnivore's time/space coordinates: "People will tell each other about the Carnivore. They'll say, 'Here's a shoe that represents the aggression of sports'" (DK 159). The aggression takes on another meaning in Pusan, South Korea, where the Carnivores were made. The Carnivores would be one of factory T3's last production runs in 1993 as Nike moved still more production to Indonesia, China, and Vietnam. The name of the shoe is a fitting metaphor for Nike's labor practices: by the end of 1993, 3,500 T3 workers, mostly women, had been laid off. The graffiti on the factory walls included the demand: "We want to be compensated for working our brains out!" (DK 165) They were not.

Meanwhile back in Beaverton, a price structure was worked out for the shoe. Before they were fired (or disavowed in my schema), the T3 workers were paid about $4.50 for every pair of Carnivores made. (This labor cost was considered too high alongside the margins available from workers like Sadisah and Sukaesih elsewhere in Asia.) Nike paid the subcontractor about $29.50 for each pair of Carnivores (60 percent of the price went to product materials). "Landing" the shoe in the consumer market would take another $7.40 (including duties). After taxes and another $15 for running the operation at Nike World Campus, the company would have a $5.50 profit built into the shoe. The retailer would pay about $70 for the Carnivore, the consumer up to $60 more than that depending upon demand and promotions (if the line becomes coveted, the price can soar—a little retail hoarding can exacerbate this effect, as it did with the infamous Air Max '95 whose margins expanded by up to 40 percent). While the women in Pusan look for employment in the emerging service industries, Nike will chase "nations farther down the developmental ladder" (DK 168)—places where a $130 pair of sneakers can still be made, not worn.[64]

The Air Carnivore looks like it could eat jobs and dollars as fast as it creates them. It is predominantly green (when first pitched at an annual sporting goods show in Atlanta the Nike salesperson barked "Vegetarians beware") and appears to abjure the natural contours of a foot. The bulkiness of the shoe is an illusion, since the synthetic materials used render it quite light. The sole is purple and black, and deeply striated into "pods" of supporting rubber. The upper of the shoe is deformed by several straps of Velcro which, like the advertising images, hold the shoe together around the foot. These straps are part of an "anti-inversion" collar which is both heavily indebted to technobabble and to a desire to prevent the ankle from turning should this cross-trainer actually be used for cross-training. The top of the shoe is dominated by a third Velcro strap which sticks, rather than stitches, the subject in the shoe (to complicate the metaphor so heavily analyzed by Derrida and the series of allusions I have made thus far). The inside of the shoe sports a Neoprene sock. This "Dynamic Fit Sleeve" allows the foot to move and breath inside a shoe whose outside suggests completely the opposite—anti-inversion indeed. We are far removed from Van Gogh's peasant shoes here, but other peasants are not completely erased: in the belly of the Air Carnivore a tiny label testifies "Made in South Korea."

The belly of a shoe? Worthington, the designer, is unequivocal: "This shoe is like an animal. It's like a living, breathing thing instead of an inanimate consumer product" (DK 127). Just as the Greeks anthropomorphized a symbol of military success, so our young designer gives life to the fetish of his desire. And what inspired this fearful symmetry? Worthington, like other Nike designers, is a self-professed "culture pirate" and, unlike most others at the World Campus, the designers often draw their imagery from outside the world of sports. The Air Carnivore owed its animal nature as much to the films *Jurassic Park* and the *Alien* series as it did to man's "natural" aggression (when Katz interviewed Worthington, the latter's office featured stills from *Alien*). Worthington also drew up a cartoon character to "image" the shoe's effect on its owner. An average kid, "Bert Starkweather," becomes "Bolt Stingwater" (Luke Skywalker?) in his Carnivores and proceeds to "win drag races on foot and step on people's faces" (DK 128). Could it be that this creativity never leaves the shoe, but becomes part of its affective image, its commodity aura, its product-being?

Obviously, the suggestion is not that merely by buying into the image one becomes the character that the designer projects but, nevertheless, if the main point of such consumption is not in fact the practical utilization of sporting technology for sport, then how the shoe is made and marketed stands in for (and contradicts) a corporate claim that is otherwise "ethically neutral." In contemporary capitalism, the violence of representation is also, and always already, the violence of production and consumption. To separate off the moment and malevolence of Image from the Being in production and consumption is to collude with precisely those avatars of this epoch who claim that image is everything and representation is, in itself, the sole arbiter of debates about the mode of production in and outside culture. The chronotope of the shoe suggests that the time and space of athletic shoe production across the globe curve toward simultaneity but in fact maintain context-specific criteria that appear to render them incommensurable. The inside/outside of commodity production, like the inside/outside of the shoe itself, is indeed inseparable, but how easy has it become to reduce the sign of worker presence/absence in production to a label tucked away from view? Two examples may elaborate the cycle of violence that is endemic to the production and circulation of commodities at the moment when fetishism must disavow its responsibility to the real, and indeed, to Reality.

Nike is taking greater control over its production and distribution operations in Asia as a result of the bad press it has received about the labor practices it fosters. (The Code of Conduct it trumpets still sidesteps the question of independent verification, but there is no doubt that Nike has been forced to reveal more detail about its day-to-day operations in Asia—it has even printed the addresses of some of the factories where it subcontracts.) Yet responsibility is a very relative state of mind in Nike's corporate ideology, since when accused of crass exploitation of its Asian workers Nike's spokespeople continue to maintain a dogged moral neutrality. This line of argument proposes that either problems occur because of the nature of the market or that Nike can hardly be held responsible for the internal socioeconomic (and political) conditions of the countries where it bases its production operations. The record, as I have already implied, underlines that Nike, like many TNCs, actively seeks and supports conditions of this kind. In addition, a program Nike describes as "Futures" exacerbates poor labor relations because, by securing future orders from retailers six to eight months in advance, the tendency is to speed up production quotas in Asia and reduce flexibility in the hours of work on the line. Other spinoff practices within this mode of production include the nightly confinement of young women workers to the dormitories within the factory grounds.[65] The apex of these violations is, of course, the wage itself, and here violence begets violence. In Serang, near Jakarta, in 1992

Nike workers went on strike and demanded a 15 percent pay increase. While this may sound excessive to some, in fact it amounts to only 24 cents a day at 1992 exchange rates. When the local subcontractor, a South Korean, refused to bargain, the women workers smashed windows at the factory and overturned furniture. Rather than jeopardize the production cycle, the owner caved in.[66] But, as the Korean workers in Pusan testify, workers take a risk with such activity: Nike can "just do it" elsewhere. In the five years leading up to this strike the company had closed twenty of its Asian factories and opened another thirty-five. And anyway, the TNC can say that any industrial action is the result of the contractors' malfeasance, not the company that pulls their strings.

But if the violence of production has material effects on workers like Sadisah, then there is a concomitant violence in the culture of consumption that accompanies it. Nike's psychographic approach to the market has had another valence in the symbolic of the shoe: for American inner-city youth racked by unemployment and the lure of drug culture, the athletic shoe offers *status*. Again, the athletic shoe company will claim that the imaging of a particular desire is not an endorsement of its consequences, which are, in the first place, overdetermined by a host of other causal factors. But when Nike's cofounder William Bowerman proclaims that one should "play by the rules, but be ferocious" the difficulty is believing that the second emotion can be contained by the civic duty of the first. Nike themselves have not "played by the rules" to the extent that (according to *Swoosh*) they have used bribery in the past, kited checks, "dumped" inventory, and avoided custom duties.[67] And, if Nike's labor practices are anything to go by, the rule in athletic shoe production is that there are no rules, at least none that need strict compliance. One reason the slogan "Just do it!" is so enticing is surely that it imagines a world bereft of rules, a world in which "being ferocious" is some Darwinian compulsion. Do we really believe that the slogan "Just do it by the rules" would have the same effect in the competitive frenzy that is the athletic shoe market? And even if the desire to win in athletic competition can be characterized as "ferocious," is that the same desire communicated in such Nike models as "Air Stab" and "Air Carnivore"? The goddess of victory is smiling.

In 1989 Michael Eugene Thomas was strangled to death by his friend David Martin for his $115 pair of Air Jordans. The same year Johnny Bates was shot to death for his Air Jordans, and Raheem Wells was murdered for his Nikes. In Chicago in 1990 there were, on average, fifteen violent crimes committed per month over athletic shoes (up to fifty a month if one includes warm-up jackets and other sports-related garments).[68] Jordan and Spike Lee have been singled out in the past for their Nike advertising campaigns of the late 1980s in which "Just do it!" became a street knowledge that dovetails with the "ferocious" reality of urban crime. In their defense, Nike played the race card by suggesting that it was typical of race bias in the media that African Americans were being blamed for contributing to the violence already heaped at the doorstep of low-income African American communities. To the extent that white celebrities are not routinely singled out for their contributions to cultures of violence (dozens of Hollywood names immediately come to mind), Nike's point is well taken, but the company's race relations contain their own history of bias. As we have seen, while Michael Jordan made $20 million a year for footwear endorsements, Nike's predominantly white American marketing managers pitted Asian workers against one another (Korean versus Indonesian, Indonesian versus Chinese) in a game of wages tag in which the only defining qualities of racial esteem are the profit margins that accrue to their location. In the United States, Operation PUSH, the Chicago-based civil-rights group, mounted a campaign against Nike because of its poor record in minority hiring in the United States and because of its failure to provide support in the communities where a disproportionate amount of Nike products are sold (disproportionate in terms of income to sales, not total sales). PUSH also discovered that, at the time, Nike had no African American executives and did not use a single African American–run company to promote its products. Nike was cashing in on the image of African American athletes while cashing out on any responsibility to African American communities in general.[69] Naturally, Nike's public-relations department has worked on these issues. (TNC's usually have philanthropic programs—which in some cases provide tax breaks—to ward off the accusation that they are in the business of economic exploitation.) Nevertheless, the larger issue remains whether a transnational corporation should be held accountable for the forms of identification with its "global power brand."

The fetish is a lure. Nike spends millions of dollars each year to cultivate an "emotional tie" (as Phil Knight describes it) to the athletic shoe but disavows this connection at the point where its psychography facilitates an irrational logic of possession. Yet this is intrinsic to the commodity form and does not resolve itself in fine-tuning an image attached (with Velcro) to it. To murder someone for their Nike shoes is irrational in the extreme but is symptomatic of, among other socioeconomic factors, the culture of possession in general. Van Gogh's shoes may well have symbolized the eclipse of valorized peasant communities (certainly this is Heidegger's belief), but the fetishistic overinvestment in the athletic shoe is no less significant: it conjures the madness and malevolence of a particular form of globalism that is itself deracinating peasant communities in different parts of the world *simultaneously and in the same affective space.* In the chronotope of the shoe, pricking stitches Sadisah to Thomas: the maps must be redrawn continually to account for this time/space continuum.

Commodity fetishism is not the same as the psychological compulsion sketched by Freud, but the centrifugal aura of the athletic shoe within contemporary transnational capitalism shows how one may be dialogically implicated with the other. Branding accentuates this overlap in the psychic and economic coordinates of the newest World Order—a relationship that is crucial to athletic shoe culture. Violence, epistemic and real, is not an accidental by-product of the matrix of contemporary commodity production but is vital to it, while the "costs" of production and consumption are necessarily rendered invisible or inconsequential. For Nike, the desire to expand sales far outweighs the use-value of their athletic shoes. In 1993, 77 percent of American young men said they wanted a pair of Nikes (even if they could not afford to buy them); some knew more than a dozen of the models available that year; others even knew the stock numbers. In the "teenager to young adult male" bracket, Americans owned more than ten pairs of sporting footwear *each*. In 1997, 350 million pairs of athletic shoes were sold in the American market alone (although increases in sales have slowed and, in some markets, have actually shrunk).

Michael Haines has a Nike obsession. When interviewed by Katz he had already collected almost forty pairs. Interestingly, his "fetish" (as his mother calls it) began in the early 1980s when he first spotted the see-through air sole of the Air Max. His desire, piqued by the appearance of absence, became at one point almost uncontrollable—he was forced to hide new pairs around the house and, when that aroused suspicion, he persuaded his father to buy them instead. Most of the shoes have never been worn and are revered almost solely for their associative effects. To read what Haines has to say about his shoes is to face the superaddressee of commodity production: "They have to face backward on the shelf because they're so much more . . . beautiful from behind"; "if I could have a new pair every day"; "I still love to come home during school breaks and come up here to open the doors" [of the cupboard that houses his collection]; "I love them. I love thinking about opening the box for the first time. I love taking them out. Just talking about them gets me . . . I don't know" (DK 262–63). The sexual dynamic of Haines's attachment may be exaggerated and frankly bizarre, but few CEOs in the athletic shoe business would be upset by a desire directly connected to a company's advertising machine. How much commodity desire is enough desire? Can this be calibrated, or is the love of these shoes incalculable such that the violence of the sweatshop and the street is an inadvertent by-product for which responsibility is an empty concept? Nike does not merely satisfy a need for athletic footwear, it deliberately creates a need far in excess of what is necessary (this, of course, is one of the meanings of capitalism). Yet conventional wisdom would have it that Haines hurts no one by coveting his shoes. In truth, his personal fixation has been purchased and in that exchange his desire is globally localized (to borrow once more from contemporary TNC lore) just as Sukaesih and Sadisah's labor has been interpellated in an international network of capital exchange. The names and the products may change, but as long as the logic of these connections remains predominantly unimagined, then the commodity fetish will continue to be naturalized: the ontology of the commodity, the Being of the shoe, will present itself as a normative Being of culture. And what seems like an adjunct to cultural discourse is in fact what silently defines it.

Sadisah does not speak to us in these pages, and neither does Sukaesih (even through reported speech).[70] The shoes don't speak either (although, on this point, the Nike designers are close to the philosophy of art proposed by Heidegger, Jameson, and Derrida[71]). Even by acknowledging Sukaesih's presence in the United States and foregrounding the immense, and generally successful, campaigns to defamiliarize the governing tenets of global sneaker production, this record does not undo the cognitive fix in "Just Do It!" The athletic shoe will pass out of TNC production exploitation not because people will stop running but because the "victory" invoked is not about running.[72] Indeed, the chronotope of the shoe is only about the essence of the shoe at all to the extent that such a commodity is a narrative about the international division of labor. Similarly, Indonesia is not miraculously mapped (even as it is integrated into global circuits of commodity production and exchange) by the affective points of time and space that I have sketched above (and no handy reference to shadow theater will wrest it from that chiaroscuro). Shoe production does not give us the magic key to the intense vicissitudes of Indonesian history since independence. All I argue here is that the athletic shoe industry has inscribed itself in a particular form of nation building that is nevertheless uninterested in the Subject that such a process confers. To imagine the links in the aura of the shoe is what must be risked if criticism is to be responsibly positioned in global analysis. For the commodity, the chronotope becomes something of a heuristic device, "the place where the knots of narrative are tied and untied," but a place that is always displaced by the logic of desire in the marketplace and by the desire for a logic that is not stitched by authoritarian regimes of truth. The imagination required is less surefooted not only because the product-being of the contemporary commodity is dispersed fantastically, but because there is no language adequate to the global representation of the worker. While Nike has global imagery, there is yet no global imaginary that can transform the developmental ladder that the TNC typically exploits. So even when activists counter corporate tokenism by organizing independent labor watchdogs like the Workers Rights Consortium, there remains a tremendously powerful ideological machine that says such efforts are blind to the good that economic exploitation brings. Nicholas Kristof and Sheryl WuDunn, for instance, blithely contend that sweatshops are the economic linchpin of Asian modernization. ("They're dirty and dangerous. They're also the major reason Asia is back on track.")[73] In the nineteenth century, a similar paucity of global imagination allowed the British to believe that the opium trade was performing the same miracle. If antisweatshop organizations head off the descent into cynicism, smugness, and glibness, the structural logic of commodity production and consumption weighs heavily on counterhegemonic discourse. Indeed, merely by detailing the deaths that result from a psychic overinvestment in the commodity, one does not break the production of desire that informs it. What then, is the point of chronotopic critique?

I have borrowed chronotope from Bakhtin as he borrowed it from Ukhtomsky (and, indeed, Einstein), "as a metaphor (almost, but not entirely)"[74] to draw together seemingly disparate elements of the world system attached (artists, workers, philosophers, inner-city youth, and cultural critics alike) by affective responsibility. We have no alibi for this responsibility (the boycott of selected consumer items is ultimately beside the point) because, as Bakhtin reminds us, we cannot claim to be anywhere else but where we are in Being. Cultural criticism must do much more than express concern for the wasted humanity of capitalist production (a somewhat sentimental, humanist answerability) by making the deracinated Being of the commodity form imaginable. But this responsibility is also about meaning, which Bakhtin suggests can only become part of our social experience when it takes on "the form of a sign." The shoe is not perhaps the "hieroglyph" that Bakhtin had in mind and that is partly why his formulation has been refigured in my argument by the "hieroglyph" that Marx identified. Just as our philosophers overlook the maker, so Bakhtin's hypostatization of the novel placed formal limits on the range of social experience imaginable. That the novel can conjure the world of commodity culture is undeniable; the test of a geopolitical imaginary is whether it can imagine how the commodity can conjure in the opposite direction. This is not ultimately about the cognitive abilities of the cultural critic (or his or her humanist inclinations) but, more importantly, about forms of collective reciprocity disrupting the aura of the commodity that anxiously purports to embrace a world economy with its own cultural transnationalism. This kind of answerability does not exclude individualist efforts like Keady's to dramatize the human costs of globalizing capitalist consumer desire, since he evokes a responsibility that can catalyze collectivity across borders. To imagine the world otherwise continues to be the challenge, not by individual volition, however, but by alternative forms of socialization. Only then will the shoe be on the other foot.

6

Joe:
The Architectonic of
a Commodity

What is fiction in particular is truth in general.
—Multatuli, *Max Havelaar*

The task of cultural transnationalism is not to comprehend commodities as
hermeneutical objects; in the contemporary situation, it is their incomprehensibility that needs to be comprehended.[1] This reworking of Adorno's typically
aphoristic (and perhaps impossible) approach to aesthetics and the artwork is not
a way to glaze, rather obviously, the banalized world of capitalist commodity
production with the rarefied discernment of bourgeois affect; it is, rather, to set
forth a necessary challenge to our understanding of the real and the reified in terms
of globalization. Certainly the compulsively incomprehensible has been a constitutive feature of capitalist commodity production all along—that inexorable
contradiction between being human and having objects that Marx elucidates in
the early part of *Capital*. Yet the mystery of the commodity has been compounded
by globalization's false narrative of integration in the modern epoch such that
incomprehensible objecthood has become so matter-of-fact as to make the commodity's opacity a deadening quotidian translucence. Of course, it is not enough
to give the lie to the commodity's naturalization, that its thereness is bound up
with centuries of exploitative socioeconomic relations, for even revelation has
become a stock commodity. We might push, however, some of the more forceful issues of aesthetics, even those numbing paratactic profusions of Adorno, to
stave off the inevitable doxa that the circulation of commodities beyond national boundaries (and nationalism) is somehow the goal of human existence.

The terrible beauty of commodity aesthetics is that it is a pharmakon for both.
The aesthetician finds the sublime aura of the artwork poisoned by the bitter doses
of the commodity: Surely all that is precious in the experience of art cannot share

the crass logic of quantification and exchange value? Similarly, the commodity broker wants to believe in taste and pleasure but would not submit these vagaries to those of supply and demand where there are laws, we are told, that can be calculated. To kill the commodity would kill the aesthetic only to the extent that the specific grounds for the commodity's incomprehensibility would no longer obtain. The mortality of one is secreted in the glorious manifestations of the other, which, sutured by much more than the serendipity of history, are condemned to expire, the one from the very logic of the Other. Just as, *pace* Benjamin, there is no document of civilization that is not a document of barbarism,[2] so there is no commodity that does not bear, in its incomprehensibility, a transcendence of things that threatens its very thingness. The ethereal that extends the life of the commodity is precisely what condemns it, for it lugs around the lie that it must be more than what it is, a touchstone for the extraction of surplus value. As Adorno notes, for most people aesthetics are superfluous and the art of the commodity is the proof: The commodity circulates an irrationality that seems out of sync with the plod of profit and loss that motivates it.[3] Transnational commodity transactions do not just mimic the general principle of the incomprehensible, they intensify its substance by making the mystery using an elsewhere, a somewhere else, not just off the map but off the cognitive, perhaps even off the sensate. The charge is not to resuscitate a lost origin for the commodity the better to confirm its titular thingness, but it is rather to come to terms with the logic of making itself, which, for the aesthetic and the commodity, has always entailed a concrete materiality. We will see that this making is neither a universal nor an endless variable based on the commodity at issue; it is what escapes the real that, paradoxically, only the real itself can transform.

I am going to approach the incomprehensible in the transnational commodity from three disparate but troublingly connected coordinates in making: the commodity as history, the commodity as philosophy, and the commodity as culture. This will do justice neither to the commodity in question nor to the fields of inquiry invoked, but the following might usefully be read as a problem of critical praxis in general rather than a judgment of the particular paradigm for which these few pages are a surrogate. It seems to me now that the commodity that appears at once as eminently comprehensible and yet so obtuse in its commingling of the sensate and the suprasensible is coffee. "This coffee," Honoré de Balzac famously reminds us in his "Traité des excitants modernes" (1838) (translated as "Treatise on Modern Stimulants"), "falls into your stomach . . . everywhere there is agitation. Flashes of wit arrive in skirmishing order. Figures arise, the paper is covered with ink; for the struggle commences and is concluded with torrents of black water, just as a battle begins and ends with black powder."[4] The battle to which Balzac alludes is primarily physiological (he drank coffee to work through the night), but it is simultaneously epistemological, economic, and political (the "agitation" that the nineteenth-century aesthete typically condemns to amnesia). Coffee is as old as capitalism and colonialism and, unlike spices, which were a crucial catalyst in the initial conditions of transnational exploration and expropriation, it has continued to grow as an integer of commodity trade. William Ukers's veritable Bible of coffee, *All about Coffee* (originally published in 1922), states the case for this centrality:

> Coffee is universal in its appeal. All nations do it homage. It has become recognized as a human necessity. It is no longer a luxury or an indulgence; it is a corollary of human energy and human efficiency. People love coffee because of its two-fold effect—the pleasurable sensation and the increased efficiency it produces.
>
> Coffee has an important place in the rational dietary of all the civilized peoples of earth. It is a democratic beverage. Not only is it the drink of fashionable society, but it is also a favorite beverage of the men and women who do the world's work, whether they toil with brain or brawn. It has been acclaimed "the most grateful lubricant known to the human machine," and the "most delightful taste in all nature."[5]

The language of this view, with Ukers's allusions to "democracy," civilization, and the universal, has a class purview that links taste to trade and necessitates an approach that can account for both. That coffee may have the most delightful taste in nature only partly explains its material ground. Coffee is the world's second-largest (legally) traded commodity and, after oil, it stimulates a massive proportion of global trade. Eighty percent of all coffee is traded internationally rather than intranationally—this wholesale trade alone is worth $14 billion a year with paper trades and futures worth five times that figure. United States retail sales in *one* segment, specialty coffee, generates more than $5 billion a year. By value, it is the largest food import to the United States (some $2.5 billion worth of wholesale beans). Although coffee consumption in the United States is in decline, Americans still consume more than 20 gallons per person per year (20 percent of all coffee consumed is downed by Americans).[6] Economies of the so-called developing world are venerated and vilified according to the performance of their bean, snared, as they are, in what is traditionally known as the coffee cycle. The cycle is characterized by typical contradictions between supply and demand, further overdetermined by time lags in the cultivation process and the danger of frosts for the major producers (Brazil in particular). Second-guessing nature has also made the futures market in coffee one of the biggest in the world.

Historically, coffee's inscription in the narrative of colonial expansion is voluminous, but the aura of that brutalization did not end with independence or much-vaunted experiments in democracy. The coffee market is still a cartel, and the coffee elites who lorded over the immiseration of millions during colonialism find many of the their bloodlines in the agribusiness and brokerage systems of today throughout the coffee-producing regions of Asia, Africa, and Central and South America. Apart from a few pockets of ecologically sound production and worker-friendly farm formations, most coffee production is done the old-fashioned way, by paying pickers a few cents per pound for their labor. With so little expended on labor costs (or on protecting the environment), the landowners, the wholesalers, the vendors, the brokers, the roasters, and the retailers enjoy some of the greatest margins available in commodity production and consumption (although prices are volatile and betting on coffee futures makes millionaires and misery in equal proportions). After water, tea may still be the most consumed beverage in the world, but coffee beats both hands down for return on investment. This is why in Central America the coffee elites remain close to the corridors of dominion. Those who trade with them keep them there. As Jeffery Paige has underlined in his book *Coffee and Power,* the social struggles in El Salvador, Guatemala, and Nicaragua in the modern era are directly related to fissures caused by coffee plantation exploitation.[7] American involvement in these crises was multifaceted but cannot be adequately understood without reference to the coffee business and a desire to be tapped into the closest and cheapest source of bean production. Both the elites and the American traders deny or suppress this fateful connection, but few would argue now that communism was ever anything but an alibi in the successive crises that beset the foundations of U.S.–Central American geopolitics in the 1970s and 1980s. This history can be "comprehended" according to my initial formulation and indeed is in the process of being written and rewritten yet does not embrace the ineffable which itself allows the aesthetic to become a material force.

How, for instance, do we make coffee? I do not simply mean whether one brews using drip coffeemakers, vacuum pots, presses, and the like, but what larger process of making is deployed in the production of coffee as commodity and culture? And why would "Joe" now be an appropriate and forceful term to characterize the process at issue? The answers that I provide below may be deemed so fanciful as to be a product of overzealous coffee consumption, a supercaffeinated coffee delirium with a jittery logic all its own. That characterization may be appropriate, but it is not quite the architectonic of coffee I have in mind. Here we are interested primarily in the materialization of commodities, their effect and affect for the imaginary, and the determinate relations they conjure. (This at least has been my attempt so far with athletic shoes.) When coffee is overextracted it becomes bitter; similarly, there is a danger in this form of critique that the commodity is overabstracted and may leave an objectionable aftertaste that detracts, ultimately, from the imaginative grasp at stake. As one commentary puts it, we tend to be "passionately subjective" about coffee,[8] and so the risk of disparaging discernment will remain, however finely the process is calculated. My basic premise is this: Coffee is not just a social beverage but the name for a very specific logic of socialization, with a philosophy, pharmacology, political economy, and culture that is peculiarly modern. There are many ways to make coffee; in this argument coffee is not a function of the modern but is axiomatic—it is steeped in an epistemology and ontology that sutures nature to Being in the modern era. Making coffee is not symbolic of this process: it is the process. But why call this "Joe"?

Call me Joe. Joe. Joe Six-Pack. GI Joe. Joe Blow. The average Joe. Joe Black. Joe Camel. Whichever way you brew it, American Joe runs deep in the cultural unconscious of the United States and all who have come into contact with it. Wherever Joe goes, so goes America. In parts of the Caribbean, Joes are simply Americans; Pacific islanders have also called any American a Joe. But not every Joe is intrinsically Joe American. Joe is everyman, and Joe is the unknown, the incomprehensible, the otherwise unnameable. Joe is an imaginary character, he who stands in for what is otherwise denied a fleshly counterpart. Joe is a particular relation, a logic of connection and disjunction, the threads of an architectonic, the making wholes from holes, the disturbance in the field of the Other that is always about the human capacity to make and make otherwise. Joe in this sense is the scene of intense identification and contestation about what a Joe can be in American states of liberty. Joe, here, is coffee (Java Joe, cup of Joe), a linchpin in an American architectonic, for there is no moment in American history when coffee has not also been about American power and the economic discourse that feeds it. From the first settlers to the house that Maxwell House built, the ideology of Joe is that it is "good to the last drop" (a phrase apparently coined by Teddy Roosevelt, a consumer of massive amounts of coffee). Joe is the coffee connection between powerful subjugation and the auspices of "free" trade, the bridge between bitter colonialism and the full-bodied aroma of neocolonialism, the kinder, gentler latte cup of late capitalism. Even when Joe is in decline at home, he is ready to go abroad as a mark of "being American" (again, the association of Joe with coffee principally emerged during World War II as a metonym to describe American presence, especially in Asia). Joe is also about workplace speed-up, or time/space compression in capital's chronotope. It is about consumption aesthetics and that wonderfully bourgeois reflex that loves buttery Sulawesi over the instant blue-collar necessity of freeze-dried Joe, a dark puddle desired for kick not connoisseurship (I should qualify this by adding that "instant Joe" was originally developed and popularized by Nestlé, the European conglomerate, whose infamous Nescafé is now downed globally at the rate of more than three thousand cups a second). Instead of reading Joe as the imaginary person, let us consider Joe as an imaginary, a geopolitical Joe but a passionately aesthetic (and subjective) Joe, the creative force in making, and making strange across national borders. This is but one strain of Joe as relation that I will later reinvoke by reference to the specialty coffee industry in the United States. Such an architectonic is called "Joe" not because America is coffee's biggest culprit (it is a truly global commodity), but because the United States currently deigns to define the contours of transnationalism. Yet the mystery of arabica complicates even the arrogance of pax americana.

How did coffee come to occupy this dominant position in commodity culture? Coffee's cultivation obviously has much to do with the contact zones established through imperial dominion and trade.[9] But beyond this truism is the fact that coffee oiled the actual processes of identification we now associate with modernity. And the pharmacology of coffee is intimately connected to the philosophical disposition of the modern, which not only guarantees a worldview but also cultivates its transformational possibilities. In the Pharmakon of Western desire, coffee inspires more than the regulative rationality it is held to embrace, which in turn only intensifies its commodity allure. But what has cleared the ground, philosophically, for the modern Joe? One trajectory takes us back to Europe and a memorandum from Immanuel Kant to E. A. Christoph Wasianski (embellished, perhaps, by Thomas De Quincey in his version of Wasianski's biographical sketch of Kant) about Kant's conditions for dining with him "that there was to be coffee."[10]

Although Kant was said to have craved coffee his whole life, he demanded the brew only at the end of it. One can only imagine what would have happened to the rigors of critical philosophy had Kant succumbed to his desire at an earlier age. He did permit himself a cup of tea or coffee at breakfast (an amount creatively underreported by the abstemious Kant) and a pipe of tobacco, but for the rest of the day he answered the call of coffee with the iron will of abstinence. Coffee was introduced into German drinking culture in the seventeenth century, and coffeehouses soon followed.[11] By the time Kant is imbibing the brew, coffee was even supplanting warm beer as the beverage of choice at the German breakfast table. Frederick the Great had attempted to restrict coffee consumption because of the large number of foreign merchants who were profiting from it. Specious claims were made regarding its effects (sterility, etc.), and most coffee histories now gleefully record how Bach was spurred to draft his *Coffee Cantata* (1732) as a more notable protest against such bunkum. In 1781 Frederick issued an edict that created a royal monopoly over coffee roasting that subsequently provided the court with handsome revenues. Given the exorbitant costs of coffee roasting licenses in Germany, coffee consumption became the domain of the bourgeois and aristocratic classes. Frederick even went so far as to create a small army of "coffee sniffers" who spied on the populace and issued fines for those found to be roasting coffee without licenses. The effects of aristocratic absolutism over coffee and its culture would not be lost on the emerging bourgeoisie. German coffeehouses, like their French and English equivalents, were meeting places for the merchants and culturati who were reshaping the country through intensities of trade and disputation. As Schivelbusch points out, it is not hard to see why coffee became a keystone among capitalist commodities of the Enlightenment: "It spread through the body and achieved chemically and pharmacologically what rationalism and the Protestant ethic sought to fulfill spiritually and ideologically. With coffee, the principle of rationality entered human physiology, transforming it to conform with its own requirements. The result was a body which functioned in accord with the new demands—a rationalistic, middle class, forward-looking body."[12] The aristocracy was certainly interested in the rituals of coffee consumption (some even went as far as dressing up *à la turque* in order to do so), but it seriously miscalculated the importance of substance over style at that moment in bourgeois coffee culture. There was to be coffee. That the German petit bourgeois had to settle for ersatz coffee, chicory, for so long was a continual reminder of aristocratic folly.

Kant, of course, did not flee Frederick's authoritarian largesse (his *Universal and Natural History and Theory of the Heavens* was dedicated to the old disciplinarian). But, in what amounts to a historical contradiction, Kant takes aristocratic rule and makes it a philosophical virtue—his self-restraint and rigorous approach to daily life mirrors the historical conditions of Prussia while producing a systematic thinking that must sublate it. Given his objective idealism and his deep distrust of empiricism, we may assume that Kant's desire for coffee was not spurred by its status as an objective phenomenon, as a pleasure linked to an object that denies the essential ends of reason. But what reason is at stake in coffee that requires Kant's use of the imperative? Here I do not mean to philosophize by invoking simply the associative effects of coffee consumption, although these are even more important than what is practical in Kant's approach; there is, however, something of the order of rationality in Kant's demand that reflects not just the obsessively regimented nature of his practical Being (neighbors could set their watches by Kant's daily routine), but also the suprasensible, or noumena, of what is beautiful in coffee. Certainly, this is a reading, an interpretation of representation, not a philosophy qua philosophy, and may be as fantastic as Kaldi dancing with his coffee-chewing goats (one of coffee lore's more prominent mythologies). Let us suppose, for a moment, that Kant's demand is invested in a law that coffee derives in nature. We know that coffee in the seventeenth and eighteenth centuries is embroiled in debates in Europe about sobriety and ethics. These are not necessarily the concern of critical philosophy (although they are features of, say, Lutheran reform and new Protestant discourses on discipline and industriousness, against which Kant's early experience of Pietism chafed until this too lost its luster by authoritarian devotion). By the time, however, that Kant is taking his coffee, the Age of Reason constituted a definably bourgeois order in which rational calculation was a justifiable end, economically and socially. For Kant, such a formula might have value if it could demonstrate a superadequation to metaphysical morals; that is, if its process were motivated by more than individual will or the mere fact of experience of the empirical real. While such a demonstration is at the heart of Kant's critiques, its relevance to coffee appears to lie most forcefully in terms of the Third Critique, on judgment.[13] Why?

In the beautiful and the sublime Kant wants to offer an apparatus that might bring a mirror to the autonomous Subject without the power of representation merely being reversible or relativized beyond substance. Make no mistake, the Subject has authority, but this power of authorizing or making must have a principle beyond itself as a phenomenon, or the Subject will be known and the game will be up, the trick of omnipotence will dissolve into unreflective *doxa*. That "there was to be coffee" is an unusual imperative that links discernment or taste to an a priori, that which is not subject to the simple truth or falsity gambit, but remains as a condition of judgment in the first place, as a free association. Just as the Subject herself or himself is noumenal, beyond what is sensible in knowledge, so the object of aesthetic judgment is wonderfully disjunctive, in that the thing-in-itself, the *Ding-an-sich,* subjectively combines the imagination and reason by representing them, paradoxically, as an unrepresentable limit. Disinterested to its core, aesthetic pleasure is not out to possess the object but, like moral law for Kant, demonstrate the nature of its compulsion. There must be coffee because, well, there must. The categorical imperative is also a commodity compulsion, one in which the effect of coffee as object is extracted as an immanent universal. Note, I am not claiming that Kant thought coffee to be beautiful, nor that he ever employed it to demonstrate the harmonizing attributes of the sublime. Yet Kant's bold pronouncement at the end of his life is particularly striking in that the referent is clearly something from which he derives pleasure and is most assuredly a commodity that conjoins the suprasensible with the sensuously particular via a desire that Freud, in his Oedipal reading of Kant on the sublime, would call wish fulfillment. The conditional in Kant's assessment is an acknowledgment of the commodity's status for the living. Kant is not interested in this objecthood yet knows that his very discernment is tied to it. The transcendental in his attachment is bound by a rather earthly contingency, mortality. Kant comments: "Well, one can die, after all; it is but dying; and in the next world, thank God, there is no drinking of coffee and consequently no waiting for it" (De Quincey, 347). The sublime cannot be willed (for it exists only in nature), but what the object makes can be projected beyond the fact of rational calculation, a sense that actually proposes a limit to our imaginary zeal. The deconstructionist leaps in here (armed with Heidegger's formidably idiosyncratic reading of Kant) to opine that the old codger from Konigsberg is bound by the paradoxical force of textual play to narrate an affect that critical philosophy would deem is otherwise beyond the capacities of narration (which is also Adorno's concern with the incomprehensible). Derrida's own reading of the Third Critique hinges on "economimesis," a rather brilliant concept that dissolves the bourgeois antinomy of high and "mercenary" art by reference to the distinction accorded salary in the production of art in Kant's schema.[14] This mimetic *mise en abŷme* stays with coffee and its making, even as Kant's demand would sublimate the principle of trade that has supplied it. However much Kant underlines the indifference of the referent in what is sensed, the radical skeptic will always sense a signifier raging against the dying of the light. But there is another aspect to Derrida's reading that is provocative in the current context. Derrida suggests that Kant's schema in the Third Critique depends on a privileging of speech (particularly in what is sublime in poetry) and the function of the mouth in sensing the suprasensible. Obviously, his target is logophonocentrism, but Derrida connects this to Kant's elaboration of the senses in his *Anthropology*. Coffee aficionados often associate coffee's taste with a sense of well-being, but what is sublime in coffee is perhaps what remains negative in the *os* of logos as a mouth. As subjective senses for Kant, taste and smell do not allow for cognition of the object by themselves—they always require the intervention of one of the other senses. Nevertheless, they are senses of pleasure and are closely linked to what Kant describes as an inner sense, where feeling conjoins with disinterestedness in the judgment of an object. Derrida argues that Kant's critique is constrained by its analogical approach to the sensate, so that, for instance, intellectual food, like food that disgusts, can be regurgitated, expelled, vomited. While Derrida's philosophy of vomit would require a very different argument, the question of taste and disgust he raises is particularly important in understanding what Ukers calls the "lure" of coffee. The subjective aura of coffee has been historically vital to processes of discernment and identification in the modern era precisely because of the intensity with which it engages the subjective in the sensing of an object. Or, as one coffee handbook puts it: "While there are ways to describe and categorize coffees objectively, the

actual experience of coffee will always be subjective. . . . Describing taste sensa-
tions is not unlike poetry in both process and result: Sip and be inspired."[15]

The literary, the question of tropes, similes, metaphors, and the like, is one
way to defamiliarize the methodological plod of Kant's sentences, but would we
need coffee if the literary were, by itself, the sole arbiter of truth, beauty, and (to
disturb the mantra) ideology? The commodity imperative articulates a free accord of the faculties, as a law of the sublime, but it is not simply a linguistic effect, in the same way that death reminds Kant that Being, if not ontology, cannot remain an entirely arbitrary consideration for living. It has recently been
suggested that perhaps Kant could have benefited from De Quincey's advice regarding Kant's failing health in old age (a typically opiated opinion), since then
he would have understood that the physiological demands of the body themselves
have a purchase on metaphysical need. But one could argue that the aesthetics
of the sublime enact such necessity, not through cognitive force (or indeed a ty-
rannical signifier) but in the form of an ideological reflex that, faced with the
disastrous calculations of the rational, finds solace in a sense of the universal as a
paradoxically material condition. Kant's demand for coffee is not a betrayal of
the ideological underpinnings of the aesthetic, nor is it a simply incontrovert-
ible proof; it is, however, a properly bourgeois antinomy that the commodity can
so effortlessly elide the conditions of its interpellation as a necessary ground of
Being. If there was to be coffee, then cerebration must make it, confident that
its concrete specificity will not detract from the universality that is its aesthetic
substance. But, of course, this is only modern philosophy making coffee (as coffee, most assuredly, inspires to make it).

Perhaps the demand of a coffee fiend can be clarified by reference to a tea
demon. Michael Holquist has noted the central role that architectonics plays in
Bakhtin's philosophical thinking (including those neo-Kantian inflections of *Art
and Answerability*).[16] Although architectonics has a specific meaning for Bakhtin (in terms of aesthetic consummation), it is clear that it is also a founding
principle (*arkhē*) that helps us to understand the relationship between the world
and the mind, or in this case, coffee and the cognitive. Rather than read this only
in the Kantian sense of a relation that is at once transcendent in its coupling of
sensibility and understanding, Bakhtinian architectonics urges a radical specifi-
cation of the sensate with thought by attending to the logic of the imaginary in
the everyday. This capacity now is trendily assigned to the virtual worlds of postmodernity (indeed, the coffeehouse has devolved into the virtual chat room of
the Internet), but, while this affect of identity has a powerful hold on the terms
of actually existing globalization, I want to maintain the imaginary of the commodity in architectonics as making. The problem of agonistic forms of the trans-

national is not necessarily that they are dominated by precious invocations of corporate capitalism, but rather that their determinate Being is unhinged from the capacity to make that lies in the production of culture *and* things. It is easy to celebrate tenacious border crossing without addressing the ability to make that is deeply inscribed in the process itself (the creativity of the novelists I discuss is also about making). This "making" is not the real meaning of globalization today as if, once more, you scratch the palimpsest of capital to reveal its lurid truth below. No. The point is both about the historicity of making, and the extent to which this process can be thought and comprehended. The impasse is not over-reached by desire (the desire for a commodity—"there was to be coffee"), but that socioeconomic limits and the liminal worlds of the imaginary both work to make up social Being, and that it is the very mark of the architectonic process involved that fosters the potential for change. Indeed, the question of architectonics reasserts the trans of transformation in the trans of·transnationalism at the very moment when the latter's "truth" has become dogma, that capital is the natural way that we make (coffee).

Coffee, then, appears to Kant as already made (we must thank philosophy for averring that there can be something more instantaneous than instant), but for every jouissance in the self-presencing of the object, a process of making is at stake, just as in the provocative formulation of the disinterested there nevertheless remains a trace of interest. To borrow from Marx, one does not make coffee alone or under conditions of one's choosing, so let us push the somewhat astringent proclivities of the categorical imperative toward the wild infusions of commodity aesthetics. The emergence of coffee as a massively valuable and traded commodity is conventionally read as an integer of power political and power economic, deeply embedded in the projects of imperialism and colonialism and obstinately in step with the structural inequalities that define global political economy itself. Coffee has also given rise to an industry in lifestyle critique and cultural patterns of consumption never far removed from bourgeois predilections in the development of taste in Kant's sense (or "distinction," to borrow from Pierre Bourdieu[17]). The disjunction between these levels in coffee's meaning should surprise no one: It is integral to the processes of production and reproduction of capitalist social relations that the commodity leads just this kind of double life. Architectonics not only connects these realities and their attendant fateful synergy but looks to explicate such a mutual dependence as a ground for Being, an ontology for the aesthetic and the economic crucial to any project interested in producing a logic of making otherwise, a world of making difference differently. Bakhtin, like Kant, tends to privilege the aesthetic itself in the making he explores (as an end in itself), but the principle of answerability or responsibility he deploys might have a still greater significance: It urges an examination of the will to saturate the world with a logic of making that eschews answerability whenever it challenges the value coding of the commodity form.

Commodity aesthetics concerns the desire to link the production of pleasure to a specific regimen of production in general.[18] Most recreational drugs, for instance, tend, in their very name, to promote a false dichotomy between leisure and work, a binary that has functioned to divide naturally those who labor from those who derive leisure from control over the means of production themselves or its cultural attributes. Yet the histories of the coffeehouse and coffee culture continually assert the imbrication of pleasure with modes of production, whether as an adjunct to productivity or as an effect of the deleterious components of productivity.[19] The largest coffeehouse in England in the eighteenth century was Lloyd's, a place where "coffee rationality" came to catalyze the business of marketing commodities and underwriting the process of their commerce. Coffee not only intensified debate about business strategies but became the industry in which these strategies were most engaged. The same might be true for tea and more recently soft drinks where caffeine is concerned, but coffee has been the benchmark for making management rationality bind itself to pleasure in production time, and not just the leisure time that needs recreational escape from the drudgery of normative socialization. Commodity aesthetics is, then, whatever else it is, about redefining the prohibitive as a block on the inhibitive in the workplace. This is also, by the bye, a definition for Americanness under the sign of globalization.

Clearly, this is an abstraction about the extraction of surplus value but one that has concrete physiological attributes. When Marx notes that the commodity is a "very strange thing," he is well aware that the thingness of the commodity depends on a metaphysical presence and that this magic (for it must present itself as absent in the finished article) is vital to value and the logic of circulation (in *Capital,* that coffee appears in Marx's calculation of the general form of value is not incidental to my argument). What if the physiological capacities of the commodity instantiated the general logic of production for the socialization of Being? The revolution of capitalism was (is) the revolution of productive desire under the sign of a general equivalence. No sublation of capitalist production can occur that does not attend to the necessity that grounds the freedom at stake. The conundrum of coffee is the doubled kernel of a determinate historical form in human activity.[20] Coffee enacts in a profound way the overlap between the physiological and the pharmacological in the production and reproduction of everyday life. Of course, there can be capitalism without coffee (for no one should underestimate the powers of metonymy, even in the most cursory sense—in commodity history, the British substitution of tea for coffee comes to mind, a function of coffee rust in Ceylon, as does the aforementioned German switch to chicory at one point) but no commodity illustrates so vividly the challenge of thinking desire differently from its distillation in the commodity form.

The antinomy of the commodity imperative *as* coffee suggests, for instance, that Indonesia is not made only for shoes. How does the commodity get related within a specific history of colonial expansion? This detour, like that on Kant, will be used to track the circulation of coffee into late capital's coffee logic, specifically as it is constellated within what "America" can mean. But this trace of "making" is also dependent on the characteristics of coffee itself, which should not be read as separable from its production within the meaning of commodity desire. The commodity character of coffee is so bound up with the reach of modernity it might be a better name for that era precisely because of its fanciful association. (Schivelbusch has gone so far as to say that coffee is "*the* beverage of the modern bourgeois age."[21]) But coffee remains a serious business, as likely to subjugate regional peasantries as it is to inspire "commotion" or wild flights of creativity.

It is not surprising that Indonesia's most prominent author, Pramoedya Ananta Toer, would identify with the achievement of Eduard Douwes Dekker, better known as Multatuli (Latin for "I suffered much," or "I endured much"). Both writers indeed suffered much for the intensity of their convictions and for the fear they struck in regimes of authoritarianism and repression. Multatuli is the author of *Max Havelaar; or, The Coffee Auctions of the Dutch Trading Company* (1859), a searing novel of social critique that satirically reveals the sordid history of Dutch machinations in Indonesia from the seventeenth century on.[22] While Pramoedya's claim that Multatuli's novel "killed colonialism" is hyperbolic, he nevertheless draws attention to the interventionist potential of the literary where colonialism and commodification are at stake.[23] Pramoedya's own contribution to this form of intervention, the Buru quartet, is itself an important articulation of decolonization in the face of neocolonial desire, which sits obliquely in the interstices of authoritarian statehood in the worlds that Bretton Woods has made.[24] But there is something else at issue here, and this is a little harder to grasp in the making and remaking of economic and social injustice. Commodity desire requires both an episteme, a functional knowledge of rational attachment, *and* that Kantian aesthetic of excessive identification, an overreaching of the symbolic by the affective embrace of the imaginary. This is not some Lacanian chicanery, nor is it an assertion that Pramoedya is simply wrong to believe in the power of literary displacement. What cultural studies gestures toward but cannot actively embody is a critical framework that would simultaneously disable regimes of knowledge that reproduce the subject for subjection *and* facilitate a vibrant and conflictual imaginary that sees desire itself as the maker and *mise en abŷme* of commodity aesthetics. The study of material culture, which is growing by leaps and bounds in the United States, too often grants the material object a logical consistency (logical enough to secure the logos of she or he who is performing the study), as if the object itself is only a distillation of the desire that made it (and is thus always already a Freudian projection). But the mystery of the commodity is that it harnesses desire while suspending the capacity of thought to trace the architectonic of its possibility from one moment to the next. In this sense (and sense, as Kant reminds us, is crucial), Pramoedya is absolutely right to invoke the centrality of Multatuli's novel in the disarticulation of a colonial machine based on commodity cultivation, for it dares to say that the sophistication of the coffeehouse rests on the barbarism and brutality of expansionism and remains a measure of injustice in the *present* (as D. H. Lawrence implies in the introduction to the English edition, *Max Havelaar* cannot be out of date until the logic against which it grates has been destroyed[25]). Yet although we must continue to challenge the universality of the commodity relation, the difficulty of its attenuation lies in the faculty of desire and disavowal it encapsulates (something that I have already connected to athletic shoe production), which is no less vital than the air we breathe.

The trace of Havelaar's intervention remains relevant to coffee history, including coffee in the American imaginary (Java Joe) and indeed on the limits of that imaginary in the worlds we make. Even the appearance of Multatuli's book underlines that desire is too important to be left to the avatars of social hierarchization and, concomitantly, that the literary is no simple adjunct to the philosophical imaginary. This makes coffee both wonderfully symptomatic and hopelessly paradigmatic. It evokes the complex vistas of affect in human socialization just as it mind-numbingly betrays the synergy of civilization and exploitation of the last few centuries in particular.

Certainly the mystery that Marx invokes and that Kant aestheticizes does not perturb Max Havelaar to any great degree. Just as Kant posits a coffee imperative without implicating the economic that is its ground, Multatuli's novel addresses the structural inequities of colonial coffee production without figuring the commodity itself in the making of machines of misery. This, I would argue, is why *Max Havelaar* demonstrably did not "kill colonialism." It is bound by an ideological contradiction for which it has no solution, one that constitutes its political unconscious. E. M. Beekman has suggested a much simpler explanation, that Multatuli's most famous work is compromised by the author's immensely problematic romantic reverie—one that rails on behalf of the oppressed yet overflows with an egotistical embrace that cancels out its appreciable political identification.[26] If *Max Havelaar* is anticolonial, it yet betrays a desire for power and authority rarely out of step with colonial dominion, in the same way that Dekker's antibourgeois predilections often produce the image of a rebel tastefully in keeping with bourgeois nonconformism. Yet the more important problem is the absent/presence of the business of coffee as commodity from a narrative that otherwise embraces it. Here the literary seems to stage the elision at the heart of Kant's imperative.

Multatuli believes himself to be writing a satire, while his narrator, Batavus Droogstoppel (as in "dry stubble"—there is a Dickensian ring to Multatuli's characters), a coffee broker, believes himself to be writing about Max Havelaar and coffee auctions. Even in a form that so obviously favors the author, we might take D. H. Lawrence's own admonition that we never trust the artist but trust the tale on these matters. Droogstoppel wants to write a tract on the business of coffee auctions, a project spurred by the fact that a person nicknamed "Scarfman" (Droogstoppel decides to protect his reputation by supplying him with a pseudonym whereas Dekker uses one to enhance his) has given him a crazy quilt of a manuscript that, in return for an earlier favor he had done the coffee trader, he wants published to alleviate his dire economic circumstances. Ever cognizant of the alibi in his own Being, Droogstoppel gets a surrogate, Ludwig Stern, to write his book and includes elements of Scarfman's manuscript that illuminate the whole business of coffee trading and what "most threatens it." The satirical element is wonderfully conceived, since it appears that Droogstoppel's expertise in coffee grading has not prepared him to cup the novelistic and poetic aspirations of Scarfman's text. He personifies the business through Max Havelaar, during the latter's tenure as assistant resident in the division of Lebak in Dutch-controlled Java in the 1850s. This, of course, parallels Multatuli's own duties at that time, and so the reader is snared between Droogstoppel's awkward and insistent professional rectitude (punctuated by the repetition of a bizarre mantra "I am a coffee broker, and I live at No. 37 Lauriergracht, Amsterdam") and the problem of author and hero in aesthetic activity. Now we may seem a long way from life-style American coffee consumption in all this, just as nineteenth-century Dutch colonial expropriation appears distant to the practices of the coffee cartel today, but the elision of the commodity in Multatuli's narrative is as good an example of the commodity imperative as an aesthetic dilemma in the architectonic, one that renders otherwise insubstantial the violence of value extraction in the commodity form. Since such an approach requires time/space coordinates, it is not unrelated to the chronotope discussed earlier in relation to Indonesia. The difference lies chiefly in its meaning for production aesthetics, which is an extension and qualification of the way the chronotope analyzes the ruse of consumption. This is the subtext of Pramoedya's claim that "the world was colonized by

Europe because of Indonesia's Spice Islands,"[27] for, by tracing the variously in-
tertwined trajectories of cloves and colonization, Pramoedya imaginatively grasps
the satire that Multatuli attempts. Such a work has its own specific context, but
there are lessons for understanding coffee today. These can be ascribed not simply to the story of coffee, which is an oft-narrated tale of interest in its own right,
but through an internal polemic that links the imaginary to affect and consummation to the consumer. Most importantly, an architectonic requires work, and
this is the aromatic allegory that coffee evokes without naming.

On a basic level, the mystery of coffee's absence in *Max Havelaar* is a function
of capital's suppression of the relations that constitute its means to narrate.
Multatuli's text insistently confirms the very contradiction that girds the colonial project and why the form of the novel is marked by satire's compulsive syn-
eciosis. As much as Droogstoppel desires an explanation of business practices that
undermine the broader aims of coffee production (the massive abuse and disavowal of coffee plantation workers in Java in the nineteenth century), Havelaar's tale
betrays the principles of commodity trading themselves as the framework for an
architectonic that is devoutly exploitative. Yet, if this would appear to be in step
with the reformist predilections of Multatuli to end the Dutch government's
pursuit of *cultuurstelsel* in Indonesia (or forced cultivation of cash crops in which
the bulk of the proceeds accrued to Holland), the representation of Havelaar
works against the independence of the Javanese by suggesting that real social
change will occur through the beneficent absolutism of the Dutch, or not at all.
Max Havelaar plays out these contradictions in its very form as a novel despite
the fact that the satire seems to fit firmly on Droogstoppel's head. ("It is decidedly not flattering for Western civilization that the ambition to create a great work
has seldom persisted long enough to see that work completed" [64].) The fragmentary nature of the novel is only partly the truth of Droogstoppel's belief, just
as its status as tract is undermined by its own logic of creativity, of making.

Ultimately, Multatuli becomes frustrated with the demands of his own conceit and the fact of commodity suppression that precipitates his intervention in
the first place. The author interjects, "Enough, my good Stern! I, Multatuli, take
up the pen. You are not required to write Havelaar's life story. I called you into
being. . . . Halt, wretched spawn of sordid moneygrubbing and blasphemous cant!
I created you . . . you grew into a monster under my pen. . . . I loathe my own
handiwork: choke in coffee and disappear!" (317). Multatuli then closes the book
in a kind of authorial ecstasy by demanding to be read in the name of the millions of Javanese who are being exploited by Dutch colonial business practices.
(For Freud this would be the return of the repressed, for Kant the reemergence
of the categorical imperative, but here it is a commodity compulsion that links

both.) Two aspects of Multatuli's narration stand out; that his literary demand asserts a moral superiority over commodity desire, and that despite his fervent opposition to the injustices of Dutch colonial rule, commodity desire has provided the Dutch with a raison d'etre to orchestrate the class relations between the *prijaji* (the gentry) and the *abangan* (peasants) with which the power of Multatuli's pen confusingly colludes. For the Batak incident, which is Multatuli's more than Havelaar's, is decidedly a *colonial* crisis over the forms of trade, one that, ironically, the coffee broker Droogstoppel knows to be a struggle of the Dutch among other European colonial powers and will only later become a countercolonial national longing within a region of intense revolutionary praxis. Today, the European colonial regimes have "choked and disappeared," but coffee, most assuredly, has not. (There is even a Max Havelaar brand for the socially conscious consumer.) Indonesia, although still known for its Javanese arabica, has become a huge producer of poorer-quality robusta, the major portion of which is grown in East Timor, over which Indonesia has exerted its own form of forced cultivation, and which may extend beyond East Timor's recent independence. Kant finds in philosophy a means to demonstrate an epistemology that correlates the world of objects and experiences. Multatuli might appreciate the power of imagination required of such judgment, but he favors the literary itself and its symbolic attributes as the medium for articulation. While hardly complementary, both views evolve through, and not in contradistinction to, specific conditions of commodity production. The fact that we still separate culture from cultivation (of commodities) is not just a testament to the persistence of philosophical and literary aesthetics but to the principle of separation itself that commodity logic requires for its reproduction.

Coffee, of course, does not emerge initially in Indonesia, but in Ethiopia as the energy food of the Galla. The myth of origins that all commodities require but need not narrate also links coffee to Islam and the supposed revelation by the Angel Gabriel to Mohammed of the medicinal properties of the coffee berry (interestingly, these are the opposite of the German warnings about impotence). Given the lack of reference to coffee in the Koran, and the coffee controversies among Islamic scholars (the most notable being the "incident" in Mecca in 1511), this myth ranks somewhat lower than the satanic verses. What is clear is that coffee use by Sufis in Ethiopia and Yemen piqued the interest of Arab Muslims eager to sanction some pleasurable beverage that might compensate for the strict prohibitions governing alcohol. This is one constant to the present: Despite periodic attempts to limit coffee consumption, it is easily the most socially acceptable intoxicant available on the planet. And the explosion of its availability is obstinately weaved with commodity culture and colonial dominion from the Ottoman Empire on.

Because of coffee's tropical habitat, it is embroiled in imperial struggle over control of the tropics and the social function of its use in imperial centers. (The vagaries of the North/South dichotomy only begin to touch on this struggle, but even a cursory look would show the importance of coffee-producing nations in that relationship.) That Arabs initially preserved the secrets of coffee's cultivation had the twin advantages of monopolizing the market and feeding the culture of the coffeehouse in Istanbul and beyond. By the time Droogstoppel is considering these connections, the logic has been long established, but the question of control has been opened by European trade and the rapacious transnational transplanting of the coffee tree wherever invasion and the ecosystem allowed. (The Dutch were the first to use colonial lands for coffee production—interestingly, Pendergast maps this narrative as "coffee migration.")[28] Indeed, by the nineteenth century coffee had become a mark of political and economic prowess. Whoever harnesses the power in the coffee trade puts their stamp not just on a lifestyle but on a mode of value extraction in the world system.

Joe's philosophical and literary disposition then, is deeply embedded in a commodity imperative. So far, we have said little about this imperative as it comes to mean within coffee production for capitalism, although I have been trying to suggest that the process at issue is synonymous with what coffee represents at that level (coffee instantiates the process of economimesis). The logic of making is extrapolated and recoded according to the needs of, say, philosophy, or culture, or indeed history but, to recall Adorno's warning about the incomprehensible, such objectification necessarily masks what does not conform to the hermeneutical rule of thumb. Ostensibly, the coffee industry is a transparent case of "peripheral" commodity production ending up in "advanced" industrial and postindustrial states. Coffee plantations take up about 27 million acres on the planet (mostly in the tropics), yielding approximately 14 billion pounds of coffee, of which the United States consumes almost 3 billion. The emergence of the coffee plantation precisely follows the trajectories of slavery and colonialism among the European powers because the "rational, forward-looking body" needed cheap or "free" labor to sustain it. Coffee workers, like any other exploited class, have strongly resisted repressive labor practices and historically they have mounted opposition both locally and nationally to the coffee elites. This activism has sometimes turned bloody—the most famous incident being the insurrection of early 1932 in El Salvador, in which coffee workers joined with Salvadoran Communist party forces to fight state-sponsored barbarism. The response was barbarism of almost unparalleled ferocity, and up to twenty-five thousand peasants, mostly Indians, were savagely massacred. There was to be coffee. Today, some twenty million laborers work on coffee plantations, despite rapid "technification" of the industry and the shaving of production costs. Although some of these workers receive "adequate" pay (for subsistence or more), many labor in conditions of abject poverty. Slavery may be gone, but the incidences of forced labor and "payment in kind" in the coffee industry are of such a scale as to make it one of the world's most exploitative businesses. More than half of world production is still done through small-scale farming involving families and local communities. Unfortunately, these growers are subject to the whims of exporters who have a lock on distribution and "special" relationships with agribusiness and large-scale "coffee dynasties." The result is often that small farmers are paid below market prices for their beans and must rely on credit from the same people and organizations that restrict market access. The three largest producers of coffee are Brazil, Colombia, and Indonesia, countries with not exactly long traditions of democratic negotiation between farmworkers, landowners, and the state. But any "transparent" narrative of repressive and reprehensible labor practices would also have to address the geopolitical interpellation of coffee-producing nations, because transnationalism is not beyond a little "enforcement" of its own.

To understand something of the power at stake, consider for a moment that during three periods in the twentieth century alone, Brazil has dumped billions of pounds of coffee into the sea or burned them to prevent a glut in the international coffee market.[29] The problem of coffee for capitalism is a very basic cycle of overproduction, long periods of depressed prices, followed by rapid price increases precipitated by frosts in Brazil, and subsequent overproduction. Since you cannot store coffee beans indefinitely, it is difficult to stockpile against the possibility of crop failure. Increased prices encourage the planting of more coffee trees, but they take at least one year to bear fruit, by which time prices may well have stabilized and the resulting overproduction forces prices down. Producers can attempt to manipulate supply (just as coffee brokers like Droogstoppel can overprice a temporary shortfall in imports), but the big buyers and roasters will exert their own forms of influence in response. Following a frost in Brazil in the mid-1970s and the largest increases in coffee prices in industry history, the United States held congressional meetings to discuss the price structure of the world coffee market. Questions were raised about who determines coffee prices in response to consumer outcry in the United States about double-digit increases in the cost of Joe. In general, the investigations were inconclusive (since both producers and traders determine price levels), but behind the scenes the *political* economy of the industry asserted itself. The International Coffee Agreement (ICA) instituted in 1962 to assign production quotas and maintain power relations in favor of the advanced industrial nations began to strain under the gyrations of the coffee cycle. As coffee analysts have long held, the original agreement recognized two basic factors: that the United States was by far the largest consumer of coffee, and that the geopolitical concerns of the cold war must not allow coffee production to be transformed by the possibility of communism in any producing countries. The ICO (International Coffee Organization) was set up to administer the ICA, and for a while the tradeoff between adequate supply levels and "development" packages worked quite well, at least for the coffee cartels, the major U.S. roasters, and, indeed, the American government. What the coffee crisis of the mid-1970s underlined, however, was a systemic change in the industry. New players, like Costa Rica, were trading outside ICO membership, and an awful lot of good quality arabica was ending up in the Eastern Bloc at comparatively discounted prices. At the same time, overall U.S. consumption of coffee was in a downward spiral from its highs in 1962 as the soft drink industry gripped American consciousness. True, large soda conglomerates like Coca-Cola were also involved in the coffee industry (because of the healthy returns on "instant coffee" and the desire to source directly caffeine), but in general what was regulating the industry was out of sync with the trade flows of the world system. The only way American roasters and distributors could get into globalization and the rapid increase in coffee imports in Asia and Europe was to cut loose from the ICA, a process dutifully delivered by Reaganism in 1989. The resulting drop in wholesale coffee prices devastated the economies of Brazil and Colombia, but "free trade" was highly prized by TNCs like Procter and Gamble, particularly since its margins on coffee could be hidden among a vast array of product lines. Indeed, immediately following the demise of the ICA and the collapse of wholesale coffee prices, retail coffee prices generally held their ground, yet no governmental organization could prove that the consumer was being gouged because within conglomerates the pricing of coffee is basically a "trade secret." This, however, is not the only aspect of the incomprehensible in our coffee architectonic.[30]

Coffee trade is usually represented as a commodity chain divided by the relations between coffee-producing and coffee-consuming nations. As work like John Talbot's shows, income distribution along these chains bears close scrutiny.[31] His research reveals, for instance, that while the ICA was in effect, TNCs like Nestlé and General Foods (a subsidiary of Philip Morris) were bound by strategic rents (a basic price-regulating strategy) that protected producers and distributors from spikes in overproduction and underconsumption in the coffee cycle. Econometric analysis shows that quotas maintained average prices above equilibrium levels, or the "normal" vagaries of supply and demand. At their zenith, Brazilian producers in the 1970s could claim up to 40 percent of total coffee income with the quota system in full force, yet when quotas were suspended in the spring of 1986, for instance, 10 percent of total income shifted back to the consumer conglomerates of the First World. It was that lesson that hastened the demise of the ICA and, when the quotas ended, another 10 percent of total coffee income shifted to consumer industries. A newer cartel, the ACPC (Association of Coffee Producing Countries) formed in 1993 to orchestrate strategic restrictions of coffee supplies into the world market. The following year, ACPC activity, exacerbated by yet another Brazilian frost, enabled major producing companies to regain about 10 percent of total coffee revenues from the North. This victory may be Pyrrhic, however, because five TNCs and a handful of green coffee importers now dominate retail sales in almost all the major consuming markets. Whatever the national cartels, monopolistic rents are actually being achieved in transnational trade. The importance of this development is hard to exaggerate. Since World War II coffee has been a major primary export commodity of the so-called Third World, with approximately 90 percent of that production being consumed in the core, or so-called First World. While not all surpluses necessarily accrue to the TNC's country of origin, for these incomes are redistributed with transnational investment strategies, it is hard not to see the coffee industry as a commodity chain that favors the economic infrastructure of the First World. On the whole, "value migration" flows from South to North.

Commodity chain analysis of this kind certainly pinpoints income distribution variations in production and consumption. But, just as Kant could remain blissfully unaware of the rational kernel in his coffee bean, so development studies suppress the mystical shell in commodity production and consumption. Coffee production certainly reveals a chain that binds the Third World to the First, but it does not necessarily attend to the logic of making we have invoked, particularly in the space that marks the imbrication of desire and necessity in the geopolitical unconscious of transnational trade. The simplicity of the commodity chain not only belies the nodal pricing variations that Talbot discovers but also the complexity of making in even a primary commodity of the modern era. I want to maintain the value of Talbot's approach about where the dollar goes on a pound of coffee alongside something of the organic and physical peculiarities of coffee itself, which are also part of its value. Rather than the schematic diagram of economic critique, I would suggest a model that follows something of the microscopy of *Coffea arabica* itself.

How does this look? Most coffee fruit consists of two parts, each one containing a bean (actually a pit) that, flattened on one side, fits against another. The fleshy fruit that holds the parts together is called the pericarp, while the endocarp within is a tissue-like parchment that more rigidly binds the beans in place. Each bean is covered with a silver skin, or spermoderm, some of which remains with the coffee bean even after processing (particularly in the cleft that riddles its flat side). The bean itself is a seed that contains both soft and hard endosperm that provide food for the embryo within. The latter is microscopic but features two tiny leaves (cotyledons) and even a root. Like most angiosperms, the coffee shrub has both an angeion, a box or "womb," and a sperm, or seed. A coffee commodity architectonic is not a reflection of nature, but struggles through catechresis to name that which is denied in nature. In this case, the nature of coffee, its botany, offers some lessons for the commodity chain that, metonymically, stands in for the process of making that governs it. The standard commodity chain splits coffee between growers and consumers, between periphery and core, between exporters and importers, between Third World and First. Such a model skips over any number of factors that enable coffee to be made: the collusion between regional producer cartels and green bean importers, coffee cultural practices *within* the producing nations, more rhizomatic maps of desire, the symbiosis of modes of production across national borders and North/South dichotomies, geopolitical alliances that pit core against core or periphery against periphery (I am thinking here of the function of capitalist competition and postcolonial neocolonialism like Indonesia's recently ended occupation of East Timor), and, of course, the reality of trading in coffee futures where coffee production and consumption may themselves be negligible (hedging on coffee now means that 500 percent more coffee is traded on paper than is actually grown). The coffee berry rather than the coffee chain offers a better sense of the process to which it is subject. Obviously, the aim is not simply to find an objective correlative in nature for a peculiarly human activity, but to stretch the cognitive where commodities are concerned.

The pericarp and endocarp of the coffee fruit trace the logic of economy and culture that holds what is produced and consumed, the beans, in their commodity form. These aspects are inside and outside what coffee represents in the same way that there could be no more flesh without the embryo to reproduce our shrub. Perhaps a traditional infrastructural/superstructural model of capitalist production still obtains, but only if its inversion can also be cognized. At a very basic level, what holds the fruit together also divides it and it is this divisibility that stays with coffee as a commodity: Processing sunders the beans, the one from the other, and yet who is to say that these bereft beans might not percolate together some day? The beans, of course, do not know of their function as commodity, but their form is an indication of their proximity and, rather than existing in diametric opposition or some teleological chain, their dialectical tension is immanent to coffee's effulgence. The wonder of mimesis here suggests that whatever the autonomy of the producer and consumer (each to its own bean), no element that exists for one is beyond or outside the capacity of the other. This is not unique to coffee's botany but points to what Adorno calls an "enigmatical-ness" that he ascribes to the artwork.[32] Here the enigmaticalness is less how the coffee bean comes to be, but how it expresses a potential for commodification and its solution. What is hermetic in the berry is demonstrably enigmatic in the beans. Their divisibility hides their symbiosis and what is common to both is lost through pulping and hulling that marks the annulment of their nature. The econ-omy of coffee as commodity has never thought this enigmaticalness, not for want of aesthetics (the passionately subjective, as we've noted), but because its fulcrum inexorably divides producer from consumer in what allows the commodity to circulate. The symbiosis remains, as does its lesson for value extraction and sur-plus accumulation; that is, what is economic justice for one is economic justice for the other. But this, most certainly, is "incomprehensible."

Coffee beans in the market easily conceal their botany and, as commodity, the form of their social value. They are merely beans, ripe with "equivalence," green or roasted, in bags, in sacks, in jars in the freezer; or ground in cans or bags bear-ing the paradox of "shelf life"; or processed beyond recognition into powders that announce their presentism in the lifelessness of being "instant." What is missing in the Kantian imaginary and the literary (my example from Multatuli) is effort-lessly confirmed by coffee as commodity: Surely it was conjured by desire and not by nature's subjection to socialization in human practice? I am not suggest-ing that we merely think of the ecosystem of the bean to break the coffee cycle and the chains that bind, primarily, 20 million pickers in or close to poverty. It is a marvel of the liberal imagination that it believes the transnational to be a problem of tinkering here and there with certification (of organic farm produc-tion, "Please no pesticides") or a "livable" wage that eases the conscience and arrogance of its own divine surpluses. Reformism does not alter the initial de-mand that there was to be coffee; it simply confirms the persistence of inequity by any means necessary. But why is this compulsion, well, so compelling?

In part, it is the pharmacology of coffee linked to that bourgeois desire for the "forward-looking body." Certainly, the smell and taste of various coffees stimu-late the powers of discernment, but nothing quite stimulates as much as the caf-feine in coffee. Caffeine is easily the most consumed psychoactive drug in the world. Eighty percent of Americans ingest caffeine in some form daily, and the primary delivery mode is coffee. (True, Americans drink more soda, but not all that soda is caffeinated. Regular cola contains about half the caffeine of coffee.) Caffeine belongs to a family of alkaloids that include strychnine, nicotine, mor-phine, mescaline, and emetine. (The last is what Socrates took and is known bet-ter as hemlock.) Of these, caffeine and nicotine are the only ones that are not con-trolled substances (although there are usually age limits on the consumption of the latter). Once in the body, caffeine is mercilessly attacked by enzymes. (The body treats caffeine as poison, which is another lesson about the Pharmakon of desire.) Smokers, interestingly, need twice the caffeine hit because compounds in tobacco stimulate enzyme production, so their bodies use up caffeine more quickly.

The key to caffeine in the body is adenosine, which regulates the firing of neurons in the brain, particularly in two areas in the brain stem. This is vital to our understanding of commodity thinking in a neurological framework (or what Derrida would call a general economy: adenosine is *différance* in the brain). The more neurons fire, the more adenosine is released, which dampens activity and eventually leads to sleep. The caffeine molecule is very similar to that of adenosine, but binds to adenosine receptors in a different way. It manages to block adenosine without mimicking its calming effects, so while adenosine puts on the brakes, caffeine sits behind the brakes like a block of wood. Caffeine not only speeds you up but won't let you slow down. Yet there is also a natural brake in caffeine: Beyond one to four cups of coffee it generally ceases to have any additional stimulant effect, perhaps because large doses attack and bind to other molecules that actually depress neural activity. Unlike most alkaloids, it is almost impossible to overdose on caffeine. A fatal dose through coffee consumption would require 40 cups drunk in quick succession, and the body has a simple cure for that—you vomit uncontrollably (although injecting caffeine in high doses might cause catastrophic liver failure). The importance of caffeine to Joe as an architectonic is its function for speed. Studies show that caffeine improves mental ability in tasks requiring speed, but not work requiring power. Now before we jump to the idea that caffeine has its own division of labor built in just as the coffee fruit has its own divisibility, I should add that power here means higher reasoning (complex arithmetic or reading comprehension), not physical exertion. Yet, as the ubiquity of the coffeemaker would attest, the availability of caffeine in the workplace speeds up passive or automatic brain functions. Thus, caffeine oils basic productivity, particularly in the morning when brains hooked on caffeine ingestion respond to it most favorably. (In the daily cycle, the same amount of caffeine ingestion in the evening produces the opposite effect, because neurons have already slowed beyond recall. Similarly, night-shift workers can stay awake on caffeine, but it does not help their productivity in basic brain functions.) Caffeine is great for work, but not so significant for "sexual play." It has been shown to speed up the swimming ability of spermatozoa, but the dose required is so large that a real possibility of chromosomal damage exists. Coffee for work, sure. Sex, doubtful. It remains however, the single most used doping agent in sports.[33]

The speed-up capacity of caffeine obviously works well within current work regimens. Workers in late capitalism work longer hours to achieve pay levels of twenty-five years ago. Maintaining this output in a work environment marked by anxiety (the concept of disposable labor intrinsic to flexi-local production) produces tension, both mental and physical (particularly in the neck and head muscles). The result is often headaches. Enter caffeine. Caffeine helps blood vessels to contract, thus limiting cerebral blood flow and keeping headaches at bay. The problem is that once caffeine wears off, the body overcompensates and the infamous caffeine-withdrawal headache ensues. Take a pain killer? Good idea. Almost all of them contain caffeine (equivalent to about a cup of Joe), so the miracle of the analgesic is often just a hair-of-the-dog fix. Caffeine does, however, enhance the effects of many prescription and more than two thousand nonprescription drugs by as much as 40 percent even when the ailment is not caffeine withdrawal.

Socially, caffeine is not viewed as an intoxicant. Rather, it is often read to normalize human activity (that "forward-looking body"). Whereas most recreational drugs are hazardous to one's health, caffeine ingestion is a relatively harmless facet of the everyday. Again, this is where the social function of Joe becomes complex. I have suggested that coffee in the workplace can help productivity levels if one tracks the importance of adenosine in neural firing. Such consumption patterns can be read to complement an economic necessity for increased productivity from labor. Yet the problem is that caffeine is a psychoactive drug, and as with all psychoactive drugs, the brain responds by calculating a normalizing level based on drug ingestion. That is to say that within seven to ten days of a prescribed caffeine intake, the brain develops a tolerance for that level. The tolerance means that users experience no real kick from the dose that used to provide it. Since most caffeine users do not inexorably increase their doses over time, studies show that they exhibit the classic symptoms of drug tolerance. The reason most everyday coffee drinkers experience a mild euphoria from their first cup of Joe each day is because they are already in the initial stages of withdrawal (low-level depression and grogginess) and the joy is in reversing that unpleasant fug. A couple of cups later the brain may well have reestablished the normalizing line and the user has reached her or his plateau. (It takes about six hours for the enzymes in the liver to break down caffeine.) It is possible that there are other parts of the brain that resist the tendencies of tolerance and allow the user to get an extra buzz, but in general most caffeine intake is keeping people in place. The coffee industry attempts to manipulate this plateau (and not simply "taste") by relying upon quotidian caffeine consumption. (The same is true for chocolate makers although the caffeine levels are considerably smaller.) But caffeine is very big business, and over the years coffee retailers have been losing their share of overall caffeine consumption to soda in the American market. How does one maintain or increase profit levels in the United States if overall coffee consumption is in decline?

Call me Starbucks. The basic idea behind Starbucks is very simple: Make lifestyle coffee consumption more upscale and you can offset the deleterious effects of all that big-gulp soda guzzling. Embrace modern America's love of (or dependence on) caffeine but niche-market the delivery medium. Tenacious marketing can take wholesale Columbian Supremo beans at less than two bucks a pound and get nine bucks for it at retail. Specialty coffee marketers can prattle all day about taste testing and batch roasting, but the techniques employed are basically the same for any coffee retailer. Yet the song of the siren has an incredible allure, which is the point of invoking the production of desire in Joe as architectonic. I would argue, for instance, that the specialty coffee company is a prime model of contemporary American capitalism—that which takes a consumption or lifestyle aesthetic and welds it to specific modes of surplus value extraction. Interestingly, the chairman and CEO of Starbucks, Howard Schultz, has suggested that the company most like Starbucks in structure and marketing techniques is Nike. This rich perception has a complex aftertaste.[34]

Starbucks would not seem to be an obvious miscreant in the structure of late capital. Indeed, Schultz's Brooklyn working-class background and charitable inclinations have tended to soften the labor/capital nexus in the business of coffee. (The story of Starbucks is a fairly precise enactment of the liberal reflex in commodity consumption.) But this belies the class character of niche marketing and the necessities of expansion. Like Nike, Starbucks succeeds through vertical integration (to a point), nonunion production (although in Canada Starbucks lost a battle for a nonunion shop), low wages, and fierce competition. Like Nike, Starbucks now franchises and licenses to broaden brand recognition and market base, but this inexorably strains quality control (as those who have had Starbucks coffee in an airport or on United Airlines will attest). Most importantly, like Nike, Starbucks has concentrated its efforts on branding, since you cannot get someone to part with four dollars for something that takes just a few cents to produce without an association beyond simply money. Interestingly, the marketing guru was the same for both companies—Scott Bedbury was the man behind "Bo Knows" at Nike. He also brought flexi-local consumption strategies to Starbucks in a big way. Tailor the product to local consumer "tastes" while maintaining a flat or branded store feel. Result: Consumers will shell out extra money because the coffee costs more, not because it actually costs more to produce (just as Nike's top-of-the-line Air Max costs about the same to produce as its entry-level models). One other connection between Starbucks and Nike is Indonesia. (Indeed, it was a Dutch tea and coffee trader, the offspring of the colonial days, Alfred

Peet, who introduced the United States to the class-coding of arabica over robusta—the latter had been, until the 1950s, the staple of American coffee consumption. Schultz showers Peet with glowing praise in *Pour Your Heart into It*.)
Starbucks is big: By the end of 1997 it had more than thirteen hundred stores
(by 2001 close to 3,500) and coffee sales well over $1 billion. It has more than
25,000 employees (who are euphemistically called "partners" because of stock
options—these, by the way, are unavailable to pickers). Over a six-year period
Starbucks revenue increased at 50 percent per annum, as did profits. Starbucks
also knows how to play partnerships: Given soda's need for caffeine, its deal with
Pepsi-Cola to produce Frappucino was a godsend (a caffeine-bottling swap). It
also has an agreement with Anheuser-Busch to put coffee extract in Redhook
stout. To date, Starbucks shares remain a darling of NASDAQ.[35]

An architectonic is about form, about how we put things together, how we
make. Joe here is a coffee architectonic, about how coffee is built into culture and
economics. Joe has a philosophical and aesthetic disposition that is well symbolized by Starbucks' emblem, the siren. Part woman, part bird, the siren is a typically masculinist symbol overinvested with phantasms of desire and fear. The siren is a lure, and the bean puts the Pharmakon back in pharmacology: The drug
you need is always already the sign of your socialization. The lure is both poison
and cure but hierarchies of socialization mean different identity formation depend-
ing on where you are positioned and position yourself through coffee. As I have
indicated, the coffee of enlightenment philosophy is also the coffee of colonization. But if we think about this in terms of coffee workers on the plantation, the
siren is displaced by the song of the coffee picker, in this case, Rigoberta Menchú.

> Mothers are very tired and just can't do [the picking]. This is where you see the sit-
> uation of women in Guatemala very clearly. Most of the women who work picking
> cotton and coffee, or sometimes cane, have nine or ten children with them. Of these,
> three or four will be more or less healthy, and can survive, but most of them have
> bellies swollen from malnutrition and the mother knows that four or five of her
> children could die. We'd been on the finca (plantation) for fifteen days when one of
> my brothers died from malnutrition. My mother had to miss some days' work to
> bury him. Two of my brothers died in the finca. The first, he was the eldest, was
> called Felipe. I never knew him. He died when my mother started working. They'd
> sprayed the coffee with pesticide by plane while we were working, as they usually
> did, and my brother couldn't stand the fumes and died of poisoning.[36]

Despite the fact that Menchu's testimonial has been challenged for its dubious veracity, certain aspects of Guatemala's truth for commerce still obtain. Forty percent of Guatemala's labor force is in coffee production, and 70 percent of
the children in these communities are malnourished. (Many of them, of course,

are also in the labor force itself.) In 1994 Starbucks was confronted by a U.S.-based Guatemalan labor organization about the conditions of coffee workers. Schultz was defensive and opined that the group had falsely suggested that Guatemalan coffee workers were on Starbucks' payroll. US/GLEP never claimed that connection, but this is another characteristic of Joe today; that is, even with a much-trumpeted code of conduct for companies like Nike and Levi's, in general corporate culture conveniently separates itself from the labor practices that often mark capital accumulation, particularly in companies that grow through crass exploitation of the third or "developing" world invisible to the consumer whose consumption is based on status. Starbucks' code for dealing with the basic problem of *finca* practices is called a "framework," which boldly declares that ultimately it has no control over plantation practices and could not possibly inspect the hundreds of plantations that constitute the fibrillar network of its production base. Let us call this "acidity"—the palate-cleaning quality of high-grade coffee that is often confused with bitterness. The point is to draw attention to the logical constraints and compulsions within capitalist culture. Boycotting Starbucks is futile, a liberal petty-bourgeois compensation for a fix in lifestyle consumption. And besides, what does the drug addict do when the dealer is busted?

No. Joe here describes a specific fix in a multibillion-dollar American industry. How can one possibly imagine an alternative to a commodity culture when that imagination itself is already predicated on the very principles of desire and disavowal from *finca* to filter? The short answer is that you cannot, at least not in terms of dislodging the synergy between coffee elites and those who fight for retail control. Resistance is never futile, as the long history of coffee farmer activism attests. Accepting that even solidarity is a mark of lifestyle liberalism, the prospect of a union in the coffee retail business that embraced and actively encouraged unionism among the pickers would present a major challenge to the feel-good platitudes of the coffee-ati, while on the plantations themselves workers continue to provide their own moments of freedom from necessity. The difficulties of transnational solidarity are immense, but in part depend upon a capacity to think the simultaneity of the commodity in its divergent and diverse forms of making. The separation of economic rationality from aesthetic affect colludes in the production and reproduction of mystification in the commodity form. This is where the commodity can be comprehended, as long as this does not wish away what remains incomprehensible as a cognitive limit on understanding. That is one reason why the literary is not irrelevant to commodity critique.

Starbucks was formed in 1971 by two teachers and a writer (two friends from San Francisco State University and a next-door neighbor after they moved to Seattle). Gerald Baldwin, the English teacher, came up with the name of the first mate on the Melville's *Pequod* after the *Pequod* itself was rejected as a moniker. Schultz notes that the name "evoked the romance of the high seas and the seafaring tradition of the early coffee traders." *Moby-Dick* is the quintessence of Americana, a novel of whaling, the first broad industry of America. Like all books with claims on the Great American Novel, *Moby-Dick* is revered for its heavy symbolism and creeping universalism. It is much more complicated than even coffee tasting. Starbuck himself is a stolid fixture of American grit, prudent with perseverance and a wife and child to confirm his family foundation (although like others on the good ship *Pequod,* he is not outside the more developed aura of homoeroticism in the tale). On the second day of chasing Moby Dick, Starbuck implores Ahab to give up before they all perish. Ahab's reply is typical of his obsession: "in the matter of the whale, be the front of thy face to me as the palm of this hand—a lipless unfeatured blank." Without recounting the huge commentary on the whiteness of the whale and the prescience of blankness to what makes America, let us say that the lipless unfeatured blank that is the face of Starbucks yet has a logic carved into its very possibility. Joe is the measure of its capacity, Joe the condition of its featureless omnipresence, and Joe a means to address its otherwise pallid opacity. Joe, according to this interpretation, is a means to trace in the everyday what remains unseen, the sireneal charm of contemporary consumption. In the interstices of caffeine, compression, and coffee capitalism you do not find the bean of America (or any other country), but the blend that binds it in the blindness and the blankness of its "I." Joe is part of the narrative that makes up America from moment to moment, cup to cup. The logic of the quotidian itself allows oppression to proceed. Like caffeine, it is connected to the way we think.

Given the literary associations of the coffeehouse, it is no coincidence that America's premiere specialty coffee retailer is named after a character in an epic of American consciousness, but that conjunction is not the final truth of Joe as an architectonic, just as Kant's coffee fetish does not undo the free association of the sublime. Nevertheless, it may be an important catalyst in rethinking the scope of how we make, and obviously not just coffee. Everybody loves to hate Starbucks as a kind of coffee leaf rust on the collective consciousness of America and Americanization (the latter a register of its transnational scope not just in terms of tropical production but also its export potential of a particular form of coffee culture). The reaction is generally well earned, particularly if one views not only the production system involved, but the effect that large-scale specialty coffee vendors have on local café cultures. Given that Starbucks increasingly links this to grating goodwill and corporate charity (its addition of once drug-enhanced Mark McGwire to promote literacy only deepens the double-think) makes the griping symptomatic of broader struggles over what is left to commodity activism. The typical Starbucks outlet drips with the flattening out of all that is provocative in coffeehouse history. Despite the warm, earthy tones, the occasional stuffed armchair, and world music or jazz that aspires to break its function as Muzak, the atmosphere is unabashedly sales-oriented (40 percent of revenues come from noncoffee items) with nary a corner for creative expression or fervent disputation (typically postmodern, the latter exist as a collective nostalgia for a past that has not been). Schultz has claimed that Starbucks (among its various universal charms) fulfills a need in America for community—a "third place" apart from the home or office for relaxation and positive interaction. The case has been made for countless third places—the bar, the mall, the stadium, the park—but rarely with such paternalistic gusto. Inspired by Ray Oldenburg's *Great Good Place,*[37] Schultz has encouraged larger Starbucks stores with more seating and even live music. This is undeniably a good thing but need not be read as the ward of feelgood capital accumulation. Starbucks abounds with this contradictory positioning, daring to call its servers *baristas* (enough to make an Italian blush) and insulting general intelligence by calling a small coffee a "tall." Even so, Schultz's *Weltanschauung* is not outside the bizarre conjoining of the aesthetic and the political (at least in terms of my idiosyncratic elaboration of the coffee fruit) that marks the modern.

I have surmised that while Kant coveted coffee for much of his life, he indulged in the fetish of his desire only toward the end of it. This did not change the course of European philosophy (as opposed to Kant's own Copernican revolution), but the process of the coffee architectonic has its own compulsion, and this commodity aesthetic is not unrelated to the epiphanic proportions of the sublime. It is highly appropriate that Schultz, the man who now sits atop the world's fastest-growing coffee retail outlet, has his own coffee epiphany in Italy in 1983, as he watches a *barista* prepare espresso in a local café: "This is so powerful! . . . This is the link. The connection to the people who loved coffee did not have to take place in their homes, where they ground and brewed whole-bean coffee. What we had to do was unlock the romance and mystery of coffee, firsthand, in coffee bars. The Italians understood the personal relationship that people could have to coffee, its social aspect."[38] The mystery of coffee is indeed its social aspect, but this means much more than providing a third place for people and coffee to interact; it means, more precisely, making a third space where the incomprehensible in the commodity form is not simply a mask for pietistic demands for reform, nor for bourgeois individualism's romance with rationalistic physiology. Similarly, the third space in the cognition of commodities is not about mythologizing the commodity with the handy palette of aesthetics, but trusting to aesthetics that making itself can transform the immanence of the object that denies understanding. Dicum and Luttinger have remarked on the emergence of a "conscious coffee" movement, one which dutifully acknowledges the social aspect of coffee with the ecological and economic components of its architectonic.[39] Certainly, any moves toward greater use of shade-grown coffee varieties or fair-trade production are to be applauded. Coffee as commodity, however, also circulates according to a coffee unconscious, a struggle in valuation between objecthood, profits, socialization, the pleasure of narcotics, and desire. These are not set in parallel, nor do they surreptitiously mirror each other like beans in a berry. Together they constitute something of the formal imaginary of coffee as currently constellated, a "feeling" of coffee as commodity and culture. An architectonic is a fiction that, in its narration, attempts to elaborate that a philosophy of making is at stake. We cannot trust the commodity for this knowledge, nor the platitudes of its retailers (again, the slogan for *Joe,* Starbucks' magazine, is "Life is interesting. Discuss!"), but transnationalism demands that cultural critique looks further than the moment of consumption for the ruse of commodity logic. The riddle of incomprehensibility for Adorno remains, yet it does make the modern more answerable for its failures, an answerability that every cup of Joe necessarily contains. The process of making coffee, its architectonic, is an arena of struggle over the social in making itself, an imaginary that remains with coffee and its transnational states. This is the source of its dissonance in valorization.

Conclusion:
Culture and Globalization

I began this work with an exploration of the prospects of cultural transnationalism, a collocation of theoretical tools with which one may broaden yet complicate our approaches to the myths and material realities of cultural integration on a world scale. The case studies that followed on the literary and the commodity have not been offered as a formal grid for cultural/transnational critique. Indeed, the studies themselves do not line up side by side in any easy or unproblematic way. The question of expertise, for instance, is not resolved by the readings I have provided, and the flattening out of cultural difference and difficulty remains at the forefront of the approaches gathered here. Most obviously, I have attempted to preserve the tension between the materials that form the kernel of each chapter rather than seek some type of hermeneutical continuity in their progression. That should not be taken as a virtue, but as a comment that the umbrella approach of cultural studies cannot escape the contradictions of its cultural interest. In a sense, cultural studies can only live with the impossibility of its transnationalism; it cannot transcend it, but neither can it afford to turn its back on the challenge of globality. John Tomlinson has suggested that "the huge transformative processes of our time that globalization describes cannot be properly understood until they are grasped through the conceptual vocabulary of culture."[1] This would seem a natural reaction of the culturalist, unless we add the caveat that the vocabulary at issue questions the very graspability that is its aim. We can therefore frame the argument somewhat differently. The problem with globalization is not only the nefarious economic system it represents, but also that it lacks a coherent or logical basis for its apprehension. Within the time/space compression of the moment, with all the presentist tendencies of postmodernity, and with all the loud trumpeting that because of technological and economic integration the world is a smaller place, there is relatively little discussion about how globalization can be understood without expounding on some cognitive, imaginative, or sensate means to do so.[2] The ever laconic *Spectator* noted in 1962 that "globalization is, indeed, a staggering concept," and so it has turned out to be. How does one address a concept that does not appear to be one? Of course, culture is the primary means through which we currently understand globalization (we may qualify that to technologies of culture for those who wish to include McLuhan's model of the global village) but it is not its essence, its primum mobile. Indeed, what is staggering about culture in this instance is not its irrefutable difference but its consummate inability to provide a transformative knowledge of the primary motor of globalization. Globalization does not offer up this knowledge with the ease of a Lonely Planet guide, or even with the electronic certitude of the information superhighway, precisely because it is grounded in a cognitive and epistemological impasse: There is no order of thought identical with the process of globalization as currently construed, no language adequate to the universalizing totality it is held to express, no subject that could embody the posthuman manifestations of its reach, no culture that could fully come to terms with the nonrepresentational excess of its Being. What is truly staggering about globalization is that in forty years of pontification about the term (which describes a process at least five centuries old) we are only just beginning to come to terms with the most basic ground of its deadening opacity. Paradoxically, globalization is not an allegory of the process of acquiring newly inclusive vistas of cosmopolitan knowledge (which is the obvious irony in the title of Timothy Brennan's book, *At Home in the World*[3]) but is instead an allegory of ignorance, of asymmetrical ignorance as Dipesh Chakrabarty would say, that stands as an indictment of the crippling and disastrous inequalities of the world system.[4] What makes culture stagger, perhaps, is the prospect of association with something as tawdry and contaminated as the narrative of globalization now on offer.

While there may be good reason to address the philosophical and cultural grounds of globalization, the idea that the work of Mikhail Bakhtin can help in this endeavor may strike one as either precious or absurd. I would like to indicate, however, by way of conclusion, how Bakhtin might further contribute to the provocation that cultural transnationalism must foster. This is not an attempt to summarize all the issues that come spilling out of the previous case studies, nor is Bakhtin being invoked to provide a litmus test for the questions about Nation that I initially raised. Yet I do hope to provide some reasons why Bakhtin may help us to understand further the role of the imaginary in a globalization that is so hugely transformative. Bakhtin is revered for many reasons, his contributions to the theorization of the novel, his elaboration of the festive and the popular, his materialist exegesis of language, his philosophy of the author and authoring, and his novel approach to questions of speech and speech genres. He is not, however, best described as cosmopolitan when considering economic structures or international cultural relations, and there is no point in berating him for this, since they simply did not occupy his otherwise intensely active mind (even in such heady lectures as "Stalin and the English Bourgeoisie"!). But Bakhtin is often discussed in terms of global concepts[5] or his obsessive concern for "the plenitude of differences in the world"[6] which, while it does not make him a social scientist of culture or globalization, does suggest that his conceptual apparatus might usefully be deployed in linking and thinking the difference of both. Why?

Such a prospect should not frighten since, for one, the provocation of Bakhtin's work is usually to be found in his theoretical constructs rather than the readings that he provides to elaborate them. In *Art and Answerability,* for instance, all that intricate philosophizing on author and hero in aesthetic activity cannot possibly be supported by the decidedly thin analysis of Aleksandr Pushkin's poem "Parting" that follows it.[7] Similarly, the rather brilliant chapter 5 of *Problems of Dostoevsky's Poetics* is only ostensibly about Fyodor Dostoevsky and works much better as a grid for the critique of novelistic discourse in general.[8] To extrapolate from this note on Bakhtin's theorizing does not mean, of course, that the use of *world* and *global* in discussions of Bakhtin is the equivalent of the *global* in globalization, although there is a universalizing tendency in both. What I would argue is that Bakhtin often took up the question of the individual's relationship to the world as a philosophical and aesthetic problem of some import and that this "world," as such, is no more abstract than that proposed in the "real" world to which globalization usually refers. To some extent, the test of Bakhtin's "global concepts" is the degree to which they denature and defamiliarize the new orthodoxy of globalization taking hold of transnational debate. But more than this, the actual limits they place on thinking globally opens up a pertinent discussion between globalization as an economic moment and transnational culture as its albeit contradictory and contributory symptom. Far from being irrelevant to this fateful conjuncture, elements of Bakhtin's thinking throw a trenchant light on the artifice of globality as well as the impasse it represents for more worldly exchanges on egalitarian social relations. Wary of the scandal of invoking Bakhtin in this way, I would first like to clarify the basic problems in the rhetoric of globalization as currently construed.

The conventional mantra announced in the term *globalization* is of an economic sea change in capitalism characterized by flexible accumulation, flexi-local production, corporate transnationalism that flouts state affiliation or obeisance, and a post-Fordist integration of production forged through the free flow of capital around the globe.[9] Without doubt there is validity to all these claims; the problem is that the term itself masks the difference in intensities of the qualities portrayed. Simply put, these features do represent a qualitative difference in formations of capital, but they only constitute a fraction of economic activity, not just globally but in terms of capital itself. The rhetoric of globalization exists first under the sign of hyperbole.

Most critics of globalization usually preempt the timing of the conditions of its emergence (for instance, there are dozens of references in Karl Marx's work that already point to the axiomatic nature of capital's transnational proclivities in the nineteenth century) and/or detail the sinister collusion of this economic form with that somewhat more pedestrian edifice, the Nation State. (I will return to Marx below.) In addition, and no less damaging, economic data itself undermines the case for globalization. For example, the ratio of exports to GDP in advanced industrialized nations is not that much greater than it was before World War I when it stood at about 16 percent.[10] Similarly, the balance sheets of most multinationals show that the bulk of their trade is overwhelmingly national or regional, where they (in tandem with the state) can best protect their market interests. The second word in the rhetoric of globalization is *localization* (or, for the neologists, *glocalization*).

Personally, I am taken with such critiques of globalization, particularly since the loudest discussants of the subject often indulge in a kind of capitalist triumphalism from the Right, or cynical defeatism from the Left. Accepting all the criticisms, however, some important qualifications should be made. First, the data fiends need to differentiate the type of company being treated as transnational. The model for contemporary globalization is not the old stalwarts of heavy industrial production like General Motors or Boeing but organizations that primarily use semiskilled or unskilled labor through subcontracts or outsourcing.[11] As recently as 1997, Nike had by some estimates more than 100,000 people, mostly in Asia, making shoes and sports-related clothing with the ubiquitous "swoosh" (the mark of sorrow) upon them. But, as we have noted, the transnationalism here is in the contract between Nike and the small to medium-sized companies that are licensed to make its products, like the Tae Gurang Industrial Company in Korea, Samyang Tonsang, or Sung Hwa Corporation in Indonesia. Yes, there is some foreign direct investment involved, but the bulk of the economic activity is up to local companies who scramble around the labor markets of Southeast Asia subcontracting to meet Nike's twelve- to eighteen-month production cycles. Despite the "swoosh" on the products, most of the workers in Asia never see Nike on their pay slip, much less an American in the factory. The true face of globalization is precisely its facelessness. Sure, the behemoths of capitalism have trouble moving productive capital, but subcontracted sweatshops can move all the time. Using productive capital or plant as a measure of global-ization for steel production, for instance, will obviously show that fixed assets remain relatively fixed (although even then, whole steel plants have moved around the globe, as even the residents of the Rust Belt will attest), but those who can-not see globalization should compare Nike's annual report with what actually happens to capital where its products are made. Nike sells most of its product in the American market, and therefore fits the criticism of glocalization. Yet half a dozen countries are involved in landing that product even though their import/export figures rarely get itemized in the Nike equation on sales of $9.6 billion in 1998 alone. Within the rhetoric *of* globalization the formula *for* globalization is itself at stake.

In chapter 5, I have used Bakhtin's trenchant sense of time/space relations to analyze the Nike phenomenon. Here I want to focus on why the *global* in *globalization* is so difficult to fathom by taking up Bakhtin's thought on the borders of I and Other and on the liminal difference between the subject and the world. Globalization is first and foremost an economic regime whose prob-lems require economic and political solutions. But they also necessitate a vig-ilance about the conditions of apprehension of globality far beyond what defines a transnational corporation, an attention to the question of understanding the globe that itself informs possible solutions to the brave new world (order) that globalization represents. Let us consider, for a moment, the world according to Bakhtin.

In his early years, Bakhtin often reads the question of the human subject's relationship to the world in terms of the aesthetic. This is an immediately alarming prospect for Marxists because the aesthetic has often been a bourgeois provenance deployed precisely to cover the real foundations of the subject's existence. While Kant casts a long shadow over Bakhtin's early philosophical musings, the realm of the transcendent is not quite the substance of Bakhtin's aesthetic, which is context-specific and surprisingly social. How does the author "author," thinks Bakhtin, without imbricating both the internal logic of her or his art with the logic of the world that informs it?

> All of the world's values enter into the aesthetic object, but they do so with a partic-ular aesthetic coefficient, and the author's position as well as the artistic task he has set himself must be understood in the world in conjunction with all these values. What is consummated or formed into an integral whole is not the material (words), but the comprehensively lived and experienced makeup of being. The artistic task organizes the concrete world: the spatial world with its own axiological center—the living body, the temporal world with its own center—the soul, and finally, the world of meaning—all in their concrete interpenetrating unity. (AA 190)

The author is a maker whose art is dependent upon an ability to complete or consummate (the religious cognate is not uncommon in Bakhtin) wholes from disparate worlds. Again, Bakhtin's sense of the world here is not the one considered in the boardrooms of Beaverton, Oregon, where Nike plots marketing, nor is Bakhtin's notion of value the equivalent of surplus value that is vital for capitalism. And yet, there are lessons in Bakhtin's invocation of "interpenetrating unity" in terms of the ruse and reality of globality. What the artist holds to be the world cannot be the world that she or he represents, but neither can the artist abjure that world that gives the "whole" of art its meaning. Bakhtin understands that when one is in art, one is not in life, and yet he attempts to elaborate the terms through which both are answerable or responsible for one another. Neither the world nor art is taken as an intransitive given; they are both for Bakhtin created in the ongoing event of Being. The whole in Bakhtin's argument is not a stable entity yet must be in the event of Being for the subject whose existence depends on it. Several elements are at stake, then, in the relationships of author to creativity (and author to hero, but this need not detain us here), to the world, and to existence. The artist can live in art, but only to the extent that the artist and art are mutually responsible to each other and the world. The cultural workers I have considered make art according to this sense of answerability. This interpenetration also textures what constitutes being in the world for Bakhtin. You cannot step outside this obligation according to Bakhtin: You have no alibi for Being, you cannot claim to be anywhere else than where you are in Being. But isn't this horribly individualist, as if the world hinges upon a monadic consciousness?

Not so, says Bakhtin. Our obligation to existence in art and life (as people, as artists, or as social scientists, for instance) precisely depends upon a coordinating vector in the nonrepeatable events that constitute our Being. The uniqueness of the individual is not the product simply of their self-recognition: The "whole" of their existence is dependent on the Other. Again, this requires clarification. On one level, the aesthetic event depends upon coexperiencing the aesthetic object itself, whether a human, an object, a color, or a line, as Bakhtin suggests. This is not a pure identification, however, which would negate the place from which such experience is possible. (An absolute identification with the other is not just a fiction, but a form of psychosis.) Coexperiencing, for Bakhtin, must be sympathetic for aesthetic activity to have meaning as an event: "what is *constitutive* for such events is the relationship of one consciousness to *another* consciousness precisely as an other. Events of this kind include all of the *creatively* productive events—the once-occurrent and inconvertible events that bring forth something new" (AA 86–87; emphasis in original). Ultimately, it is not the Other as object that is important to Bakhtin's definition, but the Other as another consciousness, as another Being who is productive in the eventness of events (the capacity for co-Being in events). The world, as such, is participative to the extent that the aesthetic activity required in apprehending it is an acknowledgment of I and Other. And yet, the world as it is remains nonparticipative to the extent that either aesthetics is read as individualist or that the world of culture itself is split off from the world of life as it is lived in all its once-occurrent eventness. There are many philosophical issues that spin out of Bakhtin's thoughts on authoring and on action in *Art and Answerability* and *Toward a Philosophy of the Act,* some of which pertain to a Husserlian phenomenology and others that take up the general challenge of deconstructing Kant's ethical imperative. What I want to develop are those threads of Bakhtin's philosophy that affect how the world can be understood and whether this indeed might make culture a greater aid in coming to terms with globalization's claims to "being" in the world.

The world according to Bakhtin requires a differentiated notion of culture, but this in turn is dependent upon a certain impasse in modes of cognition. At a most basic level, for instance, one might ask how the Other (the other human, the other subject) has access to that unique once-occurrent eventness that the "I," in its Being, must continually live? The answer that this uniqueness is coparticipative begs the question of whether it can be actually cognized by the Other. On this point, Bakhtin forces the issue. The moment of cognition in all its uniqueness is what constitutes the event as aesthetic. The realization of co-Being is the ability to cognize the world we inhabit by living aesthetically. To put it bluntly, if we do not live aesthetically, the world, as such, cannot be actively cognized.

> Aesthetic activity collects the world scattered in meaning and condenses it into a finished and self-contained image. Aesthetic activity finds an emotional equivalent for what is transient in the world (for its past and present, for its present-on-hand being), an emotional equivalent that gives life to this transient being and safeguards it; that is, it finds an axiological position from which the transient in the world acquires the axiological weight of an event, acquires validity and stable determinateness. The aesthetic act gives birth to being on a new axiological plane of the world: a new human being is born and a new axiological context—a new plane of thinking about the human world. (AA 191)

There is much that is right and wrong about this formulation. First, the history of aesthetics is not exactly unencumbered by ideologies, particularly those that justify the existence of some people's activity over others (whether such people are artists or those who make a fetish of art in the face of their own barbarism). Second, although Bakhtin is careful to invoke aesthetic activity as the operative principle, it is hard not to sense the artist "acting" within it and, in particular, arbitrating the "emotional equivalent" that fends off or organizes all that scattered meaning in the world. Indeed, it is not too hard to imagine this world as the world of modernism, with the artist as disaffected god quietly paring fingernails, incognito, over the abstruse planes of existence that characterized a good part of the twentieth century. (The allusion is to James Joyce, of course, but for political and other reasons, Bakhtin's primary example is Dostoevsky.) On the positive side, Bakhtin knows that the event he describes is not simply the equivalent of the world or some representational surrogate. He is trying to explain how the world, as such, might remain fleeting and abstract and can only be given form for cognition through an activity that makes truth and value from its inconstancy. Bakhtin neither denies the latter nor celebrates it; he merely acknowledges that what is given in the world is not directly the means to apprehend it.

Now this still falls far short of an adequate explanation of the world, and particularly the world of globalization, which is our chief concern. Yet I would argue that the narrative of globalization wants to situate an activity that would cognize the world but ends up forwarding itself and the world as an alibi of existence that is precisely the object of Bakhtin's criticism. The partial truths of globalization as an economic integer, like its fraction of overall economic activity, are often projected as a global dominant. As an activity, it may acknowledge the world "scattered in meaning," but it obstinately refuses the cognitive risk (and coparticipation) inscribed in eventness and the axiological function of answerability or responsibility that this necessitates. While the guardians of globalization may court the aesthetic (which have taken my earlier arguments into the nether worlds of commodification, corporate identity, and the engine of advertising), they would prefer to empty out meaning at the point that it questions the world to which globalization actually refers. They would surely appreciate the idea of "newness" that Bakhtin embraces (for this year's "new human being" is a catchy consumable) and the metaphor of birthing that is often Bakhtin's own alibi for getting people into the "natural" creative act. But the process of meaning that Bakhtin analyzes is somewhat thornier, and so too are the values or axiology that it implies. Indeed, whatever the gestures toward the aesthetic within the rhetoric of globalization, under the terms of the aesthetic that Bakhtin examines, globalization is not aesthetic enough. It fails in its sweep to acknowledge the difference and responsibility in cognition that threaten what might otherwise pass for its logical integrity. Not surprisingly, this ruse in accumulation was something of which Marx was well aware.

For most, the idea that Marx was an aesthetician is intolerable or at best an acknowledgment of a certain humanist philosophical disposition before that now infamous epistemological break. Certainly, the 1844 manuscripts argue forcefully for an aesthetic provenance within materialism, for which Terry Eagleton provides a pertinent gloss:

> Marx is most profoundly "aesthetic" in his belief that the exercise of human senses, powers and capacities is an absolute end in itself, without need of utilitarian justification; but the unfolding of this sensuous richness for its own sake can be achieved, paradoxically, only through the rigorously instrumental practice of overthrowing bourgeois social relations. Only when the bodily drives have been released from the despotism of abstract need, and the object has been similarly restored from functional abstraction to sensuously particular use-value, will it be possible to live aesthetically.[12]

Again, this is different from Bakhtin's articulation of the aesthetic, but nevertheless a similar role for aesthetics emerges. Like Bakhtin, Marx understood the givenness of the world as something that had to be worked; a human's sensate fulfillment does not exist in the mere fact of our bodies or the world in which we live. Indeed, our recognition of an externally verifiable world does not obviate our role in constructing it but becomes the very basis of our answerability—a responsibility that is socialized. The world according to Marx has developed an economic system in which the body's sense of itself has been sundered, as Eagleton points out, by "abstract need," as if the world of "having" under capitalism was the purest expression of a human's sensate being and surplus value the axiological ground of activity. Marx is not arguing for art for art's sake but for a sensuous particularity that provides a ground for meaning, and not just see-through soles, to invoke that infamous god of victory once more.

In the early philosophical manuscripts, Marx is grappling with several issues simultaneously, but in general his attention to human sensate experience is a means of understanding the process of estrangement that is intrinsic to the capital relation. I do not want to belabor this point, but Marx's aesthetic predilections are concerned with what happens to human activity under the sign of capital. He asks, "what is life but activity?" Marx then proceeds to elaborate how labor is separated from the products of its activity and how this literally denatures human activity in general: It is

> in his working-up of the objective world, therefore, that man first really proves himself to be a species-being. This production is his active species-life. Through and because of this production, nature appears as his work and his reality. The object of labor is, therefore, the objectification of man's species-life: for he duplicates himself not only, as in consciousness, intellectually, but also actively, in reality, and therefore he contemplates himself in a world that he has created. In tearing away from man the object of his production, therefore, estranged labor tears from him his species-life, his

real species-objectivity, and transforms his advantage over animals into the disadvantage that his inorganic body, nature, is taken from him.[13]

This split in Being, being human, is calamitous, for those who labor are presented with an external world in which their activity is effectively nullified as a relation between a human and nature (as "man's inorganic body"). The estrangement of the worker under capital is not wrong simply because somebody else gets rich; it is fundamentally wrong because it denies labor the very substance of life activity, that which constitutes a human as human in relation to the world. This is a crisis in activity that globalization seeks to globalize (again, under conditions that Marx clearly understood as a structural compulsion of capitalist productive capacities). The young Bakhtin, like the young Marx, takes up the philosophical problem of the changed circumstances of the world that humans make:

> The contemporary crisis is, fundamentally, a crisis of contemporary action [*postupok*]. An abyss has formed between the motive of the actually performed act or deed and its product. But in consequence of this, the product of the deed, severed from its ontological roots, has withered as well. Money can become the motive of the deed that constructs a moral system. In relation to the present moment, economic materialism is in the right, although not because the motives of the actually performed act have penetrated inside the product but rather the reverse: the product in its validity walls itself off from the actually performed act in its actual motivation. But the situation cannot be rectified from within the product: it is impossible to break through from here to the actually performed act. It can be rectified only from within the act itself.[14]

For Marx, of course, the solution is to make that practical activity of humans revolutionary because this is the only way to take back the objective world that is now expressed as the relationship between things. (Like Bakhtin, Marx abhors the fact that products have taken up the motives of human existence and can make tables dance like that hideous example from the commodity chapter in *Capital*.) The answer then to the philosophical problem inscribed in the capital relation is to change the nature of activity. Bakhtin also wants change, but he places a heavier burden on interpretation than perhaps Marx's Eleventh Thesis on Ludwig Feuerbach would allow. Nevertheless, his solution, that activity must be made answerable or responsible, is not a metaphysician's dream. Bakhtin does not read the world as an abstraction from the reality it presents; rather, he attempts, at least in *Toward a Philosophy of the Act,* to understand the "fundamental moments in the architectonic of the actual world of the performed act or deed—the world actually experienced, and not the merely thinkable world" (54). Thinking globally, in this sense, would require a unity of thought with the practice that produces it, and yet "thinking globally" is the emptiest slogan within the rhetoric of globalization because its economic logic has already granted the product sway over the life activity and species being of those who produce. The idea that the world can be thought under this regimen is not simply an idealism, it is a concrete expression of the banalization of human activity in the contemporary epoch.

Aesthetics alone, thankfully, cannot untangle this knot in Being, because in itself it cannot encompass every aspect of the answerable deeds we perform. It demonstrates the principle of activity without constituting itself as an agential discourse (or, for Marx, the actually performed deed of revolution). It does, however, raise significant issues about cultural critique that waxes global at this juncture, and here again Bakhtin may be of use. The expansion of capital along global trajectories has always entailed a concomitant cultural dynamism. Often this has been of a negative valence, as the connections between imperialism/colonialism and, for instance, orientalism have amply illustrated. The new intensities of capital have not bucked this trend, although the actual conditions of global cultural difference exceed the simplified confines of the cultural imperialism gambit. The homogenizing tendencies of global cultural flows (like those discussed by Arjun Appadurai[15]) have been met by the difficulties of differentiation, so that while the world has been "given" a Coke (obviously, it has been sold it), "coca-colonization" (as Salman Rushdie, among others, has characterized it) does not quite encapsulate the processes of resistance and delinking that take place in the same time/space or chronotope of commodity culture. Even if one limits one's argument to items of mass culture, it is clear from cultural studies and other approaches that consumption cannot extinguish creativity and/or radical activity. (Indeed, it can provide examples of it.) Furthermore, if globalization is not just about the economics of space, but also the cultural dynamism of space (the subject of my section on Caribbeanness), the exploded borders of its logic open up the possibility of greatly expanded transnational activity in cultural and in political formations. Yet, just as we can learn a lot from studying the complex contradictions in the long history of capital's will to globalization, so the possibilities of transnational cultural and political practice would also have to be read against the achievements and failures of anticapitalist internationalism of at least the last 150 years. The pretensions of globalization do not necessarily make it easier to oppose (as even the laudable protests against the WTO in Seattle in December 1999, underline), nor do they guarantee in advance that the expiration of capitalist social relations is at hand. (Whatever was wrong or misguided about the *Communist Manifesto,* Marx and Engels were certainly right to stress that historical change is dependent upon historical context and not simply wish fulfillment).)[16] But what is there in globalization that might make culture a pertinent cornerstone of critical inquiry?

As I have suggested above, we will always find a cultural representation for globalization, whether it is a Coke bottle, Windows XP, or a Sony television, but the task remains to unravel the cognitive limits on globalization, not so that those limits disappear (for they are intrinsic to its very possibility), but rather so that no system, economic or cultural, might stand in for global difference. The opacity of globalization is that it uses difference for undifferentiation; it congeals culture as a conduit for stasis; it renders the local merely a fragment of its larger picture; it promises freedom via a worldliness that means oppression for those who are not among the "golden billion." Accepting that cultural globalization does not simply express the dubious power relations of globalization as a history of dominance, one must continue to doubt the relative weight of struggle it carries and whether heterogeneity itself defies the machinations of expansion into globality. Here, then, I will schematize cultural globalization as distinct from economic globalization before returning us to the world according to Bakhtin and how it may be sensed. Cultural globalization's multicultural manifestation is primarily in the form of recognition by accretion achieved in a wonderful flourish by adding the letter *s* where necessary and eschewing the uppercase: literatures, not Literature; americas, not America; traditions, not Tradition. The cultural accretionist will laud almost anything as long as it represents variety. The point is rarely the position of adjudication of those who hunt and gather this vibrant multiplicity but the fact that there are all those marvelously intricate names out there that can be added to the gumbo, or the masala, or the culinary mixture of the day. The cultural accretionist is not just an academic, literary type, but any liberal humanist who banks on multiplicity sui generis as cultural capital. Obviously, multiplicity or heterogeneity is absolutely vital (one only has to think of one's own manifest plurality) but there are ways to conceive the *s* in an interventionist rather than simply accretionist fashion.

The second form of cultural globalization is very similar to the first but works on the principle of consumption. Here globalization is an index of intensification in the conversion of quality into quantity, but it also foregrounds the act of consumption itself. The cultural consumer is here a subject that uses up culture as a condition of worldliness. It is not the addition of culture that is at issue, but its availability to be ingested that strikes the consumer as a very global thing to do. The act of consumption is spurred by the production of desire, globalization as desire, and comes with desire's intricate dependence on lack—a lack that remains in excess to the moment of consumption and thus requires still more of that global fix. Given the psychosexual provenance of such consumption, it is perhaps small wonder that its most visible displacement is in a kind of ethnicist frenzy for global cookery. Indeed, the global city is defined by just this division of gastronomic labor—the migrant worker, or subaltern, or racial "minority" cooks so that one might have "a taste of China" as my local restaurant puts it. If you eat the world, then, of course, you must be part of it. I have tried to complicate this model considerably by putting transnationalism to work in the process of commodity production and circulation themselves. The revelation of commodity chains does not dissolve the moment of consumption in the global imaginary, but it does test the limits of the commodity's quotidian pervasiveness by questioning whether this consumption can occur without reproducing economic conditions of oppression.

The consumption and accretion models of globalization represent Global Lite but are nevertheless vital components of globality, the way economic globalization itself gets naturalized in everyday culture. If there is something inescapable about their reach, it is because there is very little that is obviously disturbing about their practice. It should also be added that such cultural globalization does not just feed on a process but is a very active feature of it. These forms produce identities in the global imaginary. They are easily the most prominent models of global citizenry, yet we need to delve further into the processes of selving at issue. Clearly, there are already emergent critical forms of cultural globalization.

Postcolonialism, in some of its more agonistic manifestations at least, describes a significant paradox in historicizing globalization. Postcolonialism is about the disjuncture and difference wrought by the experience and subsumption of the colonial moment. Here globalization is a ready index of displacement, diaspora, migration, *and* intense forms of localization, national reformation, and independence. The same doors that open out onto the bright lights of globalization close in on a detailed history of expansionism, resistance, revolution, and readjustment. There is no space here to detail all the pitfalls of postcolonialism as a concept (some of these, at least, are evident in every chapter), but it seems to me that it usefully functions as an interrogative pause about the logic of connection in globalization. The postcolonial subject has its own alibi, yet there is in this aura a problem for those heady narratives of integration. Just like the inedible concoctions of the multiculti mix, the hybridized or interstitial identities of the postcolonial flutter more than philosophies of the Same. Postcoloniality is not just the name for what cracks the colonial State, but also what confounds a logic of assimilation by projection ("you're really like me underneath"). It is the desire for that unveiling that postcoloniality questions, and thus it tends to thwart the idea that the world is simply there to be revealed in all its commonality.

The fourth and most theorized form of cultural globalization, the one that seems to partake of every other (and every Other), is also the one that frequently substitutes effects for causes (and indeed constitutes the metaleptic majority) that has made it all the easier to proclaim it as the dean of discursivity or signifier of signifiers. This is postmodernism. Like postcoloniality, postmodernism focuses on a certain irreducible play across the field of difference, that identities multiply beyond their putative tactical essences. (Class is striated or fractured by race; gender exceeds the substance of race matters, etc.) This is where that troublesome *s* becomes interventionist. The subjects of histories never quite congeal into a subject of history, so one lesson of postmodernity for globalization is that there are subjects and worlds that resist recuperation within the oneness of the world (a multiplicity that is built into Bakhtin's notion of the cognitive/ethical). As Aijaz Ahmad has pointed out, we live in one world not three, which is a materialist injunction about the deleterious modes of global integration that the pomo/poco theorist bends to as well as against.[17] But that *s* ensures or at least encourages an attention to how identities get articulated, so that, although the postmodern has been contaminated by the zeal of its own profusion, it nevertheless grapples in the space between the aesthetic and the political, never too tongue-tied to pronounce its own importance but ever dubious about whether one side or the other might render it effete. But all its irony and pastiche is much too patronizing about the possibilities of social praxis in the face of material contradiction. People really don't have to go through the eye of the postmodern in order to change the material circumstances of their lives. This does not mean that such people simply live outside postmodern effects or its notorious "condition," but that the ebullience of pomo stylization must, according to its own logic, fall short of a devoutly wished globalization.

Globalization is about power, but not a power that accrues to all, a comment that cancels through the effortless *we* in many of my sentences. How could cultural globalization possibly disable the will to power that is integral to its worldly pretensions? If it now parades the diversity of representation, then who or what arbitrates the hierarchies of representation intrinsic to plurality that, after all, is no "blinder" than Teiresias? If cultural globalization negotiates the differentiation of identity, then does it have a politics of identity? What if globality itself negates this identitarian formula? This is, I hope, where cultural transnationalism emerges as a critical reflection on the cultures of globalization. Recall, once more, Bakhtin's modest proposal. The apprehension of a world is not the product of training or expertise, or sensitive analogies from advertising campaigns. Cultures are ways to live, but if Bakhtin's thoughts on aesthetic process and the relations of I and Other remain provocative, it is because the recognition of another culture does not necessarily constitute a global event of answerability. Living the differences of the world, like living aesthetically, would require a different relationship to other cultures than the accretionist and consumption models. So within cultural transnationalism, what is Bakhtin's lesson for cultures of globalization?

The Bakhtinian shorthand for productively thinking the world in this way would be "dialogize"! Yet this too would have to be qualified, since there is already plenty of evidence that overexuberance about the "dialogue" in dialogism can just as easily jump over real difference and hierarchy in the world as a smile from Ronald McDonald. Cultural globalization often wants the Other to talk back, but only on terms constructed by the "I" (or let us say, the North or the Western hemisphere of the globe, to give it geopolitical context). The invocation of dialogism, then, will continue to be an empty gambit if the axiological function of the Other in the answerable act remains an object and not a coparticipant (and this would require a much greater dialogical imagination than that which globalization embodies at this time). A culture of globalization should, on the one hand, be understood in the way it engages the contradictory sense of the world resplendent in the economic logic of globalization characterized above and, on the other, be cognizant of the modest yet important role it can play in actively thinking differences in the world. The assumption of differences is not enough because dialogism is agonistic: It refers to dynamic struggles over difference, something that does not necessarily melt borders but throws into relief the logic of their construction and interaction.

The world according to Bakhtin does not, then, solve the impasse in cultural globalization and certainly does not present a blueprint for cultural transnationalism in dismantling the daunting machinery of global capital. Bakhtin does, however, alert us to the constitutive contradictions of the world that are common to both culture and the economic. These can be read both as logical contradictions in how the world is rendered for globalization and as a provocation to analyze more seriously the terms of cognition and imagination in the worlds we make. The failure of globalization is not only the horror of economic hierarchy it brings, but the absence of a cognitive correlative for its apprehension. This cannot be conjured out of the philosopher's hat, just as culture cannot simply be retooled to be virulently anticapitalist (there are obviously concepts of culture that are coterminous with the development and expansion of capitalism itself), but Bakhtin's warning is that the world is not realized by naming it. His world has chronotopes (the time/space of comprehension), bodies and borders, and conditions of answerability that have yet to be met by anything like the world according to globalization. And so any scientific critique of the historical emergence of globalization as a social force (which Bakhtin demonstrably does not provide) might usefully be tempered by Bakhtin's thoughts on how we might ground art and activity as something more than an alibi for being, or being "glo-bal" in this age. Far from being a distraction, such thinking keeps alive capaci-ties for change that don't simply mirror the imaginary relations of globalization as currently construed. It actively presages a world according to a different sense of participation and responsibility, but a world that is not just predictive or final-ized. At the very least, it is a world to win.

Notes

Introduction

1. While social being determines consciousness, how that being is imagined is also part of socialization. The point is not to reverse a founding principle of Marxism in favor of idealism, but to understand critically the role of imagination in what social being can become.

2. Arjun Appadurai, *Modernity at Large* (Minneapolis: University of Minnesota Press, 1996), 31. Of course, how central imagination is to agency is the crux of the matter. The danger is always that a discourse of agency can devolve into agency *tout court*. Certainly, discourses are agential, but what makes them social also makes them subject to action about, even from the nondiscursive.

3. Briefly stated, Appadurai's "flow" analysis is an initial theorization of the dynamics involved in transnationalism that, in its urge to "scape" the complexities of the world system, often underplays the value of economic and sociological critique in such a debate. That lack of emphasis does not necessarily negate the terms of Appadurai's argument but, in the absence of a fully articulated engagement with the limitations of, for instance, materialist understandings of globalization, one might be forgiven for thinking that the "largeness" of modernity has been radically truncated. It is partly in recognition of the daring of Appadurai's approach that his critique continues to be fiercely debated. Aihwa Ong, for instance, questions whether the "flows" that Appadurai proposes can be so independent of national and Nation configurations, with the power structures that they imply. See Aihwa Ong, *Flexible Citizenship: The Cultural Logics of Transnationality* (Durham, N.C.: Duke University Press, 1999), 11.

4. The question will immediately arise whether cultural transnationalism is simply a synonym for cosmopolitanism. The latter is a highly contentious zone of engagement that struggles to free itself from the contaminated history of colonial and imperial knowledges of the other. That postcolonial subjects "on the move" have been interpellated and interpreted as the new cosmopolitans has only intensified the problematic status of cosmo-

politanism today. Cultural transnationalism is not outside such debate and, given my own subject position, is not intended to escape the culpability of "Western" criticism in setting the terms of transnational cultural analysis. The attempt is to build culpability or answerability into the critical model itself so that it might attend more closely to the actual power relations that obtain. For a lively discussion of cosmopolitanism, see Pheng Cheah and Bruce Robbins, eds., *Cosmopolitics: Thinking and Feeling Beyond the Nation* (Minneapolis: University of Minnesota Press, 1998). For a more polemical intervention on cosmopolitanism, particularly with regard to the location of the United States in new transnationalisms, see Timothy Brennan, *At Home in the World: Cosmopolitanism Now* (Cambridge, Mass.: Harvard University Press, 1997).

5. Edward Said, *Culture and Imperialism* (New York: Knopf, 1993), 330.

6. See, for instance, Jon Stratton and Ien Ang, "On the Impossibility of a Global Cultural Studies: 'British' Cultural Studies in an International Frame," in *Stuart Hall: Critical Dialogues in Cultural Studies,* ed. David Morley and Kuan-Hsing Chen (London: Routledge, 1996), 361–91. The introduction to the volume is also recommended in this regard. It should be noted that Stuart Hall and his work have often been a cornerstone for this reconsideration, or "retranslation" as he would say, of cultural studies from the position of transnationalism.

7. For an incisive critique of the confluence of the Nation as idea and as ideology, see Étienne Balibar and Immanuel Wallerstein, *Race, Nation, Class: Ambiguous Identities* (New York: Verso, 1992), especially chapter 5. For an examination of the Nation's demands on the aesthetic, see Antony Easthope, *Englishness and National Identity* (New York: Routledge, 1999). For a wide-ranging collection on this topic, see Homi K. Bhabha, ed., *Nation and Narration* (New York: Routledge, 1990).

8. For more on this concept of Being, see Mikhail Bakhtin, *Toward a Philosophy of the Act,* trans. Vadim Liapunov, ed. Vadim Liapunov and Michael Holquist (Austin: University of Texas Press, 1993). Again, this does not serve as an excuse regarding transnationalism, but as a determinate condition of being in the world at this juncture. Being, for Bakhtin, is an "event" for which we are continually answerable. He stresses the once-occurrent nature of individual being not to proffer the prospect of humans as hopelessly separated monads, but to forward a sense of being that is not simply contingent, but based on the "world of inescapable actuality" (44). It is the actuality of transnationalism that necessitates theorization of being in the world.

9. This concept is inspired by Fernando Ortiz's immensely important *Contrapunteo cubano del tobacco y el azúcar* (Cuban counterpoint). Ortiz's cultural analysis of commodity relations in Caribbean history holds enduring lessons for the way the aesthetic can be thought both historically and spatially. This is also why Ortiz's study is a cornerstone in Benítez-Rojo's equally prescient reading of the Caribbean, *The Repeating Island.* See Fernando Ortiz, *Cuban Counterpoint: Tobacco and Sugar,* trans. Harriet De Onis (New York: Vintage Books, 1970). See also Antonio Benítez-Rojo, *The Repeating Island: The Caribbean and the Postmodern Perspective,* trans. James E. Maraniss (Durham, N.C.: Duke University Press, 1992).

10. A formative text here is Benedict Anderson, *Imagined Communities: Reflections on the Origin and Spread of Nationalism,* rev. ed. (London: Verso, 1991).

11. See Smadar Lavie and Ted Swedenburg, eds., *Displacement, Diaspora, and Geographies of Identity* (Durham, N.C.: Duke University Press, 1996).

12. Lavie and Swedenburg are using Sandoval's concept as part of a broader critique of transnational consciousness. See Chela Sandoval, "U.S. Third World Feminism: The Theory and Method of Oppositional Consciousness in the Postmodern World," *Genders* 10 (1991): 1–24. While one might quibble with the automatic ascription of "postmodern" to such differentiation, Lavie and Swedenburg usefully link the consciousness debate to resistance of transnational capitalist formations.

13. Thirdness of this kind is not meant to rekindle a form of unreconstructed "Third Worldism"; rather, the legacy of Third World politics and positioning is simultaneously displaced and reinscribed within the geopolitics of the transnational. See, for instance, Homi Bhabha, "Third Space: Interview with Homi Bhabha," in *Identity: Community, Culture, Difference,* ed. Jonathan Rutherford (London: Lawrence and Wishart, 1990), 207–21. See also Edward Soja, *Thirdspace* (London: Blackwell, 1996). Soja's "Thirdspace" is a flexible concept, part Foucaldian, part Lefebvrean, and resolutely postmodern that seeks to spatialize experience and critique beyond the binaries of yesteryear (chiefly the opposition of material and mental geographic constructs). It is at once an enriching and troubling text that, while critically engaged, never once questions whether its playful exuberance ("*the*" postcolonial critique, "*the*" paradoxical face of feminism and geography —definite articles for the indefinite in his prose) is itself a symptom of location (Los Angeles in particular) well known for solipsism in the face of competing orders of knowledge. The strengths of *Thirdspace* far outweigh its weaknesses and the flourish of its poetry, but rather than accept its carefully arranged chaos, one might take it as a challenge to think beyond its scrupulously ordered synchrony of names and self-referentiality toward other productions of space inspired by its logic, if not layout.

14. The most notorious example of this tendency remains Francis Fukuyama, *The End of History and the Last Man* (New York: Free Press, 1992). Interestingly, Fukuyama's perception of a perpetual modernism is not that far removed from the perpetual state of digression in postmodern theory often meant to displace it.

15. Raymond Williams, *Keywords* (London: Fontana, 1983), 153–60.

16. Perry Anderson, "Components of the National Culture," *New Left Review* 50 (July–August 1968): 3–58. This view was a more or less standard interpretation of establishment ideology which Terry Eagleton gave an Althusserian twist a few years later. See Terry Eagleton, *Criticism and Ideology* (London: Verso, 1976).

17. The reader must decide whether my invocations of commodity critique are themselves a symptom of this rejection or a means to reexamine the prescience of the literary.

18. Here I mean to invoke something of the constitutive ambivalence written into the Nation as idea. Homi Bhabha has attempted a similar deconstructive turn in "Dissemi-Nation: Time, Narrative, and the Margins of the Modern Nation," in *Nation and Narration,* ed. Homi K. Bhabha (New York: Routledge, 1990), 291–322.

19. I have explored this sense of a politics of positioning in *Dialogics of the Oppressed* (Minneapolis: University of Minnesota Press, 1993).

20. Although, that said, Clifford's use of travel seems to trope the two together, if not always in step. See James Clifford, *Routes* (Cambridge, Mass.: Harvard University Press, 1997).

21. Aijaz Ahmad has made the case provocatively in *In Theory: Classes, Nations, Literatures* (London: Verso, 1990). Among other points, Ahmad explores the "Third Worldist" reflex of suppressing the importance of nation formation in the process of decolonization. For this piece of materialist insight, Ahmad's book often became the focus of heavy-handed criticism, although, given the relative silence of the argument in terms of gender and postcolonial subjectivity, some of the attacks were justifiable. Timothy Brennan's *At Home in the World* provides a judicious corrective, as does the work of Neil Lazarus. See, for instance, Neil Lazarus, "Postcolonialism and the Dilemma of Nationalism: Aijaz Ahmad's Critique of Third Worldism," *Diaspora* 9, no. 3 (Winter 1993): 373–400.

22. Indeed, with the waning of the cold war the rise of postmodern media simulacra has seemed to aid rather than retard the "realities" of nationalist sentiment. There is no neat division between Nation and modernity on the one hand, and transnationalism and postmodernity on the other. It is the political ramifications of their contradictions that provide the challenge for global critique.

23. Here I must take issue with Anthony Easthope's otherwise astute analysis of Nation. He criticizes Benedict Anderson's theory of Nation as an "imagined community" for its stark reliance on an empiricist division between the prenational authenticity of face-to-face contact and the impersonal and therefore imagined collectivity of Nation. Indeed, he goes on to link Raymond Williams and Eric Hobsbawm to the same tendency, which is roundly dismissed as a Marxist exercise in nostalgia and sentimentality. I think this misses the point (although the humanist inclinations of these Marxists are well documented). Even if Anderson is guilty of the dreaded "b" word (as in binary) in his thinking, the major thrust of his approach remains pertinent. Of course, all collectivities are imagined, but to accuse Anderson of rendering Nation as an ideology, and one that is simply false consciousness, distorts the nuances of his invocation of the imagined and the imaginary. To argue for Nation as a discourse or array of discourses as Easthope does makes good sense, but discourse analysis does not exclude the governing tropes of Anderson's critique, and neither does it exempt itself from traces of empiricism. The value surely of both approaches is that if the Nation can be imagined, it can be imagined otherwise, even out of existence. Nation is a historical idea, and as such can die as a means for humans to sustain their social being, unless, again, we believe that we have reached the end of history. See Anthony Easthope, *Englishness and National Identity* (New York: Routledge, 1999), especially part 1.

24. Michael Taussig, *The Magic of State* (New York: Routledge, 1997).

25. See Kamala Visweswaran, *Fictions of Feminist Ethnography* (Minneapolis: University of Minnesota Press, 1994). Part of the importance of Visweswaran's argument is not just that fieldwork has tended to elide the material conditions of the ethnographic "I," but that the traveling theorists have often forgotten the masculine privilege in their move-

ment, which is constitutive and not tangential to the critical framework elaborated. I will say more about this under the rubric of "crossing" in chapter 1.

26. A pertinent work in this regard is Forest Pyle, *The Ideology of Imagination* (Stanford, Calif.: Stanford University Press, 1995).

27. Obviously, I'm thinking of my own institution in this regard. There are sincere attempts underway to retool the curriculum so that it both reflects a broader cultural archive and comes to terms with what is an extremely diverse student population. Nevertheless, questions of expertise and the logic of inclusion employed are often overlooked in the rush to be as "global" as New York City itself claims to be.

28. Rob Wilson and Wimal Dissanayake, eds., *Global/Local: Cultural Production and the Transnational Imaginary* (Durham, N.C.: Duke University Press, 1996), 6 (emphasis in original).

29. Paul Bové, "Afterword: 'Global/Local' Memory and Thought," in *Global/Local: Cultural Production and the Transnational Imaginary,* ed. Rob Wilson and Wimal Dissanayake (Durham, N.C.: Duke University Press, 1996), 385.

30. Fredric Jameson, *The Geopolitical Aesthetic: Cinema and Space in the World System* (Bloomington: Indiana University Press, 1992), 3.

31. I have explored this hesitation/vacillation as oscillation in *Oscillate Wildly: Space, Body, and Spirit of Millennial Materialism* (Minneapolis: University of Minnesota Press, 1999).

32. Clifford, *Routes.*

33. The following commentary will refer to Ien Ang and Jon Stratton, "Asianing Australia: Notes toward a Critical Transnationalism in Cultural Studies," *Cultural Studies* 10, no. 1 (1996): 16–36; Kuan-Hsing Chen, "Not Yet the Postcolonial Era: The (Super) Nation-State and Trans*nationalism* of Cultural Studies—Response to Ang and Stratton," *Cultural Studies* 10, no. 1 (1996): 37–70; and Ang and Stratton, "A Cultural Studies without Guarantees: Response to Kuan-Hsing Chen," *Cultural Studies* 10, no. 1 (1996): 71–77.

34. Ahmad, *In Theory.*

35. Williams, *Keywords,* 153–60.

36. See Louis Althusser, *"Lenin and Philosophy" and Other Essays,* trans. Ben Brewster (New York: Monthly Review Press, 1971). Althusser's essay on ideology and ideological state apparatuses remains a defining Marxist analysis of ideology.

37. Gloria Anzaldúa, *Borderlands/La Frontera: The New Mestiza* (San Francisco: Aunt Lute Books, 1987).

38. Border theory of this kind is legion, but it is important to maintain its sense of the imaginative edges of identity and not just the somewhat fictive fencing between nations. See, for instance, John C. Welchman, ed., *Rethinking Borders* (Minneapolis: University of Minnesota Press, 1996).

39. Salman Rushdie, *Imaginary Homelands* (London: Granta Books, 1991), 1–42.

40. Stuart Hall, "For Allon White: Metaphors of Transformation," in *Stuart Hall: Critical Dialogues in Cultural Studies,* ed. David Morley and Kuan-Hsing Chen (London: Routledge, 1996), 287.

41. Paul Gilroy, *The Black Atlantic* (Cambridge, Mass.: Harvard University Press, 1993), 31.

42. Antonio Benítez-Rojo, *The Repeating Island: The Caribbean and the Postmodern Perspective,* trans. James E. Maraniss (Durham, N.C.: Duke University Press, 1992). This question of repetition and difference in island identity will be discussed in more detail in chapter 1.

43. See Joan Gross, David McMurray, and Ted Swedenburg, "Arab Noise and Ramadan Nights: *Rai,* Rap, and Franco-Maghrebi Identities," in *Displacement, Diaspora, and Geographies of Identity,* ed. Smadar Lavie and Ted Swedenburg (Durham, N.C.: Duke University Press, 1996), 119–55. Research on North African and French disjuncture and difference has intensified within postcolonial and diasporic critique in recent years. See, for instance, Alec Hargreaves and Mark McKinney, eds., *Post-Colonial Cultures in France* (London: Routledge, 1997).

44. See Peter Hitchcock, "It Dread Inna Inglan," *Postmodern Culture* 4, no. 1 (September 1993): 1–24 (edited, abridged, and reprinted in *Reggae, Rasta, Revolution: Jamaican Music from Ska to Dub,* ed. Chris Potash [New York: Schirmer Books, 1997], 163–67).

45. Wolfgang Haug, *Critique of Commodity Aesthetics* (Minneapolis: University of Minnesota Press, 1986).

46. Karl Marx, *Capital,* vol. 1, trans. Ben Fowkes (New York: Penguin, 1976), 163.

47. Jameson, *Geopolitical Aesthetic,* 4.

The Agon of the Archipelago

1. This has been the subject of much debate, under the terms of *métissage* and, in particular, *creolization* (as will become evident in my subsequent discussion of Glissant and Brathwaite). Creolization obviously is not limited to questions of linguistic appropriation, imbrication, and a vibrant syncretism—but also refers to the historical and political realities of Caribbeanness within modernity. For most works on Caribbean literature, this set of relations (in which both "set" and "relation" are contestable) is positively axiomatic. See, for instance, Patrick Chamoiseau and Raphael Confiant, *Lettres créoles: Tracées antillaises et continentales de la littérature—Haïti, Guadeloupe, Martinique, Guyane, 1635–1975* (Paris: Hatier, 1991).

2. Aimé Césaire, *Discourse on Colonialism* (New York: Monthly Review Press, 2000), 74.

3. Antonio Benítez-Rojo, *The Repeating Island: The Caribbean and the Postmodern Perspective,* trans. James E. Maraniss (Durham, N.C.: Duke University Press, 1992), 37. Benítez-Rojo's book is perhaps the most exuberant theoretical investigation of what makes Caribbean consciousness both ex-ilic and ex-orbitant—that is, what is simultaneously beyond the island and the global as currently construed.

4. Peter Hitchcock, *Oscillate Wildly: Space, Body, and Spirit of Millennial Materialism* (Minneapolis: University of Minnesota Press, 1999), especially the conclusion.

5. Benítez-Rojo, *Repeating Island,* 141.

6. Ibid., 23.

7. See Paget Henry and Paul Buhle, "Caliban as Deconstructionist: C. L. R. James and Post-Colonial Discourse," in *C. L. R. James's Caribbean,* ed. Paget Henry and Paul Buhle (Durham, N.C.: Duke University Press, 1992), 111–42. Their caution resides in the difference they correctly perceive between the work of a politico-literary vanguard in anticolonial critique (Garvey, James, Fanon, Césaire, Lamming, Wynter, etc.) and the changed conditions of postcoloniality. Henry and Buhle therefore argue for a deconstructive, or "semio-linguistic" model of interpretation that is more sensitive to the textual play across and within the figure of Caliban. As we have seen in recent Fanonian studies, this makes James a more ambivalent cornerstone of postcolonial discourse.

8. Jean Bernabé, Patrick Chamoiseau, and Raphael Confiant, *Éloge de la créolité* (Paris: Gallimard, 1989), available in English as "In Praise of Creoleness," trans. M. B. Taleb-Khyar, *Callaloo* 13 (1990): 886–909, republished in a bilingual edition as *Éloge de la créolité/ In Praise of Creoleness,* trans. M. B. Taleb-Khyar (Paris: Gallimard, 1993).

9. The "poetics of relation" refers to Édouard Glissant, *Poétique de la relation* (Paris: Gallimard, 1990), available in English as *Poetics of Relation,* trans. Betsy Wing (Ann Arbor: University of Michigan Press, 1997). Relation refers simultaneously to several notions, one of which is Glissant's penchant for alterity over identity, the fragment of otherness over any kind of unitary island self. That this grates against rather than equates with Bernabé, Chamoiseau, and Confiant's sense of créolité should be clear, even as they acknowledge Glissant as a primary influence. I would argue, however, that the complex parameters of relation cannot help but take up the charge of a specific identity in creolization, although Glissant's concomitant strain of worldliness, of *Tout-monde,* clearly casts his theory into the realm of abstract globalization.

10. I have explored this poetics of vocal variation in "It Dread Inna Inglan," *Postmodern Culture* 4, no. 1 (September 1993): 1–24 (edited, abridged, and reprinted in *Reggae, Rasta, Revolution: Jamaican Music from Ska to Dub,* ed. Chris Potash [New York: Schirmer Books, 1997], 163–67).

Chapter 1: Glissant and Opaque Space

1. This is storytelling of the nation as supplement, and not simply as a reprise or adjunct of the Nation idea. It must be said that theorists too often conflate nationalism as a politics of positioning with Nation as a logos of community identity. The nationalist urges of Glissant in *Le discours antillais* (Paris: Éditions du Seuil, 1981), for instance, are not the measure of his being duped by logocentric or binary thinking, but are instead symptoms of a war of position overdetermined (but not determined absolutely) by the real foundations of Martinique as a *département d'outre mer* (DOM; overseas administrative district).

2. Édouard Glissant, *La lézarde* (Paris: Éditions du Seuil, 1958), available in English as *The Ripening,* trans. Michael Dash (London: Heinemann, 1985).

3. Édouard Glissant, *Malemort* (Paris: Éditions du Seuil, 1975), and *Mahogany* (Paris: Éditions du Seuil, 1987). Both these novels doubt whether an expressive understanding of

Martinican history can be expressed: they are, in a sense, an enactment of that struggle to express, to come to terms with, to engage with the trauma that girds the island's past.

4. *Le discours antillais* outlines some of the principles of this poetics, including (as here) the function of landscape and the importance of the oral, but see also Édouard Glissant, *Poétique de la relation* (Paris: Gallimard, 1990).

5. Aimé Césaire, *Cahier d'un retour au pays natal* (Paris: Presence Africaine, 1971); see also *Notebook of a Return to My Native Land* in *The Collected Poetry,* trans. Clayton Eshelman and Annette Smith (Berkeley: University of California Press, 1983).

6. Édouard Glissant, *Discours antillais,* 199. All translations in the text are mine except where otherwise indicated. Subsequent references will be noted as DA followed by a page number. The English translation here is from Édouard Glissant, *Caribbean Discourse,* trans. Michael Dash (Charlottesville: University Press of Virginia, 1989), 143. Subsequent references to this abridged version of the French work will be noted as CD followed by a page number.

7. For a detailed account of the nexus of slavery and plantation in Martinican history, see Dale W. Tomich, *Slavery in the Circuit of Sugar* (Baltimore, Md.: Johns Hopkins University Press, 1990).

8. Édouard Glissant, *L'intention poétique* (Paris: Éditions du Seuil, 1969), 158.

9. Ibid., 196.

10. Édouard Glissant, *Pays rêve, pays réel* (Paris: Éditions du Seuil, 1985), 7.

11. Wilbert J. Roget, "Land and Myth in the Writings of Édouard Glissant," *World Literature Today* 63, no. 4 (Autumn 1989): 626–31. This special issue of *World Literature Today* is dedicated to Glissant and is highly recommended. Roget's dissertation, "Édouard Glissant and Antillanité" (University of Pittsburgh, 1975), is also pertinent to the current discussion. The most important collection of essays on Glissant in French is Yves-Alain Favre and Antonio Ferreira de Brito, eds., *Horizons d'Édouard Glissant* (Biarritz: J. & D. Éditions, 1990). The most important resource for the study of Glissant is Alain Baudot, *Bibliographie annotée d'Édouard Glissant* (Toronto: Éditions du GREF, 1993).

12. Glissant, *Ripening,* 204.

13. The references are clear in *Le discours antillais* but also extend to Glissant's fiction. In *Tout-monde,* for instance, Mathieu links the banyan and the question of roots to both Chaos Theory and the rhizome (*Tout-Monde* [Paris: Gallimard, 1993], 55–57). Whether or not the tree bears the weight of Deleuze or Guattari's philosophical distinctions vis-à-vis Glissant's would form a separate argument in its own right. My point here is to emphasize the spatial logic which attempts to delink from the binaries that construct the colonial landscape.

14. The debate with history is common to several contexts but is particularly acute where colonial discourse begins to dissociate from the historical logic that informs it at the same time that it is actively challenged by the alterity of knowledge systems it cannot explain. The phenomenon of postcolonial discourse is testimony to the complexity of this issue although much of its impetus comes from the anticolonialist polemics of the 1940s to 1960s—the strongest and most relevant influence on Glissant's position.

15. Frederick Ivor Case, "Édouard Glissant and the Poetics of Cultural Marginalization," *World Literature Today* 63, no. 4 (Autumn 1989): 598.

16. Alain Baudot, "Édouard Glissant: A Poet in Search of His Landscape," *World Literature Today* 63, no. 4 (Autumn 1989): 584.

17. The relevant essays are Homi K. Bhabha's "Of Mimicry and Man: The Ambivalence of Colonial Discourse," *October* 28 (1984): 125–33, and "Signs Taken for Wonders: Questions of Ambivalence and Authority under a Tree Outside Delhi, May 1817," *Critical Inquiry* 12, no. 1 (1985): 144–65. The principle of ambivalence not only relates to the subject of history but also to the critic who articulates it—as Robert Young shows in his reading of Bhabha in *White Mythologies* (London: Routledge, 1990).

18. Quoted from a lecture by Glissant called "Language and Identity" in Beatrice Stith Clark, "IME Revisited," *World Literature Today* 63, no. 4 (Autumn 1989): 603.

19. Édouard Glissant, "René Char: A Tribute," *UNESCO Courier* 41, no. 6 (June 1988): 33.

20. The phrase appears in V. N. Volosinov, *Marxism and the Philosophy of Language,* trans. Ladislav Matejka and I. R. Titunik (New York: Seminar Press, 1973), 88. For more on this sense of the interpellation of the collective subject see Peter Hitchcock, *Dialogics of the Oppressed* (Minneapolis: University of Minnesota Press, 1993).

21. *La case du commandeur* (Paris: Éditions du Seuil, 1981) is Glissant's most formal experiment with a collective subject for fiction and it is no coincidence that it appears at the same time that he is attempting to theorize this collectivity in *Le discours antillais.*

22. Recall that in his essay "White Mythology: Metaphor in the Text of Philosophy," in his *Margins of Philosophy,* trans. Alan Bass (Chicago: University of Chicago Press, 1984), 207–92, Jacques Derrida is trying to show how metaphoricity functions as an undecidable in Western metaphysics: it grounds an ontology in the cognitive aporia of *relever* (to raise and preserve, but in this case what it preserves is an original *mise en abŷme*). The misuse of metaphor is built into metaphoricity and is not a question of philosophical tenacity. Metaphysics literally takes off (*relève*) from metaphor. But catachresis enters into Derrida's argument to make strange the logic of this launch—to displace the project of Western philosophy in the very moment of its inscription. The misuse of metaphor draws attention to the ruse of metaphoricity in Western philosophy, in this case its anemia, or "white" mythology.

23. Derek Walcott, "The Sea Is History," *The Star-Apple Kingdom* (New York: Farrar, Straus, and Giroux, 1979), 25–28; Edward Kamau Brathwaite, *History of the Voice* (London: New Beacon, 1984).

24. Baudot, "Édouard Glissant," 583.

25. See CD 66 and DA 134 for more on transversality. The idea would be to understand Caribbean history through a subterranean convergence, rather than linear modality. The confluence of "shock" and historical time bears comparison to Walter Benjamin's theorization of the modern in "The Work of Art in the Age of Mechanical Reproduction," although obviously Benjamin sees the "quarrel with history" from within its "Western" correlatives. I would suggest that there are traditions of autocritique within the tele-

ologies of history, perhaps even intimations of transversality, that would themselves find the homogenization of Western history suspect.

26. See Barbara J. Webb, *Myth and History in Caribbean Fiction* (Amherst: University of Massachusetts Press, 1992).

27. Bernadette Cailler, "Édouard Glissant: A Creative Critic," *World Literature Today* 63, no. 4 (Autumn 1989): 589.

28. Interestingly, Cailler, ibid., 590, also suggests that "the dream of a heroic male order includes an unconscious nostalgia in the author's psyche" but then drops the subject, pointing out instead that female characters in Glissant's fiction actually realize the narrative's popular base—its legitimacy as a "people's story." I, however, remain unconvinced that this gendered division of narrative labor functions in this way in Glissant's novels.

29. And indeed Glissant comments on Bertolt Brecht in this section of *Le discours antillais* (in *Caribbean Discourse,* 219–20). Glissant explains that "political tragedy" of the Brechtian variety is, however, not possible in a Martinican context precisely because the maroon is not deposited in Martinican unconscious as a viable hero.

30. Brathwaite, *History of the Voice,* 10. Obviously, I will be commenting more on Brathwaite in chapter 2.

31. Cailler, "Édouard Glissant."

32. Jean Bernabé, Patrick Chamoiseau, and Raphael Confiant, *Éloge de la créolité* (Paris: Gallimard, 1989), available in English as "In Praise of Creoleness," trans. M. B. Taleb-Khyar, *Callaloo* 13 (1990): 886–909, republished in a bilingual edition as *Éloge de la créolité/ In Praise of Creoleness,* trans. M. B. Taleb-Khyar (Paris: Gallimard, 1993).

33. Bernabé, Chamoiseau, and Confiant, *Éloge de la créolité/In Praise of Creoleness,* 80.

34. Ibid., 56.

35. Glissant, *Poétique de la relation,* 241.

36. Bernabé, Chamoiseau, and Confiant, *Éloge de la créolité/In Praise of Creoleness,* 36–37 (my translation).

37. Walter Benjamin, *Illuminations,* trans. Harry Zohn, ed. Hannah Arendt (New York: Schocken, 1969), 255.

38. Bernabé, Chamoiseau, and Confiant, *Éloge de la créolité/In Praise of Creoleness,* 110.

39. Édouard Glissant, "Beyond Babel," *World Literature Today* 63, no. 4 (Autumn 1989): 561.

40. Ibid., 563.

41. Case, "Édouard Glissant," 595.

42. Cailler, "Édouard Glissant," 42.

43. Françoise Lionnet, "Inscriptions of Exile: The Body's Knowledge and the Myth of Authenticity," *Callaloo* 15, no. 1 (1992): 34.

44. Bernabé, Chamoiseau, and Confiant, *Éloge de la créolité/In Praise of Creoleness,* 80.

45. Danielle Dumontet, "Antillean Authors and Their Models," trans. Suzanne Houyoux, *Callaloo* 15, no. 1 (1992): 117.

46. Prisca Degras, "Name of the Fathers, History of the Name: Odono as Memory" *World Literature Today* 63, no. 4 (Autumn 1989): 613–14.

47. Ibid., 619.

48. Ibid.

49. Pamela Mordecai and Betty Wilson, eds. *Her True-True Name* (Oxford: Heinemann, 1989), xiii.

50. Simone Schwartz-Bart, *Pluie et vent sur Télumé Miracle* (Paris: Éditions du Seuil, 1972), and *Ti-Jean l'horizon* (Paris: Éditions du Seuil, 1979); Myriam Warner-Vieyra, *Le quimboiseur l'avait dit* (Paris: Presence Africaine, 1980), and *Juletane* (Paris: Presence Africaine, 1982).

51. Édouard Glissant, *Monsieur Toussaint,* trans. Joseph Foster and Barbara A. Franklin (Washington, D.C.: Three Continents Press, 1981).

52. Cornell West, *Race Matters* (Boston: Beacon, 1993).

53. Glissant, *Monsieur Toussaint,* 110.

54. Abdul JanMohamed, *Manichean Aesthetics* (Amherst: University of Massachusetts Press, 1993).

55. Glissant, *L'intention poétique,* 139.

56. Antonio Benítez-Rojo, *Repeating Island: The Caribbean and the Postmodern Perspective,* trans. James E. Maraniss (Durham, N.C.: Duke University Press, 1992), 199.

57. Ibid., 201.

58. Bruce Robbins, "Comparative Cosmopolitanisms," in *Cosmopolitics,* ed. Pheng Cheah and Bruce Robbins (Minneapolis: University of Minnesota Press, 1998), 246–64. There are perhaps as many pitfalls in the term *cosmopolitanism* as there are in *postcolonial,* but I will explore the insertion of a discrepant political "worldliness" that Robbins advances in my conclusion in terms of "globalization."

59. Ibid., 261.

60. Ibid., 251.

61. Barbara Harlow, *Resistance Literature* (London: Methuen, 1987).

62. This possibility is explored in a different way by Suzanne Crosta in *Le marronnage créateur: Dynamique textuelle chez Édouard Glissant* (Quebec: Laval, 1991).

Chapter 2: Brathwaite, Crossing, Voicing

1. James's conception of Caribbean identity is crucial to the readings presented here. Just as Glissant takes Martinican selfhood through creole as "nonsituated," so James argues that this lack of embeddednes is itself a lesson about the ineluctable pressures of Westernization on Caribbean being. The controversy over James's view is connected to the positive role he ascribes to Western influences. Rather than posit some prelapsarian authenticity to Caribbeanness, James starts from the "bad new things" bequeathed by modernity. For cultural studies, the crux has always been whether this deracinates counterhegemonic cultural expression as a matter of course. To some extent, the symbolic recoding that James extols in, for instance, cricket, productively accentuates the proac-

tive capacities of Caribbeanness, but he, like Glissant *and* Brathwaite, does not assume that such creativity has a cognate in the political institutions of nationhood. Instead of an idealist projection (for which we often use the term *culturalism*), James deemed that the politics of nation remained set as a semiautonomous task, while acknowledging that it required an engagement in the imaginary, whatever its institutional expression.

2. C. L. R. James, *Beyond a Boundary* (London: Hutchinson, 1963). Of course, it must be said that the "window" at issue is conditioned and overdetermined by the historical sedimentations of the British Empire, but in effect this only makes the political intervention James attempts all the more necessary. Indeed, the international "play" he analyzes is nothing less than a history of the emergence of the postcolonial subject (and one replete with many of the qualifications and contradictions that we see in other modes of postcolonial critique). One does not derive a model from such articulations of subjecthood, but a better sense of the elements of struggle at stake in Caribbean delinking from the colonial moment.

3. Kamau Brathwaite, "Letter Sycora χ," *Mother Poem* (Oxford: Oxford University Press, 1977), 83.

4. The importance here of words themselves cannot be underestimated. Elsewhere, Brathwaite notes: "It was in the language that the slave was perhaps most successfully imprisoned by his master, and it was in his (mis-)use of it that he perhaps most effectively rebelled. Within the folk tradition, language was (and is) a creative act in itself" (*The Development of Creole Society in Jamaica, 1770–1820* [Oxford: Oxford University Press, 1971], 237).

5. Kamau Brathwaite, *Barabajan Poems, 1492–1992* (New York: Savacou North, 1994), 23.

6. Ibid., 77.

7. If place is space to which meaning has been ascribed, in Brathwaite's work the Caribbean has been both inscribed and envoiced. Brathwaite's vision of this place has been a work in progress spanning several decades. Individual poems have themselves been reinscribed as Brathwaite has rethought his aesthetic and political stance on Caribbean writing. Notable works include (chronologically) *Rights of Passage* (Oxford: Oxford University Press, 1967); "Jazz and the West Indian Novel," *Bim* 44 (1967): 275–84, 45 (1967): 39–51, and 46 (1968): 115–26; *Masks* (Oxford: Oxford University Press, 1968); *Islands* (Oxford: Oxford University Press, 1969); *Contradictory Omens* (Mona, Kingston, Jamaica: Savacou, 1974); *Mother Poem; Sun Poem* (Oxford: Oxford University Press, 1982); *History of the Voice: The Development of Nation Language in Anglophone Caribbean Poetry* (London: New Beacon, 1984); *X/Self* (Oxford: Oxford University Press, 1987); "Trench Town Rock," *Hambone* 10 (Spring 1992): 123–201; *The Zea Mexican Diary, 7 Sept 1926–7 Sept 1986* (Madison: University of Wisconsin Press, 1993); *DreamStories* (Harlow, England: Longman, 1994); *Barabajan Poems*.

8. Brathwaite, *Barabajan Poems*, 228.

9. *Tidalectics* reflects both Brathwaite's penchant for punning and a poetic license in his understanding of the way that ideas and words interrelate. Like Glissant, Brathwaite

balks at the notion of the dialectic, since its Eurocentric, totalizing vision is not unconnected to forms of colonial dominion. Nevertheless, Brathwaite wants to contextualize place with thought as a way of understanding the effects of Barbados, and the Caribbean sea, on his worldview and his aesthetics. While not formulaic, tidalectics reflects the physical determinants, including those of rain and sea, that condition to some degree Brathwaite's approach to his writing within the culture of Barbados. Of course, what Brathwaite does bring to dialectics is dialect, as in creative variations of everyday speech that become a primary and lived relationship in language. Taken together, *nation language* is Brathwaite's dialectic of dialect as the language of nation, or tidalectics, for short.

10. Kamau Brathwaite, *History of the Voice: The Development of Nation Language in Anglophone Caribbean Poetry* (London: New Beacon, 1984), 13.

11. Paul Gilroy, *The Black Atlantic: Modernity and Double Consciousness* (Cambridge, Mass.: Harvard University Press, 1993), 23. Gilroy, like Fanon and James, takes seriously the implications of dialectical thinking for black liberation and discourses of decolonization.

12. Ngũgĩ wa Thiong'o, "Kamau Brathwaite: The Voice of African Presence," *World Literature Today* 68, no. 4 (Autumn 1994), 677.

13. Ernest Renan, "What Is a Nation?" trans. Martin Thom, in *Nation and Narration,* ed. Homi K. Bhabha (New York: Routledge, 1990), 8–22. Renan's "absolutely cool and impartial" approach to the question of nation has spurred a number of critiques, some of which emerge in Bhabha's volume.

14. Benedict Anderson, *Imagined Communities: Reflections on the Origin and Spread of Nationalism,* rev. ed. (New York: Verso, 1991), 200. Anderson, as noted earlier, has his detractors, but the idea here that community may require an active forgetting to maintain consensus (his example is Renan invoking massacres in French history in the service of their sublimation for a higher ideal of French nationhood) at least touches on the important ideological component of nation formation.

15. Brathwaite, *History of the Voice,* 13.

16. Ngũgĩ wa Thiong'o, "Kamau Brathwaite," 678. Ngũgĩ's essay is part of a special issue on Brathwaite in celebration of his receipt of the 1994 Neustadt Prize for Literature. Notable contributions by Abiola Irele, Abena Busia, and Brathwaite himself are also included.

17. Ibid., 679.

18. This is a tricky point, since Fanon clearly believes national consciousness to be the ward of the bourgeoisie under precise and explicable economic conditions, and that the *under*-developed nature of class relations in decolonizing states undermines precisely the production of this consciousness. No appeal to the imagination can compensate for this real foundation of the actual processes of socialization, but the crux remains whether postcolonial constituencies are condemned to go through the eye of bourgeois nationhood, or not all. Caribbeanness does not exist outside the classic conditions of class formation, but neither does it simply confirm extant models of nation identity. Fanon's argument remains pertinent not just because of the systemic pitfalls he reads in postcolonial state formations, but because he has a profound understanding of the differential con-

sciousness written into such formations. The struggle over national consciousness is also about false and corrupt representations of national leadership by elites convinced of the appropriateness and appropriations that accrue to their position. And anything that imagines this formation otherwise must in some sense be revolutionary. See Frantz Fanon, *The Wretched of the Earth,* trans. Constance Farrington (New York: Grove Press, 1991).

19. Homi K. Bhabha, "DissemiNation: Time, Narrative, and the Margins of the Modern Nation," in *Nation and Narration,* ed. Homi K. Bhabha (New York: Routledge, 1990), 297.

20. Ibid., 299.

21. I am thinking here in particular of Anderson's reading of Creole in chapter 4 of *Imagined Communities.*

22. Homi K. Bhabha, *The Location of Culture* (New York: Routledge, 1994), 86.

23. Ibid., 87.

24. Kamau Brathwaite, Prelude to *Masks,* in *The Arrivants* (Oxford: Oxford University Press, 1973), 90.

25. *X* is characteristically multivalent in Brathwaite's work, simultaneously invoking a crossed-out subjectivity and its proactive decolonizing counterpoint. It can mean "out of Africa" (as in "from") but also that which is beyond or excessive to summary notions of Caribbean being as currently constellated. The creative trickster symbolism of Sycorax extends and reconfigures a long tradition of engagement with Shakespeare's *Tempest* as itself the scene of colonizing contradictions and postcolonial possibilities, not only in the rewriting of Ariel, but also most notably in an emphasis on Caliban (Retamar and Césaire). For Brathwaite, Sycorax is almost literally a mother of invention, the exorbitant muse of otherwise centered subjectivity.

26. See Brathwaite, *History of the Voice,* for more on this topos of Caribbean poetics.

27. Brathwaite, *Barabajan Poems,* 173.

28. Ibid., 173–74. In *Barabajan Poems* Brathwaite includes an appendix on Shango train-songs.

29. Brathwaite, *DreamStories,* 729.

30. Brathwaite, "Vèvè," in *Arrivants,* 265–66.

31. Brathwaite, *Barabajan Poems,* 152.

32. Ibid., 96.

33. Brathwaite, *Sun Poem,* 104.

34. Brathwaite, *Barabajan Poems,* 96.

Chapter 3: Condé, Crossing, Errantry of Place

1. Quoted from an interview between Françoise Pfaff and Maryse Condé in Djelal Kadir, "Introduction: Being at the Other End of the World," *World Literature Today* 67, no. 4 (Autumn 1993): 695. This would seem to imply a binary of sorts, but the "other" invoked by Condé is, as we shall see, closer to a space of transgressive possibility than to an absolute of normative logic.

2. Condé defines *marronnage* in a particular way as a whole series of resistance rituals to colonial rule. The familiar criticisms of maroon identity are that it partakes of binary logic (one is either a slave or an escapee) and that there is a certain masculinist mythology embedded in the history of the maroon bravado. Condé claims this space for a more general oppositional mode: "En fait, le marronnage, c'est-à-dire le refus de la domination de l'Occident, symbolise une des constantes de l'attitude antillaise" (*Le roman antillais* [Paris: Fernand Nathan, 1977], 27) (In fact, *marronnage,* that is to say, the refusal of domination by the West, is a continuing Caribbean attitude). That Condé would later infuse this sense with a feminist politics is an extension not of the binary, but of the insurgency that the general condition indicates.

3. Jean Bernabé, Patrick Chamoiseau, and Raphael Confiant, *Éloge de la créolité* (Paris: Gallimard, 1989), available in English as "In Praise of Creoleness," trans. M. B. Taleb-Khyar, *Callaloo* 13 (1990): 886–909, republished in a bilingual edition as *Éloge de la créolité/ In Praise of Creoleness,* trans. M. B. Taleb-Khyar (Paris: Gallimard, 1993).

4. In an interview, Condé notes, "You see, you're not writing only for yourself. Of course, when you are writing, you are doing it for yourself, so you are satisfied. Once your novel is finished, you have to publish it and then you have to call for other people's attention, and when you live on a small island like Guadeloupe, nobody reads on Guadeloupe. Nobody pays attention to your work. People just know you because they see your face sometimes on TV. They don't know anything about you as a writer. They have no use for you as a writer. . . . It is very frustrating to be a West Indian writer. When you go abroad, people know you and pay more attention to you. But at the same time, they are foreigners, and they don't completely understand what you wanted to put in your book, what matters for you. There is always a kind of distance between your readers and yourself, so you are never satisfied with the impressions that you give, that you make on their minds" (Barbara Lewis, "No Silence: An Interview with Maryse Condé," *Callaloo* 18, no. 3 [1995]: 547–48). Again, like Glissant, Condé's position invites the charge that she is rationalizing an elitism that appeals mostly to Western cosmopolitans. Yet one would have to come to terms with the marked differences between Condé's literary modes of identification and the alternative alienation effects of neocolonial inclusionary desire, even if the nonassimilable in both contribute to the idea of "crossing" I have invoked.

5. Typical of this approach is Wangari Wa Nyatetu-Waigwa, "From Liminality to a Home of Her Own: The Quest Motif in Maryse Condé's Fiction," *Callaloo* 18, no. 3 (1995): 551–64. Interestingly, the same special issue of *Callaloo* on Condé contains an essay that explicitly challenges this methodology: Mireille Rosello, "Caribbean Insularization of Identities in Maryse Condé's Work: From *En attendant le bonheur* to *Les derniers rois mages,*" *Callaloo* 18, no. 3 (1995); 565–78. The question here is not really about the space of Condé's geographical mobility but the teleology that structures the time coordinates. As I argue, to investigate the process in "crossing" complicates the intersection of nation and identity made almost inevitable by traditional chronologies. (*World Literature Today,* for instance, almost always provides a chronology to accompany its special issues on in-

dividual authors, which, while convenient, steps over the question of errantry of place in the imaginary.)

6. Édouard Glissant, *Poétique de la relation* (Paris: Gallimard, 1990), 13. Available in English as *Poetics of Relation,* trans. Betsy Wing (Ann Arbor: University of Michigan Press, 1997).

7. In a special issue of *Callaloo* (15, no. 1 [1992]) on the literature of Guadeloupe and Martinique, Condé provides a brief introduction where she recognizes the continuing importance of Césaire (again, this is an instructive link with both Glissant and the advocates of créolité): "This issue could as easily be called *Césaire's Legacy,* since almost all the writers of the French Caribbean acknowledge Césaire as their spiritual father, even as they contradict or oppose him. Aimé Césaire is an essential voice in the Black World, one which made French Caribbean literature visible on the international scene. One way or another modern literary movements in the French Caribbean . . . seem to relate to the movement that Césaire illustrated half a century earlier—a movement whose brilliance still captivates the intellectual today" (1). Certainly, Césaire's influence on Condé's worldview is pronounced, but this does not mean that she has not been critical of either Césaire or Negritude in general. When Condé comments on Césaire's proposition in *Cahier d'un retour au pay natal* (Return to my native land) that one should reject European assimilation in favor of acceptance of a fully black identity, she argues: "the Negro does not exist. Europe created him expressly for the purpose of legitimizing exploitation" ("Négritude césairienne, négritude senghorienne," *Revue de la littérature comparée* 3–4 [July–December 1974]: 413). This tension between identity and assimilation complicates Condé's sense of self in a French *département d'outre mer.* More recently, Condé has reaffirmed the centrality of Césaire while contrasting this with the realities of the Caribbean diaspora ("Language and Power: Words as Miraculous Weapons," *CLA Journal* 39, no. 9 [September 1995]: 18–25).

8. Aimé Césaire, *Discourse on Colonialism,* trans. Joan Pinkham (New York: Monthly Review Press, 1972), 10.

9. The special issues on Condé in *World Literature Today* (67, no. 4 [Autumn 1993]) and *Callaloo* (18, no. 3 [1995]) trace much of Condé's biography. See also the collection of interviews conducted by Françoise Pfaff in *Conversations with Maryse Condé* (Lincoln: University of Nebraska Press, 1996), which contains extensive biographical reference material.

10. Antonio Benítez-Rojo, *The Repeating Island: The Caribbean and the Postmodern Perspective,* trans. James E. Maraniss (Durham, N.C.: Duke University Press, 1992).

11. Interestingly, Condé has been accused of misogyny in her characterization of island women in her early play *Dieu nous l'a donné* (God gave it to us). In conversation with Françoise Pfaff, she notes that the criticism emerged out of perceptions of Condé's relationship to the island, "a negative rapport with the country and the island as a womb" (*Conversations,* 35). Of course, the repetition of a negative metaphor does not necessarily confirm the truth of its ideology.

12. Terry Eagleton, "Nationalism: Irony and Commitment," in *Nationalism, Colonialism, and Literature* by Terry Eagleton, Fredric Jameson, and Edward Said (Minneapolis: University of Minnesota Press, 1990), 35. Eagleton's notes on modernist errantry are focused on James Joyce but constitute a useful reminder that European cultural formations have their own versions of crossing.

13. Maryse Condé, *Guadeloupe* (Paris: Éditions Xavier Richer, 1994). Indeed, the tourist office of Guadeloupe is thanked for its support in the production of the book. Subsequent quotations from this work will be noted by page references in the text.

14. Maryse Condé, *La vie scélérate* (Paris: Seghers, 1987), available in English as *Tree of Life*, trans. Victoria Reiter (New York: Ballantine, 1992); *Ségou: Les murailles de terre* (Paris: Laffont, 1984), available in English as *Segu*, trans. Barbara Bray (New York: Viking, 1987); and *Ségou: La terre en miettes* (Paris: Laffont, 1985), available in English as *The Children of Segu*, trans. Linda Coverdale (New York: Viking, 1989).

15. Elsewhere Condé has described this as a "pedagogy of survival in a threatening environment" (*La civilisation du bossale* [Paris: L'Harmattan, 1978], 6). I have suggested a similar tactical virtuosity in Glissant in chapter 2.

16. Benedict Anderson introduces this indeterminacy in chapter 2 of *Imagined Communities: Reflections on the Origin and Spread of Nationalism*, rev. ed. (New York: Verso, 1991) by drawing explicitly from Walter Benjamin's concept of messianic time in Walter Benjamin, *Illuminations*, trans. Harry Zohn, ed. Hannah Arendt (New York: Schocken, 1969). In *The Location of Culture* (New York: Routledge, 1994), 157–61, Homi K. Bhabha has suggested that Anderson fails to understand the temporal complexity of the sign in dissemination as a disjunction in the present continuous (which is part, at least, of the messianism in Benjamin's notion). I think this has more to do with the multiple readings that Benjamin allows than a fatal flaw in Anderson's articulation of the "imagined." Nevertheless, Bhabha's reading permits a more nuanced understanding of the temporal formulae that I would argue Condé brings to her polemical brochure and her sense of "crossing" in general.

17. Étienne Balibar, "The Nation Form," in *Race, Nation, Class: Ambiguous Identities* by Étienne Balibar and Immanuel Wallerstein (New York: Verso, 1992), 93. The ambiguities of Nation are bequeathed by its imaginary status. That this truism is a shorthand explanation for the formation of national literatures need not detain us. What is more interesting is the extent to which writers disrupt the Nation idea that is at the core of the imaginary. This where Condé, Glissant, and Brathwaite problematize the otherwise tidy colonial episteme that continues to construct the Caribbean as the Other of Western desire.

18. Pfaff, *Conversations*, 65.

19. Maryse Condé, *Hérémakhonon* (1976; reprint, Paris: Seghers, 1988), 3. Not surprisingly, Condé intends some irony in such an epigraph, which is only matched by the Mande of her title, "waiting for happiness." Veronica, the main character in the novel, returns to her "roots" in Africa to find her expectations, and her perceptions as a witness to what Africa represents, seriously challenged by the experience, which is something of Condé's biography.

20. Typical of this reading is A. James Arnold, "The Gendering of *Créolité*," in *Penser la créolité*, ed. Maryse Condé and Madeleine Cottenet-Hage (Paris: Éditions Karthala, 1995), 20–40. There is much to recommend such an approach, and indeed the gendering of créolité is absolutely necessary in order to understand the alternative concerns of women writers. Nevertheless, Arnold tends to present créolité as an either/or stratagem in which women are excluded, whereas Condé appears to want to refashion Caribbean aesthetic movements according to the specificity of her artistic needs—a kind of tactical métissage.

21. Maryse Condé, *Traversée de la mangrove* (Paris: Mercure de France, 1989), available in English as *Crossing the Mangrove*, trans. Richard Philcox (New York: Anchor, 1995). For more on literary influences, see Pfaff, *Conversations*. Faulkner clearly has also been a major inspiration for Glissant.

22. When Condé was asked whether her work could be considered "postnational," however, she asserted her privilege as a writer not to be concerned with such theoretical terms. See Marie-Agnès Sourieau, "Entretien avec Maryse Condé: De l'identité culturelle," *French Review* 72, no. 6 (May 1999): 1091–98.

23. Pfaff, *Conversations,* 72.

24. Maryse Condé, *Les derniers rois mages* (Paris: Mercure de France, 1992), available in English as *The Last of the African Kings,* trans. Richard Philcox (Lincoln: University of Nebraska Press, 1997).

25. Édouard Glissant, *Poetics of Relation,* trans. Betsy Wing (Ann Arbor: University of Michigan Press, 1997), 20–21.

Chapter 4: The White of Algeria

1. Here I mean to invoke Derrida's trenchant philosophical investigation of the *parergon* in his book *The Truth in Painting,* trans. Geoff Bennington and Ian McLeod (Chicago: University of Chicago Press, 1987).

2. Assia Djebar, *Le blanc de l'Algérie* (Paris: Albin Michel, 1995). All translations in the text are mine unless otherwise indicated. The English translation of the book is *Algerian White,* trans. David Kelley and Marjolijn De Jager (New York: Seven Stories Press, 2001).

3. Jacques Derrida, "White Mythology: Metaphor in the Text of Philosophy," in his *Margins of Philosophy,* trans. Alan Bass (Chicago: University of Chicago Press, 1984), 207–92.

4. Hélène Cixous and Catherine Clément, *The Newly Born Woman,* trans. Betsy Wing (Minneapolis: University of Minnesota Press, 1986), especially part 2. This work remains a complex cornerstone for feminism's relationship to history and postcolonial subjectivity.

5. We recall here the notion that for the writer the blankness of the page is set as a task, yet I want to maintain something of the cinematic in this task—the space off is that place beyond the screen that demarcates what is seen. Djebar, of course, is also a filmmaker, and part of the challenge in reading her is to understand her use of visual absence in the process of writing itself.

6. Here I would take issue with John Erikson's otherwise erudite reading in "Translating the Untranslated: Djebar's *Le blanc de l'Algérie,*" *Research in African Literatures* 30, no. 3 (Fall 1999): 95–107. Erikson suggests that Djebar "manages to translate the language of violence, to find that 'innerness of the word' that unifies rather than destroys. Her metaphors penetrate the layers of meaning, pierce the cover that hides an invisible layer of meaning beneath it" (106). The diction here, "unifies," "penetrate," "pierce," is oddly redolent with that phallogocentrism that the discourse of difference is meant to subtend. There remains a great aesthetic and political contrast between filling in the white and deconstructing its aura. Thus, while I would wholeheartedly agree with Erikson's nuanced understanding of the question of "the translated" in Djebar's book, I would urge a reading that maintains the disjuncture of the untranslatable in what Algeria represents, particularly where it falls on metaphors of woman.

7. It is important to note that Djebar's concern for what I will elaborate as the paroxysm of the postcolony is longstanding and predates the specific crisis precipitated by the cancelation of elections in December 1991. While the latter has clearly influenced several of her recent works (*Le blanc de l'Algérie, Vaste est la prison* [translated as *So Vast the Prison*], *Oran, langue morte* [Oran, the language of death], and *Les nuits de Strasbourg* [Strasbourg nights]), Djebar's sense of history has also taken her into the archives of Algeria's past.

8. Robert Young, *White Mythologies* (New York: Routledge, 1990), especially chapter 1.

9. Marie-Aimée Helie-Lucas, "Women, Nationalism, and Religion in the Algerian Liberation Struggle," in *Opening the Gates: A Century of Arab Feminist Writing,* ed. Margot Badran and Miriam Cooke (Bloomington: Indiana University Press, 1990), 104–14.

10. The best English-language summation of Djebar's oeuvre can be found in the special issue of *World Literature Today* (70, no. 4 [Autumn 1996]), commemorating Djebar's success in winning the 1996 Neustadt International Prize for Literature. Other significant works will be noted in passing.

11. For more on exotopy, see Peter Hitchcock, "Exotopy and Feminist Critique," in *Bakhtin: Carnival and Other Subjects,* ed. David Shepherd (Amsterdam: Rodopi Press, 1993), 194–209. "Outsideness" is a key philosophical concept in Mikhail Bakhtin, *Art and Answerability,* trans. Vadim Liapunov, ed. Michael Holquist and Vadim Liapunov (Austin: University of Texas Press, 1990). For many, exotopy remains a principle of otherness, but it is important to maintain the creative aspect of this outsideness. It is not because of Djebar's geographic location that she is able to articulate a transgredience of what Algeria represents but because she explores outsideness as an aesthetic and axiological ground. Whiteness is the space of outsideness as it comes to mean Algeria in Djebar's writing. That this is a troubled aesthetic whole is a mark of her feminist dialogism. The exotopy that allows for whiteness is also what excludes woman in Algeria's name. And this is why Djebar writes "in the white" while remaining exotopic. Simply put, she cannot identify with an aesthetic object that exists by its capacity to deny her existence.

12. See, for instance, Soheila Ghaussy, "A Stepmother Tongue: 'Feminine Writing' in Assia Djebar's *Fantasia: An Algerian Cavalcade,*" *World Literature Today* 68, no. 3 (Summer 1994): 457–62; Danielle Marx-Scouras, "Muffled Screams/Stifled Voices," *Yale French*

Studies 82 (1993): 172–82; Nadia Turk, "Assia Djebar: Voix au féminin," *Constructions* 3 (1988): 89–98; and Joanna Goodman, "L'écrit et le cri: Giving Voice in Assia Djebar's *L'amour, la fantasia,*" *Edebiyat: The Journal of Middle Eastern Literatures* 6, no. 1 (1995): 1–19. What such criticism often productively explores is the dilemma of speech in writing as a feminist and not just a philosophical difficulty.

13. This topic is a huge one, but it would be interesting to track how thinkers like Derrida, Cixous, and Lyotard steer the Scylla and Charybdis of writing and voice as a postcolonial *de*-scription. While the privileging of voice within Western metaphysics has been rightfully critiqued, the question of voice in, say, Algerian culture offers a different order of "being," one with which such philosophers must surely be familiar.

14. Mikhail Bakhtin's prescient discussion of "utterance boundaries" can be found in *Speech Genres and Other Late Essays,* trans. Vern McGee, ed. Caryl Emerson and Michael Holquist (Austin: University of Texas Press, 1986), 92–94, quotation from 93. Here I use Bakhtin's discussion to interrogate the problematic borders of the Nation State.

15. Djebar, *Algerian White.* In it an extended "in memoriam" links her recently murdered fellow writers to other celebrated members of Algeria's literary history. The effect is of a deeply committed song of protest.

16. Assia Djebar, *Vaste est la prison* (Paris: Albin Michel, 1995), available in English as *So Vast the Prison,* trans. Betsy Wing (New York: Seven Stories, 1999). All translations in the text are mine unless otherwise indicated.

17. Marnia Lazreg, *The Eloquence of Silence* (New York: Routledge, 1994), 201. Lazreg's critique of women in Algerian cultural and political life is salutary and necessary. All I disagree with here is her characterization of Djebar's work. Djebar too has contributed to "women's rise to the word" as Lazreg investigates it.

18. Djebar has written a poem that ponders the space between writing and the violence of this "event." Assia Djebar, "RAIS, BENTALHA . . . Un an après," translated by Marjolijn de Jager as "RAIS, BENTALHA . . . A year later," both published in a special issue on Algeria in *Research in African Literatures* 30, no. 3 (Fall 1999): 7–14.

19. This operates at several levels, not just in the way Djebar's writing breaks from Algerian forms of masculinism, but also in the disjunction she figures in the relationship of Western and Algerian women (seen, for instance, in her short story "Women of Algiers in Their Apartment"). For more on Djebar's sense of this disjunction, see the afterword by Clarisse Zimra (which includes an interview not available in the French edition) in Assia Djebar, *Women of Algiers in Their Apartment,* trans. Marjolijn de Jager (Charlottesville: University Press of Virginia, 1992), 159–211.

20. Mildred Mortimer, *Journeys through the French African Novel* (London: Heinemann, 1990), 147–64. Mortimer argues that Djebar explores the space between two languages by writing the Arabic voice into French. This, of course, could be read into much Maghrebi Francophonic writing, but the key here is in the transposition of women's voices in the decolonization of French and, by implication, the Maghreb. Significantly, Mortimer also analyzes how this reinscription is simultaneously a struggle over women's space. See, in particular, Mildred Mortimer, *Assia Djebar* (Philadelphia: CELFAN Monographs, 1988).

21. For more on the contradictions of Arabization, see John Ruedy, *Modern Algeria* (Bloomington: Indiana University Press, 1992), especially chapter 7. What Djebar "loathes" is not only the patriarchal norms that gird aspects of the Arabic language but also the fact that the privileging of Arabic is made at great cost to Kabyle and other Berber languages. The situation is complicated, however, since historically the Kabyles themselves were the most inclined to Francophonie under colonialism and in general held higher social ranks than the other indigenous groups. Clearly, Arabization was in part aimed at the privilege that had accompanied the use of French.

22. M'hamed Alaoui Abdalaoui, "The Moroccan Novel in French," trans. Jeffrey S. Ankrom, *Research in African Literatures* 23, no. 4 (1992): 31.

23. This is a controversial topic that cannot be settled here, but it remains difficult for Maghrebi women themselves to articulate an oppositional politics without reference to the forms of oppression that structure their lived realities. Lazreg's main target is, of course, Western feminism and its religion/tradition paradigm where Arab women are concerned. The argument is a forceful one and is unresolved (if not unresolvable) within the scholarship on this issue. See Marnia Lazreg, "Feminism and Difference: The Perils of Writing as a Woman on Women in Algeria," *Feminist Studies* 14, no. 1 (Spring 1988): 81–107. See also Peter Hitchcock, *Dialogics of the Oppressed* (Minneapolis: University of Minnesota Press, 1993), especially chapter 2.

24. Assia Djebar, *L'amour, la fantasia* (Paris: Jean Lattès, 1985), available in English as *Fantasia: An Algerian Cavalcade,* trans. Dorothy S. Blair (London: Quartet Books, 1989); and Djebar, *Ombre sultane* (Paris: Jean Lattès, 1987), available in English as *A Sister to Scheherazade,* trans. Dorothy S. Blair (London: Quartet Books, 1987).

25. H. Adlai Murdoch, "Rewriting Writing: Identity, Exile, and Renewal in Assia Djebar's *L'amour, la fantasia,*" *Yale French Studies* 83 (1993): 71–92. I would read Djebar's textual practice as outlined by Murdoch as a *de*-scription rather than a rewriting, although the general strategies of displacement pinpointed are surely the sine qua non of postcolonial subjecthood. See also Jenny Sharpe, *Allegories of Empire* (Minneapolis: University of Minnesota Press, 1993).

26. Edward Blaquière, introduction to *Narrative of a Residence in Algiers* by Filippo Pananti (London: Colborn, 1818), 4.

27. Assia Djebar, *Loin de Médine* (Paris: Albin Michel, 1991), available in English as *Far from Medina,* trans. Dorothy Blair (London: Quartet Books, 1993). For an informative discussion of this book and an interview with Assia Djebar, see Clarisse Zimra, "'When the Past Answers the Present,'" *Callaloo* 16, no. 1 (1993): 116–31.

28. See Leila Ahmed, *Women and Gender in Islam* (New Haven, Conn.: Yale University Press, 1992).

29. Bakhtin, *Speech Genres,* 170.

30. Hafid Gafaiti, "The Blood of Writing," *World Literature Today* 70, no. 4 (Autumn 1996): 819.

31. Assia Djebar, "The White of Algeria," trans. Andrew Benson, *Yale French Studies* 87 (1995): 147–48.

32. Helie-Lucas, ""Women, Nationalism, and Religion," 113.

33. Ibid.

34. Djebar, "The White of Algeria," 142.

35. Djebar, *Le blanc de l'Algérie,* 271.

36. Derrida, "White Mythology," 254.

37. Homi K. Bhabha, "Introduction: Narrating the Nation," in *Nation and Narration,* ed. Homi K. Bhabha (New York: Routledge, 1990), 1.

38. Gafaiti, "The Blood of Writing," 821.

39. Clarisse Zimra, "Not So Far from Medina," *World Literature Today* 70, no. 4 (Autumn 1996): 827–28.

40. Djebar, "The White of Algeria," 142.

Chapter 5: Chronotope of the Shoe (Two)

I originally conceived this chapter as the second version of an article I had written on the fetishism of shoes. As if to underline the contradictory psychic aura I invoke in this piece, that desire also spawned several conference papers and a round-table discussion that took the study in very different directions (one of which appears in my *Oscillate Wildly*). Thus, while this version remains focused on imagination and transnationalism, the "two" remains an integer of shoes themselves (they come in pairs) as well as a specific chronology in the project.

1. Karl Marx, *Capital,* vol. 1, trans. Ben Fowkes (New York: Penguin, 1976), 163.

2. The main reason for this is primarily the shoe's contradictory status within and between commodity fetishism and its psychosocial cognates. This is a huge and separate debate in its own right, and one that dances among the lines that follow. For a wideranging and suggestive collection in this regard, see Emily Apter and William Pietz, eds., *Fetishism as Cultural Discourse* (Ithaca, N.Y.: Cornell University Press, 1993). Appropriately, the cover of this book features a pair of shoes bound tightly together—it's an illustration by Mary Kelly entitled "Supplication."

3. Here I allude to Jacques Derrida's reading of Martin Heidegger in "Restitutions of the Truth in Pointing [*pointure*]," in *The Truth in Painting,* trans. Geoffrey Bennington and Ian McCleod (Chicago: University of Chicago Press, 1987). In general, I use Lacan's interpretation of Jones on aphanisis to underline the difference between the meaning that is ascribed to the commodity and the "disappearance" of the labor that marks its very possibility. The "fading" of the worker as subject is a function of her relationship to the commodity form under capitalism.

4. The geopolitical imagination eschews the totalizing impulse of the dialectic at the same time as it resists the aestheticizing tendencies of the dialogic. If this imagination is indeed "representable," the commodity under transnational capitalism is its most prescient instance.

5. Part of this reevaluation is manifest in the work of William Pietz, particularly in a series of articles entitled "The Problem of the Fetish" published in *Res: A Journal of Aes-*

thetics and Anthropology 9 (Spring 1985): 12–13, 13 (Spring 1987): 23–45, and 16 (Autumn 1988): 105–23, and in his essay "Fetishism and Materialism" in *Fetishism As Cultural Discourse,* ed. William Pietz and Emily Apter (Ithaca, N.Y.: Cornell University Press, 1993), 119–51. I must say, however, that Pietz's general rejection of what he characterizes as "semiological" readings of Marx on fetishism seriously underestimates the significance of the imagination and the imaginary in commodity desire. The affective responsibility I explore is predicated on a materialist approach to semiosis.

6. This, of course, is not how Bakhtin uses *responsibility,* which, in his early essays at least, is a means to foreground an ethical responsibility in aesthetics that is often antagonistic to the neo-Kantian Marburg school from which Bakhtin nevertheless drew sustenance. For Bakhtin's sense of responsibility ("answerability"), see his *Art and Answerability,* trans. Vadim Liapunov, ed. Michael Holquist and Vadim Liapunov (Austin: University of Texas Press, 1990). What I will attempt to do with both Bakhtinian answerability and chronotope is reinscribe them within an economy of difference that does not resolve itself in an aesthetic "ought." The globalization of commodity culture answers traditional notions of authoring with the magic of the fetish: It "speaks" to them. But it also marks out new territories of practical engagement for the academic, for whom responsibility cannot remain an "academic" inquiry. For this sense of responsibility, see, for instance, Gayatri Chakravorty Spivak, "Responsibility," *boundary* 2 (Fall 1994): 19–64.

7. See Mikhail Bakhtin, "Forms of Time and of the Chronotope in the Novel: Notes towards a Historical Poetics," in *The Dialogic Imagination,* trans. Caryl Emerson and Michael Holquist, ed. Michael Holquist (Austin: University of Texas Press, 1981), 84–258. The chronotope has engendered intense disputes among Bakhtinians. My effort here is to accentuate its spatial possibilities in the critique of the commodity form.

8. See Michael Holquist, *Dialogism: Bakhtin and His World* (London: Routledge, 1990), 108–25.

9. Bakhtin, "Forms of Time," 253.

10. Katerina Clark and Michael Holquist, *Mikhail Bakhtin* (Cambridge, Mass.: Harvard University Press, 1984), 278.

11. Bakhtin, "Forms of Time," 280.

12. Fredric Jameson, *Postmodernism; or, The Cultural Logic of Late Capitalism* (Durham, N.C.: Duke University Press, 1991).

13. Gayatri Chakravorty Spivak, "Can the Subaltern Speak?" in *Marxism and the Interpretation of Culture,* ed. Cary Nelson and Lawrence Grossberg (Urbana: University of Illinois Press, 1988), 271–313.

14. The culture of sport is very big business in the United States: even in the early 1990s it already represented a market of more than $60 billion.

15. Donald Katz, *Just Do It: The Nike Spirit in the Corporate World* (New York: Random House, 1994), 9. Subsequent references to this work (New York: New Press, 1998), 149–53. The latter is a symptom of precisely the greater affective responsibility that this study envisages.

18. In addition to the book by Katz, Nike has been eulogized and criticized in J. B.

Strasser and Laurie Becklund, *Swoosh: The Unauthorized Story of Nike and the Men Who Played There* (New York: Harper, 1993). The "swoosh" is Nike's trademark—vaguely reminiscent of the goddess's wing but more evocative of a secret diacritic. Such is the brand recognition of Nike that it can market all manner of shoes and clothing merely by adding the "swoosh."

19. These figures are reported in Andrew Hsiao, "Standing Up to the Swoosh," *Village Voice*, 10 October 2000, 41–43.

20. Jameson, *Postmodernism;* Arif Dirlik, "The Postcolonial Aura," *Critical Inquiry* 20 (Winter 1994): 329–56.

21. While late capitalism does not display the same cultural codes as in the age of European imperialism, the objectification of Asia as a market is not far removed from such an ideology. Interestingly, Phil Knight, the CEO of Nike, is something of a collector of "oriental" objets d'art, and his office is designed and decked out in traditional Japanese style. See Edward Said, *Orientalism* (London: Penguin, 1978).

22. See Fredric Jameson, *The Geopolitical Aesthetic: Cinema and Space in the World System* (Bloomington: Indiana University Press, 1992), 2. Subsequent references to this work will be noted in the text as GA followed by a page number.

23. For instance, a Bakhtinian reading of the postmodern might find virtual reality an electronic adventure time, what Bakhtin calls a "pure digression from the normal course of life," which is "characterized by a technical, abstract connection between space and time, by the reversibility of moments in a temporal sequence, and by this interchangeability of space" (Mikhail Bakhtin, *The Dialogic Imagination,* ed. Michael Holquist, trans. Michael Holquist and Caryl Emerson [Austin: University of Texas Press, 1981], 100). Again, this is another way to read Bakhtinian chronotope beyond the confines of his own examples at the same time as it highlights the transhistorical impulse it fosters.

24. This, therefore, is not a humanist response to the inhumanity of the commodity for the worker. In *Capital*, vol. 1, Marx is quite explicit about the twofold character of embodied labor in the commodity and its connection to the socialization of consciousness. The issue of embodied labor must be kept separate from that of the worker as commodity, or as an exploitable cost of production.

25. Nike also makes/has made athletic shoes in South Korea, Taiwan, Vietnam, Bangladesh, and China. These countries may be interchangeable for transnational capital but they are not for this argument.

26. See Aijaz Ahmad, *In Theory* (London: Verso, 1992), 97. A further problem, as Ahmad well knows, is that even if one focuses one's critique in relation to a national paradigm, the necessary expertise calls into question the globalism of the critique itself, and not just the blithe country hopping of the TNC. The answerability of theory is bound by a cognitive shortfall, one that prescribes and denatures even the most ardent openness to global others.

27. The U.S. Central Intelligence Agency's role in this is still hotly debated (it was clearly involved in the civil war of the 1950s), as are the consequences for American foreign policy in the aftermath of the genocide that swept Indonesia at that time (the estimates of

murdered PKI members, sympathizers, and anti-Suharto supporters of all persuasions range from 250,000 to one million). By 1967 Sukarno's power was effectively nullified and opposition to Suharto had either "disappeared" or was languishing in prison (in the late 1960s Indonesia could boast more than 100,000 political prisoners). A critical account of the coup is provided in Benedict R. O'G. Anderson and R. T. McVey, *A Preliminary Analysis of the October 1, 1965, Coup in Indonesia* (Ithaca, N.Y.: Cornell University Press, 1971). A useful, if general, reading of the period can be found in Robert Cribb and Colin Brown, *Modern Indonesia* (London: Longman, 1995).

28. We are still too close to the events of 1998–99 in East Timor to gauge the success of East Timorese independence. At that time, the Indonesian military and its sponsored thugs, usually termed "militia," officially withdrew from East Timor and a UN peace-keeping contingent led by Australia took up positions in Dili, the capital, and elsewhere. Little, if any, mention was made of Western, particularly American, machinations in the invasion of 1975 (or, for instance, the military and economic support provided by Australia to Suharto's regime afterward). Indeed, the international community has trodden gingerly over the issue of Indonesian violence in the region in order to maintain its sinuous ties to Indonesia's far more important geopolitical economy. Again, this schema of desire and disavowal (with its attendant diplomatic amnesia) is deeply embedded in the logic of globalization. For a polemical critique of the Indonesia invasion of East Timor, see Matthew Jardine, *East Timor: Genocide in Paradise* (Tucson, Ariz.: Odonian Press, 1995).

29. To borrow from Benedict Anderson's famous formulation, the Pancasila are about as good an example of how communities get "imagined" as one could find (the principles are belief in God, national unity, humanitarianism, people's sovereignty, and social justice and prosperity). Sukarno kept them sufficiently vague to smooth over the obvious divisions that racked the Indonesian archipelago in the aftermath of colonization. If the geopolitical imagination merely replays the deficiencies of the imagined community epitomized in the Pancasila, then it must fail as an adequate critical apparatus.

30. See, for instance, D. Cherchichovsky and O. E. Meesook, *Poverty in Indonesia: A Profile* (Washington, D.C.: World Bank, 1984); and C. Iluch, *Indonesia: Wages and Employment* (Washington, D.C.: World Bank, 1985).

31. Consider the World Bank monograph *Indonesia: Strategy for a Sustained Reduction in Poverty* (Washington, D.C.: World Bank, 1990). The World Bank reports that in 1987 30 million Indonesians lived in poverty (17 percent of the population at that time). Indonesia had one of the lowest per capita incomes, lowest life expectancy, and lowest number of doctors per capita in the world (1 doctor for 9,460 people). The World Bank recommends that, because of the limited feasibility of expanding Indonesia's rice farming, the country embark on a course of light industrial, labor-intensive manufacturing. Several years later (and millions of Nike shoes), the World Bank reports (in *Indonesia: Environment and Development* [Washington, D.C.: World Bank, 1994]), that the problem is overindustrialization from the expansion and inclusion of the workforce in manufacturing (by the end of the decade, this represented 45 percent of Indonesia's GDP). The World Bank asks where Indonesia is going to get the foreign capital to sustain such an industri-

al workforce and wonders at the same time whether the severe pollution (particularly on Java) is a catastrophe waiting to happen. Income, life expectancy, and the number of doctors have all improved, but these reports reveal that the World Bank, foreign governments, and foreign corporations have all played a part in exacerbating underlying systemic problems in Indonesia. The effects of greater pollution, for instance, and indeed of industrialization in general, may well lower life expectancy in the years to come. While there is little rigidity to developmental models in Asia, the experience of urban centers like Jakarta and Taibei might give the World Bank some pause about the prospects of Beijing or Shanghai.

32. Unless the selling of a representation itself is at stake. While there is no space here to detail the intricacies of "cultural diplomacy," it is clear that the Indonesian government has attempted in the past to sell an image of the nation that provides a cultural compensation for its otherwise authoritarian operations—and that foreign governments and corporations are entirely complicit with this process (since to overlook a massacre or two might garner economic preferences). See, for instance, Clifford Geertz's trenchant assessment of the "Festival of Indonesia" in the United States in 1991 in "The Year of Living Culturally," *New Republic,* 21 October 1991, 30–36; and Brian Wallis, "Selling Nations," *Art in America* 79 (September 1991): 85–91.

33. One of the best English-language studies is provided by Benedict R. O'G. Anderson, *Language and Power: Exploring Political Cultures in Indonesia* (Ithaca, N.Y.: Cornell University Press, 1990). See also J. D. Legge, *Indonesia* (Sydney: Prentice Hall of Australia, 1980); and Leslie Palmier, ed., *Understanding Indonesia* (Aldershot, England: Gower, 1985).

34. For instance, the infamous *Cultuurstelsel,* or Forced Cultivation System (which basically paid for the Netherlands' debts, costs of war, and public works programs *in Holland* from 1830 to 1869), is an object lesson in colonial excess *and* modes of labor exploitation in Indonesia.

35. Sigmund Freud, "Fetishism," trans. Joan Riviere, in vol. 21 of *The Standard Edition of the Complete Psychological Works of Sigmund Freud* (London: Hogarth, 1961), 154.

36. Most of the innovative work in this area does not just take issue with the normative function that Freud provides for this "minor perversion" but unpicks the model of masculinity it seems to imply. This includes feminist appropriations and renegotiations that, while not necessarily complementary, have "feminized the fetish" in significant ways. See, for instance, Donald Kuspit, "The Modern Fetish," *Artforum,* October 1988, 132–40, in which he argues that some contemporary women artists fetishistically mimic the phallic mother in order to attach the power of birth to the creation of their objects. Researching the *aliénistes* (as the nineteenth-century French psychiatrists often called themselves), Jann Matlock reinterprets the phenomenon of women as clothing fetishists in "Delirious Disguises, Perverse Masquerades, and the Ghostly Female Fetishist," *Grand Street* (Summer 1995): 157–71. In a highly original reading of fetishism's economic and psychic interrelations, Linda Williams explores how ambivalent phallocentrism can structure even the conventional masculinist narratives of hardcore pornography in "Fetishism

and the Visual Pleasure of Hard Core: Marx, Freud, and the 'Money Shot,'" *Quarterly Review of Film and Video* 11, no. 2 (1989): 23–42.

37. Emily Apter, *Feminizing the Fetish* (Ithaca, N.Y.: Cornell University Press, 1991), 2.

38. And these are many, especially as they slide into and contradict Marx's metaphors for ideology. For a provocative reading of the function of metaphor for Marx's concepts, see W. J. T. Mitchell, *Iconography: Image, Text, Ideology* (Chicago: University of Chicago Press, 1986). While not subscribing to a Marxist position, Mitchell is careful to distinguish the tactical, historical deployment of metaphors in Marx's arguments. What can and cannot be seen in the commodity fetish remains vital to the present polemic but as an indication of a continuing dissymmetry between visualization and imagination.

39. Jean Baudrillard, *Simulations,* trans. Paul Foss, Paul Patton, and Philip Beitchman (New York: Semiotext[e], 1983).

40. Jameson, *Postmodernism.* Subsequent references to this work will be noted in the text as PM followed by a page number.

41. Martin Heidegger, "The Origin of the Work of Art," trans. Albert Hofstadter, in *Basic Writings,* ed. David Farrell Krell (New York: Harper Collins, 1993), 143–212.

42. See, for instance, Haynes Horne, "Jameson's Strategies of Containment" in *Post-modernism/Jameson/Critique,* ed. Douglas Kellner (Washington, D.C.: Maisonneuve Press, 1989), 268–300.

43. Walter Benjamin, *Illuminations,* trans. Harry Zohn, ed. Hannah Arendt (New York: Schocken, 1969), 255.

44. Derrida, "Restitutions of the Truth in Pointing," 256. Subsequent references to this work will be noted in the text as RT followed by a page number.

45. Marx, *Capital,* 1:163.

46. It seems to me that "pointing" underestimates the sexual economy of shoes in comparison to "pricking." True, a prick was an early form of the knitting needle, and pricking also once referred to embroidery of certain kinds, but there is more evidence in English for an excess of signification than perhaps the French word allows. Pricking, for instance, might describe the process by which leather is stitched (the result is called a "prick stitch"), but it is also a mental operation, not just in pricking one's conscience, but also in the infliction of mental pain. Similarly, a prick is a dot or metrical mark in literature and music, but also a less writerly puncture in the sole of the foot of a horse. Just in case this seem too far removed from the principle of the chronotope, one should add that a prick is both a point of space, a geometrical point, and the smallest portion of time—an instant. Indeed, in one of its meanings, prick is the precise instant at which anything happens: It is the critical moment. In the sixteenth century, prick was a vulgar term of endearment, but in the twentieth it became a particular term of abuse for a man. Finally, in the seventeenth century one could test whether a woman were a witch by pricking her until one found a spot that did not bleed, but more recently pricking could mean the magical act of writing itself. Of this surplus of signification shoes indeed might be made. See the *Oxford English Dictionary,* 2d ed. (Oxford: Oxford University Press, 1991).

47. It is highly appropriate in this regard that young males, the primary consumers of

athletic shoes, face a wall of single shoes when exercising their consumer choice. True, this is a general feature of the mass consumption of shoes (to display pairs invites shoplifting), but this will have a particular valence for the consumer of athletic shoes, as a later example will accentuate.

48. I will make more of this transparency in a moment. The function of Cinderella's foot in a phallic economy of presence continues to garner critical attention. See Susanne Sara Thomas, "'Cinderella' and the Phallic Foot: The Symbolic Significance of the Tale's Slipper Motif," *Southern Folklore* 52, no. 1 (1995): 19–51.

49. Indeed, the proletarianization of Asian women emphasizes either dexterity or eyesight and often both. For a keen analysis of the treatment of women workers under transnational capitalism, see Annette Fuentes and Barbara Ehrenreich, *Women in the Global Factory* (Boston: South End Press, 1983).

50. The disciplinary zeal of the managers is reinforced by the ideological underpinnings of the Pancasila, which encourage dutiful submission and *ibuism,* the belief that a woman should primarily act as a mother without demanding power or prestige in return. Clearly, women workers have resisted every element of this desire, despite the threat of wage cuts or dismissal.

51. Yet the higher Nike's profile, the more vocal the resistance against such business practices has become. For capitalist investors, however, Nike is an exemplary organization. In 1993 *Money* magazine included Nike in a list of six American companies who offered investors returns of up to 47 percent per annum. See Ellen Stark, "Making Money on America's Top Money," *Money,* June 1993, 114–17.

52. The conservative reinterpretation of the Pancasila as a document that supports patriarchy is detailed in Cribb and Brown, *Modern Indonesia.* For an important essay on the enlistment of young peasant women into the Indonesian industrial workforce, see Diane L. Wolf, "Linking Women's Labor with the Global Economy: Factory Workers and Their Families in Rural Java," in *Women Workers and Global Restructuring,* ed. Kathryn Ward (Ithaca, N.Y.: Cornell University Press, 1990), 25–47. In *Factory Daughters* (Berkeley: University of California Press, 1992) Wolf has written one of the most extensive and detailed analyses of the effect of globalization on Javanese women workers. For some pertinent discussion of the cultural representations of the effects of the Pancasila for women, see Tineke Hellwig, *In the Shadow of Change: Images of Women in Indonesian Literature* (Berkeley: University of California Press, 1994).

53. See Jeffrey Ballinger, "The New Free Trade Heel," *Harper's Magazine,* August 1992, 46–47. In 1993 Ballinger appeared in a special edition of "Street Stories" on CBS that focused on Nike's operations in Indonesia. Ironically, the main factory featured was about the cleanest shoe manufacturing plant on the planet. Nevertheless, the program reported that a strike at another Indonesian plant had resulted in twenty-two workers being "suspended," and it did document the practice of confining the women workers to the plant dormitories. Katz (*Just Do It*) provides plenty of details on this and other evidence of Nike's misdeeds in Asia, but his critique remains a long way from condemnation.

54. Quoted in Strasser and Becklund, *Swoosh,* 501.

55. It also reminds the business community of Nike's economic vulnerability. Michael Janofsky, for instance, recalls the misfortune of Quincy Watt, the American runner, whose Nike shoes came apart during a race at the world track and field championships in Stuttgart in August 1993. Watt, an Olympic champion, finished fourth. Janofsky uses this as an occasion to discuss a quarter in which Nike's earnings dropped. He suggests that "Just Do It" be amended to "Just Glue It." See Michael Janofsky, "Market Place," *New York Times,* 24 September 1993, D6.

56. Much of Ballinger's activism on Nike in Indonesia is recorded in Jeff Ballinger and Claes Olsson, eds., *Behind the Swoosh: The Struggle of Indonesians Making Nike Shoes* (Uppsala: Global Publications Foundation, 1997).

57. Shaw's book provides a fairly detailed chapter on the human- and labor-rights campaigns directed at Nike in the 1990s as part of a general argument on new forms of activism in the United States. See Randy Shaw, *Reclaiming America: Nike, Clean Air, and the New National Activism* (Berkeley: University of California Press, 1999).

58. This is a subtext that runs through the collection *No Sweat,* ed. Andrew Ross (New York: Verso, 1997). The campaign against sweatshop practices in the United States has achieved numerous victories, but, as Ross points out, eradicating the worst excesses of the fashion industry does not remove the tyranny of substandard wages as a whole in clothing and shoe production. And, given the sharp mobility of contemporary transnational corporations, continued vigilance must be maintained to ensure that subcontracting does not simply reproduce sweatshop conditions in a new location. The latter is a major reason for a company to go global in the first place.

59. See Hsiao, "Standing Up to the Swoosh," 43.

60. For more on the cultlike campus at Beaverton, see James Servin, "Camp Nike: It's Not a Job, It's a Lifestyle," *Harper's Bazaar,* June 1994, 46–48. In another odd twist in economic history, a psychology professor suggests that the model for the Nike World Campus was the athletic sports camps provided in Eastern Europe under Communism!

61. See Kate Bednarski, "Convincing Male Managers to Target Women Customers," *Working Woman,* June 1993, 23–24, 28. Not surprisingly, the language of this article is generally in step with capitalist consciousness. There is no recognition, for instance, that Nike had been "targeting" women workers for quite some time. In effect, the women managers disavow the women workers just like their male counterparts, although that is not the same as saying that a woman's identification with the shoe is simply the equivalent of male fetishism; it is to acknowledge, however, that male fetishism is hegemonic. For an article that reconnects the woman as producer to woman as consumer, see Cynthia Enloe, "The Globetrotting Sneaker," *Ms.,* March–April 1995, 10–15. For more on this form of global critique, see Cynthia Enloe, *The Morning After: Sexual Politics at the End of the Cold War* (Berkeley: University of California Press, 1993).

62. Katz (*Just Do It,* 130) describes a process of invention at Nike World Campus that is indistinguishable from artistic reverie and is nurtured "in a general ambience of youthful, free-associative creativity that is invariably tempered by some flavor of sophisticated wit."

63. On this point, labor is the deciding factor: "No matter how inspired a new techni-

cal design, style statement, or marketing campaign, the entire industry's productive processes were still based on how fast the women in Pusan, South Korea, and Indonesia could glue together by hand up to twenty-five pieces of a single shoe" (ibid., 174).

64. Vietnam and Bangladesh are more recent additions to this game.

65. The factory dormitories are widespread, but this has been a particular feature of Nike's Chinese operations. The retort has been that this is for "security reasons" and has nothing to do with the fear that the workers might become romantically involved, want to start families, or even choose another line of work.

66. See Mark Clifford, "Spring in Their Step," *Far Eastern Economic Review*, 5 November 1992, 56–57. The title refers to Nike's practice of hopping from one Asian country to the next in search of cheap labor.

67. None of this is particularly surprising for a capitalist organization. Nike's annual reports detail several other practices that may or may not abide by the rules of risk management for capital. The company uses both derivatives and hedging as financial instruments, both of which are subject to greater extremes of volatility than are most accounting practices. Interestingly, in fiscal 1997, Nike issued about $300 million of debt securities, the proceeds from which were swapped into Dutch guilders, ostensibly to smooth the financing of European operations. Since the company also hedges using currency contracts, it might be interesting to trace the life of these guilders. Obviously, that the Dutch were the primary colonial force in Indonesia is an irony easily missed by Nike's accountants.

68. For more on the culture of killing for sportswear, see Rick Telander, "Senseless," *Sports Illustrated*, 14 May 1990, 36–49. See also Katz, *Just Do It*, 268–70. On Tuesday, 19 December 1995, in New York a man went berserk in a shoe store after being told that the Nike hightops he had ordered had not yet arrived. He pulled out a 9mm pistol and shot dead five people. The man had been previously diagnosed with schizophrenia. While Nike cannot be blamed for individual acts of madness like this, a culture of active responsibility does not resolve itself in the mere fact of diagnosis.

69. See, for instance, Wiley M. Woodward, "It's More Than Just the Shoes," *Black Enterprise*, November 1990, 17.

70. My point here is simply that such speech does not constitute the truth of the commodity, not that testimony is irrelevant.

71. Heidegger, "Origin of the Work of Art," 161, claims the Van Gogh painting "spoke" the Being of the thing, the product-being in the shoes. Jameson's comment that Warhol's "Diamond-Dust Shoes" "doesn't really speak to us at all" implies that Van Gogh's effort does (PM 8). And Derrida's entire investigation is about how the truth "speaks" in painting. Derrida suggests that Heidegger makes the peasant shoes "speak"—once they are painted, "these shoes talk" (RT 323). My point is that these figures of speech are written into the product-being of commodity fetishism.

72. Indeed, the rise in popularity of rugged "outdoor" shoes and boots has already redrawn the athletic shoe market. Nike, of course, has switched production accordingly and expanded its focus on apparel. It also experimented with another slogan, "I can," which carries enough existential baggage to rewrite this chronotope again.

73. Nicholas D. Kristof and Sheryl WuDunn, "Two Cheers for Sweatshops," *New York Times Magazine,* 24 September 2000, 70–71.

74. Bakhtin, "Forms of Time," 84.

Chapter 6: Joe

I have adapted my title from Heinrich Eduard Jacob's *Coffee: The Epic of a Commodity,* trans. Eden and Cedar Paul (New York: Viking Press, 1935). Jacob's book (a literal translation from the German would be "Myth and the Triumphal March of Coffee") is an extraordinary account of coffee's past. Part history, part folklore, part fiction, and part cultural critique, Jacob's story of coffee raises commodity narrative to the status of a literary genre. With sections titled "The Island Realm of the Dutch" and "Soil, Empire, and the Labor Problem," there is much that is of interest for the present study. There are also obvious differences. One of Jacob's theses is that coffee is Islamic wine and that its cultural significance complements the Judeo-Christian focus on alcoholic wine. This leads him to question, for instance, the dualism in Nietzsche's Dionysus and Apollo. Here I will link coffee to a specific economic order and the emergence of transnational trade, and the philosophy at issue is Kant's. If I prefer "architectonic" over "epic" it is because of the former's function in the analysis of a global imaginary over the latter's inscription within the story of nation.

1. I am drawing here from Theodor W. Adorno, *Aesthetic Theory,* trans. Robert Hullot-Kentor (Minneapolis: University of Minnesota Press, 1997), 118. Adorno is a very unlikely touchstone for the following argument, since the commodity I have in mind is linked to the popular in ways that he might find deadening on the brain. Two points are pertinent, however: first, what Adorno says of the artwork is not outside what the commodity means in terms of spirit—the aesthetic of the modern is coterminous with commodification; second, capital obviously necessitates the projection of the incomprehensible in order for the commodity to circulate. In this sense, the task is not to understand the aestheticization of the commodity, but is rather to provide a working knowledge of that which is immanent to the commodity form and which does not allow for handy rationalization at the level of hermeneutics. Adorno's text reads: "The task of aesthetics is not to comprehend artworks as hermeneutical objects; in the contemporary situation, it is their incomprehensibility that needs to be comprehended" (ibid., 118). My suggestion is that the operation whereby the real emigrates to the imagination and becomes conscious of its own unreality, in Adorno's parlance, is the very logic of spirit that permits commodification in general to proceed. True, artistic imagination and commodity imagination must be differentiated, but not in such a way that the material embeddedness of one is lost to the spiritual waywardness of the other.

2. Walter Benjamin, *Illuminations,* trans. Harry Zohn, ed. Hannah Arendt (New York: Schocken, 1969), 256. Here I hope to brush the history of coffee against the grain or, more appropriately, against the seed.

3. Just as there is a conceit in Adorno's viewpoint in *Aesthetic Theory* (since he will make much of the superfluous in his own argument), so the incomprehensible of the commodity

is masked by its rational thingness, a thingness that is itself a composite of abstraction and extraction with an understandable materiality. (I should add that this holds true whether the commodity is a material object or something that has been commodified, like a service in a service economy, for instance.)

4. Honoré de Balzac, "Traité des excitants modernes," <http://www.bmlisieux.com>, my translation. This is a fascinating essay by Balzac whose comments on coffee are often misquoted in English translation because of the reliance on Ukers's hasty précis in the first edition of *All about Coffee* (New York: Tea and Coffee Trade Journal, 1922). Balzac is attempting to understand how the absorption of five substances (alcohol, sugar, tea, coffee, and tobacco) is altering, in an unappreciated way, the characteristics of modern society. He suggests that because civilization produces tranquility, the social "man" of civilized societies will seek excess (which is in part a commentary on romanticism and an ironic footnote to a very turbulent period in European history). If one wonders why Balzac uses militaristic imagery to describe the effects of coffee, one need look no further than his quote from Napoleon: "war is a natural state." While Balzac sometimes opts for what today would be called "pop" psychology, his treatise remains a notable historical document on the relationship between recreational substances and modernity.

5. Ukers, *All about Coffee*, ix. This and all subsequent references will be to the second edition (1935). Ukers's book is easily the most informative single-volume book on coffee (it is the *Ulysses* of coffee books), but any euphoria that one may have for its compendious extravagances must be tempered by the circumstances of its production: It is itself a symptom of the "Pan American Coffee Bureau" that facilitated its publication, a pan-American logic that is closely allied to commodity colonialism.

6. The most useful statistical data on coffee and coffee consumption in the United States can be gleaned from the regular reports of the Food and Agriculture Organization and the National Coffee Association. See also the *Statistical Annual of the Coffee, Sugar, and Cocoa Exchange*. I should add that little social or political commentary accompanies such reports.

7. See Jeffery Paige, *Coffee and Power* (Cambridge, Mass.: Harvard University Press, 1997). This is the most innovative and rigorous sociological critique of coffee in Central American history to have emerged in post–cold war scholarship. While many analysts have tracked the function of power elites in Central America, few have linked it to the economic logic of a particular commodity (although there remains a great deal of interest in the Colombia-cocaine nexus). Given what I have said so far about coffee and modernity, it is not surprising that the dynastic family elites that Paige investigates emerged in the middle of the nineteenth century, when coffee demand took off in North America and Europe.

8. K. Knox and J. S. Huffaker, *Coffee Basics* (New York: John Wiley and Sons, 1997), x.

9. For a standard history of coffee's emergence as a cash crop, see the first thirteen chapters of Ukers, *All about Coffee*. See also Andrés C. Uribe, *Brown Gold: The Amazing Story of Coffee* (New York: Random House, 1954). If one were to attempt a chronotopic critique of coffee, one would also have to account for the different ways its story gets told.

For instance, Mark Pendergast's *Uncommon Grounds: The History of Coffee and How It Transformed Our World* (New York: Basic Books, 1999) often follows the main narrative elements of Ukers's text but is situated by liberal humanist ideology in a form unimaginable to Ukers. Neither a paean to transnational coffee corporations (the three main companies, Philip Morris, Procter and Gamble, and Nestlé, all refused to provide research avenues for his project) nor a radical exposé, *Uncommon Grounds* nevertheless offers enough fieldwork to differentiate sharply monopoly capitalist versions of coffee lore from the niche marketing profusions of late capitalism. A more difficult task, however, would have been to elaborate the imbrication of one narrative in the other precisely because of the time/space of globalization. Obviously Paige's (*Coffee and Power*) polemic undermines the happy narrative of coffee in socialization. See also North London Haslemere Group, *Coffee: The Rules of Neocolonialism* (London: Third World First, 1972).

10. See Thomas De Quincey, "The Last Days of Kant," in vol. 4 of *The Collected Writings of Thomas De Quincey*, ed. David Masson (Edinburgh: Adam and Charles Black, 1890), 346. Masson notes that De Quincey's sketch of Kant first appeared in *Blackwood's Magazine* in 1827 as part of a series dubbed "Gallery of the German Prose Classics, by the English Opium-Eater." While De Quincey remained profoundly ambivalent about Kantian philosophy, he seems positively engaged by Kant's penchant for caffeine, which is, like heroin, an alkaloid. It should be noted that most of De Quincey's memoir is held to be a translation of Wasianski's—although the interest in stimulants is accentuated by De Quincey. See E. A. Christoph Wasianski, *Emmanuel Kant, ein Lebensbild,* ed. Alfons Hoffman (Halle, Germany: Peter, 1902).

11. For more on the early history of coffee consumption in Germany, see chapter 7 of Ukers, *All about Coffee*. For a general history of coffeehouses, see Ulla Heise, *Coffee and Coffee Houses,* trans. Paul Roper (West Chester, Pa.: Schiffer, 1987).

12. Wolfgang Schivelbusch, *Tastes of Paradise: A Social History of Spices, Stimulants, and Intoxicants,* trans. David Jacobson (New York: Pantheon, 1992), 38–39.

13. Such readings of Kant are not uncommon. Terry Eagleton, for instance, has advanced an argument for the *Critique of Pure Reason* as a conduit for commodity rationality: "The qualities of the Kantian moral law are those of the commodity form. Abstract, universal and rigorously self-identical, the law of Reason is a mechanism which, like the commodity, effects formally equal exchanges between isolated individual subjects, erasing the difference of their needs and desires in its homogenizing injunctions" (*The Ideology of the Aesthetic* [Oxford: Basil Blackwell, 1990], 83).

14. Jacques Derrida, "Economimesis," trans. R. Klein, *Diacritics* 11 (1981): 3–25.

15. Knox and Huffaker, *Coffee Basics,* 30.

16. Michael Holquist, Introduction to Bakhtin's *Art and Answerability,* trans. Vadim Liapunov, ed. Michael Holquist and Vadim Liapunov (Austin: University of Texas Press, 1990), ix–xlix. Stories abound regarding Bakhtin's consumption of tea and cigarettes (the tea urn often sat on his writing desk). The rumor that Bakhtin's substance abuse led him to smoke some of his own manuscript (because he had run out of papers) has never been verified.

17. Pierre Bourdieu, *Distinction,* trans. Richard Nice (Cambridge, Mass.: Harvard University Press, 1984).

18. In capitalism, of course, this process is usually given over to the world of advertising. See W. F. Haug, *Critique of Commodity Aesthetics,* trans. Robert Bock (Cambridge, England: Polity Press, 1986). I am going to read the mode of intoxication at stake a little more literally.

19. See, for instance, Ralph S. Hattox, *Coffee and Coffeehouses* (Seattle: University of Washington Press, 1985).

20. The coffee bean is actually a berry which, in most varieties, divides in two. The flatness of one side of the bean is a measure of its absent half. To my mind, this is the philosophical conundrum of "economimesis."

21. Schivelbusch, *Tastes of Paradise,* 38.

22. Multatuli (Eduard Douwes Dekker), *Max Havelaar; or, The Coffee Auctions of the Dutch Trading Company,* trans. Roy Edwards (New York: Penguin, 1967). Page references in the text will be to this edition unless otherwise noted.

23. See Pramoedya Ananta Toer, "The Book That Killed Colonialism," *New York Times Magazine,* 18 April 1999, 112–14.

24. The Buru Quartet is published in English in four separate volumes: *This Earth of Mankind, Child of All Nations, Footsteps,* and *House of Glass,* trans. Max Lane (New York: Penguin, 1990). This extraordinary epic of Indonesian nationhood was banned in 1981 by the Indonesian government. With a new power structure emerging in Indonesia, this ban may soon be lifted. Pramoedya himself was a long-time prisoner of Suharto's regime but in 1999 he was allowed to leave Indonesia on a book tour.

25. D. H. Lawrence, Introduction to Heinemann's 1967 London edition of Multatuli, *Max Havelaar,* 11–15 (originally published as the introduction to the 1927 Knopf edition). Lawrence believes that Multatuli's book is driven principally by hate, hate mostly of the powers that be. As he rightly points out, Multatuli does not just heap scorn on the Dutch colonial machine but acknowledges the role of the Indonesian aristocracy in the reproduction of relations of domination. But Lawrence also reads *Max Havelaar* as a satire and, while this form may have been sustainable in Lawrence's time, it has succumbed to a less refined cynicism in the present.

26. E. M. Beekman, Afterword to Multatuli, *Max Havelaar; or, The Coffee Auctions of the Dutch Trading Company,* trans. Roy Edwards (Amherst: University of Massachusetts Press, 1982), 372–92.

27. Pramoedya, "Book That Killed," 114.

28. Pendergast, *Uncommon Grounds.*

29. Gregory Dicum and Nina Luttinger, *The Coffee Book: Anatomy of an Industry from Crop to the Last Drop* (New York: New Press, 1999), 60.

30. Studies of the economics of coffee abound. A good basic tome is Richard L. Lucier, *The International Political Economy of Coffee* (New York: Praeger, 1988). For an interesting exercise in reading this political economy "apolitically," see Robert H. Bates, *Open Economy Politics: The Political Economy of the World Coffee Trade* (Princeton, N.J.: Princeton

University Press, 1997). Bates is good at revealing the malfeasance of producers in the world coffee trade but less adept at exploring the machinations of "First World" corporations in manipulating the surpluses of the coffee market.

31. John Talbot, "Where Does Your Coffee Dollar Go? The Division of Income and Surplus along the Coffee Commodity Chain," *Studies in Comparative International Development* 32, no. 1 (Spring 1997): 56–91.

32. Adorno, *Aesthetic Theory,* 120.

33. For more on the complex effects of caffeine, see Stephen Braun, *Buzz: The Science and Lore of Alcohol and Caffeine* (New York: Penguin, 1996). See also Cynthia Kuhn, Scott Schwartzwelder, and Wilkie Wison, *Buzzed* (New York: Norton, 1998); and Silvio Garattini, *Caffeine, Coffee, and Health* (New York: Raven Press, 1993).

34. Howard Schultz and Doris Jones Yang, *Pour Your Heart into It: How Starbucks Built a Company One Cup at a Time* (New York: Hyperion, 1997). This book follows the "business success story" genre but provides endless insights into the function of desire in coffee production along the way.

35. Although there are moments when not all that glitters is coffee. When Starbucks announced in 1999 that it was going to expand its market components into a broad range of consumables and adopt an Internet strategy (basically an e-commerce Web site), investors hammered the stock mercilessly. The wisdom was that Starbucks should stick with its specialty coffee business, even though challengers are emerging at an increasingly rapid, and caffeinated, rate. Starbucks also introduced a magazine, predictably called *Joe,* with the amazing slogan "Life is interesting. Discuss!" The premier issue was organized around a theme that is another categorical imperative for capitalism: "Trust Me." Typically, the magazine is a humdrum collection of adverts meant only to stimulate page turning of the automaton variety. The business of coffee is stylishly absent.

36. Rigoberta Menchú, *I, Rigoberta Menchú: An Indian Woman in Guatemala,* trans. Ann Wright, ed. Elisabeth Burgos-Debray (London: Verso, 1984). For an argument that criticizes Menchú's myths of self and downright invention, see the controversial book by David Stoll, *Rigoberta Menchú and the Story of All Poor Guatemalans* (Boulder, Colo.: Westview Press, 1999).

37. Ray Oldenburg, *The Great Good Place* (New York: Marlowe, 1999).

38. Schulz and Yang, *Pour Your Heart,* 52.

39. Dicum and Luttinger, *The Coffee Book,* especially chapter 5.

Conclusion

1. John Tomlinson, *Culture and Globalization* (Chicago: University of Chicago Press, 1999), 1. There is much to recommend Tomlinson's book, particularly over the earlier arguments he made in his work on cultural imperialism. Nevertheless, while there are conceptual tools at work in Tomlinson's book that are of broad appeal (his nuanced reading of deterritorialization, for instance), his argument is often buoyed by the assumption that the systematicity on one side of the *and* in his title complements or reveals the logic at work on the other.

2. This is, of course, where the case for economics runs up against the argument for philosophy. I will not be using Bakhtin to arbitrate the two in the discussion that follows but to see in what sense a cognitive/ethical principle is at stake in what globalization can become. For a related, if gestural, reading of the world according to philosophy, see Jean-Luc Nancy, *The Sense of the World* (Minneapolis: University of Minnesota Press, 1997).

3. Timothy Brennan, *At Home in the World: Cosmopolitanism Now* (Cambridge, Mass.: Harvard University Press, 1997). Brennan suggests that cosmopolitanism has been contaminated from the outside by its development within the terms of worldliness provided by colonialism and imperialism. Clearly, this represents an *unheimlich* existence for a more egalitarian world.

4. Dipesh Chakrabarty, "Postcoloniality and the Artifice of History: Who Speaks for India's Pasts?," *Representations* 37 (Winter 1992): 2. Globalization is a wonderful and frightening example of Chakrabarty's pointed critique. What could better illustrate asymmetrical ignorance than the difference between the pronouncements of the avatars of globalization and the world to which it refers?

5. Gary Saul Morson and Caryl Emerson, *Mikhail Bakhtin: Creation of a Prosaics* (Stanford, Calif.: Stanford University Press, 1990).

6. Katerina Clark and Michael Holquist, *Mikhail Bakhtin* (Cambridge, Mass.: Harvard University Press, 1984), 1.

7. Mikhail Bakhtin, *Art and Answerability,* trans. Vadim Liapunov, ed. Michael Holquist and Vadim Liapunov (Austin: University of Texas Press, 1990). Subsequent references to this work will be noted in the text as AA followed by a page number.

8. Mikhail Bakhtin, *Problems of Dostoevsky's Poetics,* trans. and ed. Caryl Emerson (Minneapolis: University of Minnesota Press, 1984).

9. I should point out that, while the proponents of globalization are concerned with what is primarily an economic logic, some of their chief critics often accept the terms of globalization in offering an alternative. It is my contention that to accept the terms of globalization is already to displace the cognitive aporia that girds globalization in the first place.

10. See, for instance, Linda Weiss, "Globalization and the Myth of the Powerless State," *New Left Review* 225 (September–October 1997): 3–27, for more on the nature of this phenomenon. Obviously, the formula for globalization looks different according to the criteria used. If, for example, one based the "existence" of globalization on financialization and currency speculation, there would be little doubt that the economic relations of the globe have seen a massive restructuring (similar, some might say, to the rise of the casino).

11. Clearly I am not arguing that heavy industry does not play a significant role in contemporary economic activity (General Motors, for instance, remains one of the largest companies on Earth) but it does not provide the best example of capital mobility under the sign of globalization. It is somewhat ironic, therefore, that Chris Harman, in an otherwise erudite analysis of the term and its condition, pivots his critique on the relative immobility of productive capital within heavy industry. It seems to me the "new ortho-

doxy" is not best undermined by reference to an old one. See Chris Harman, "Globalisation: A Critique of a New Orthodoxy," *International Socialism* 73 (Winter 1996): 3–33.

12. Terry Eagleton, *The Ideology of the Aesthetic* (Oxford: Basil Blackwell, 1990), 202.

13. Karl Marx, "Economic and Philosophic Manuscripts of 1844," in *The Marx-Engels Reader,* ed. Robert C. Tucker (New York: Norton, 1978), 76–77.

14. Mikhail Bakhtin. *Toward a Philosophy of the Act,* trans. Vadim Liapunov (Austin: University of Texas Press, 1993), 54–55.

15. See, for instance, Arjun Appadurai, "Disjuncture and Difference in the Global Cultural Economy," in *The Phantom Public Sphere,* ed. Bruce Robbins (Minneapolis: University of Minnesota Press, 1993), 269–95, reworked in Appadurai's *Modernity at Large,* which I have discussed in my introduction.

16. Some critics are more optimistic than others on this point. Brecher and Costello, for instance, have argued for a "globalization from below." Again, while I am in agreement with the production of counterhegemonic resistance formations, these cannot appear as a mirror of the operative logic of globalization. Delinking would have to be accompanied by dethinking on this point. See Jeremy Brecher and Tim Costello, *Global Village or Global Pillage* (Boston: South End Press, 1994).

17. Thus, while there is much in postmodernity that simply skips the conditions immanent in globalization, it nevertheless emerges as a critical approach to the forms of worldliness that globalization represents. This is, perhaps, why forms of postmodern Marxism are on the rise. See, for instance, Fredric Jameson, "Notes on Globalization as a Philosophical Issue," in *The Cultures of Globalization,* ed. Fredric Jameson and Masao Miyoshi (Durham, N.C.: Duke University Press, 1998), 54–77; and Roger Burbach, Orlando Núñez, and Boris Kagarlitsky, *Globalization and Its Discontents: The Rise of Postmodern Socialisms* (London: Pluto Press, 1997). The latter provides a provocative cross-cultural and transnational critique that reads peripheral economies as postmodern vis-à-vis normative modes of globalization. Whether or not such economies are to be merely swallowed up by the juggernaut of capitalist globalization is a key challenge for the twenty-first century.

Index

Peter Hitchcock is the author of *Oscillate Wildly: Space, Body, and Spirit of Millennial Materialism,* and *Dialogics of the Oppressed.* He is currently a professor of literary and cultural studies at Baruch College and the Graduate Center of the City University of New York.

■ ■ ■ TRANSNATIONAL CULTURAL STUDIES

From Here to Tierra del Fuego   *Paul Magee*

Sounds English: Transnational Popular Music   *Nabeel Zuberi*

Imaginary States: Studies in Cultural Transnationalism   *Peter Hitchcock*

The University of Illinois Press
is a founding member of the
Association of American University Presses.

Composed in 10.5/13 Adobe Garamond
with Veljovic Black display
by Jim Proefrock
at the University of Illinois Press
Designed by Dennis Roberts
Manufactured by Thomson-Shore, Inc.

University of Illinois Press
1325 South Oak Street
Champaign, IL 61820-6903
www.press.uillinois.edu